BADASS
BEGUMS

Praise for *Badass Begums*

'*Badass Begums* feels like tracing Delhi's heartbeat through the women who built it. Anoushka writes with the curiosity of a researcher archivist and the tenderness of a storyteller. Her version of Delhi is alive, and the begums do not shout for power; they just stand their ground, and they simply refuse to be forgotten.'—**Sadaf Hussain, author of *Masalamandi* and chef**

'Writing as if Delhi is recollecting its past, Anoushka lifts the purdah of history from splendid Mughal women whose sense and sensitivity produced grand architectures, only to be documented as *built during the emperor's reign*, thus casting all credit to the male rulers. Other than an academic renavigation of facts, this book paints the pain and power of "privileged" women. As an audience, I feel envious of their lustre, but simultaneously, I would never seek to own that glory!'—**Koral Dasgupta, author of The Sati Series**

'Jain's affinity with the heroines of *Badass Begums* shines through her lucid prose. She brings these long-neglected women vividly to life, turning history's hidden stories into modern-day lessons. Their contributions to society, nation-building and women's emancipation are not only retrieved from obscurity but celebrated and remembered for posterity.'—**Manish Gaekwad, author of *The Last Courtesan***

'Deftly combining history, humour and travelogue, *Badass Begums* unveils the vital role that women played in shaping Delhi's rich Mughal past.'—**Dr John Zubrzycki, author and historian**

'A charming, personal and revelatory account of the fascinating women who built Old Delhi.'—**Kavitha Rao, author of *Lady Doctors***

'*Badass Begums* unveils the audacious Mughal women who rewrote the rules. Anoushka's bold storytelling tears through history, spotlighting the enigmatic begums.'—**Tanushree Podder, author of *Bimbisar's Curse***

'These very readable stories of women familiar from history lessons show again how the centuries-old argument that women aren't fit to lead has always been pure fallacy. Here are begums who took to power with ease and style—badass indeed!'—**Divrina Dhingra, author of *The Perfume Project***

'Anoushka Jain's *Badass Begums* is a dazzling debut. It is a reclamation of women's voices from Mughal history, vividly written, deeply researched and irresistibly empowering. Each story pulses with courage, wit and defiance, proving that history's most formidable builders were often its most forgotten women.'—**Raza Mir, author of *Murders in the Mushaira***

'In this riveting, eye-opening account, Anoushka Jain raises her own glorious monument to celebrate the forgotten women of the Mughal Empire. *Badass Begums* is a clear-eyed chronicle of these schemers, dreamers, builders and rebels, written in a chatty conversational style, which effortlessly combines present-day observation with immaculate historical research.'—**Palash Krishna Mehrotra, author, editor and columnist**

BADASS BEGUMS

The
INCREDIBLE
WOMEN *who* SHAPED
MUGHAL INDIA

ANOUSHKA JAIN

HARPER
NON-FICTION
An Imprint of HarperCollins Publishers

First published in India by Harper Non-fiction 2025
An imprint of HarperCollins *Publishers*
HarperCollins *Publishers* India, Cyber City,
Building 10-A, Gurugram, Haryana – 122002, India
www.harpercollins.co.in

2 4 6 8 10 9 7 5 3

P-ISBN: 978-93-7307-651-5
E-ISBN: 978-93-7307-617-1

Typeset in 11.5 pt/15 Adobe Garamond Pro
by HarperCollins *Publishers* India Pvt. Ltd

Printed and bound at
Nutech Print Services Pvt. Ltd.

This book is printed on FSC® certified paper
which ensures responsible forest managemen

HarperCollins *Publishers*, Macken House, 39/40 Mayor Street Upper, Dublin 1,
D01 C9W8, Ireland

To,
My father, who stayed positive for both of us.
And my mother, who taught me the greatest gift of humanity is the ability to read and write.

Contents

Locating Her in the City: An Illustrated Study of Women's Architectural Spaces in Chandni Chowk

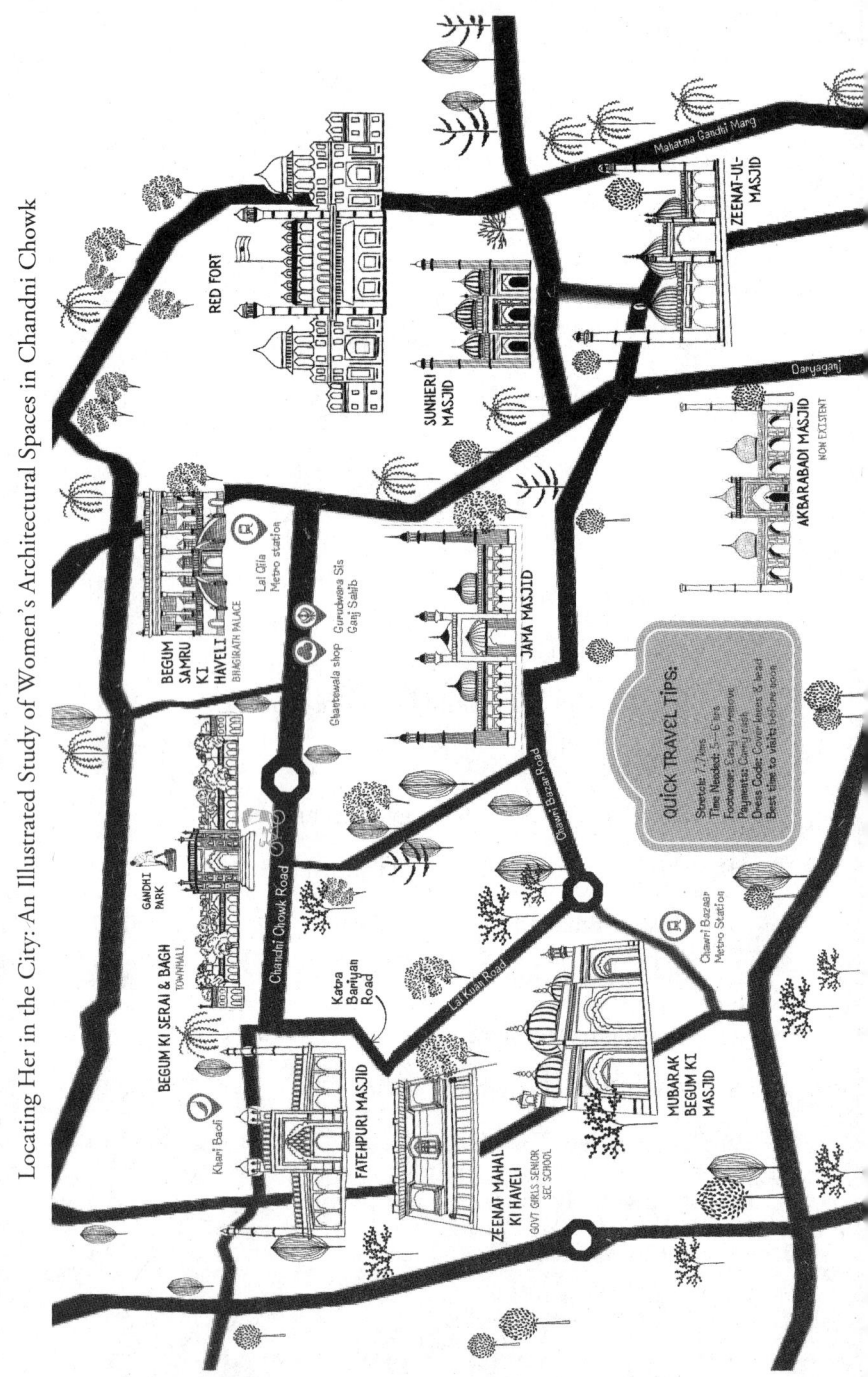

The Queen's Monument to an Emperor: An Illustrated Map of the Humayun's Tomb Complex

RIVER YAMUNA

NEELA GUMBAD

COOL FACTS

- The tomb exists because of Begum Bega (Haji Begum). A queen who dared to dream of a tomb so grand, fit for her emperor.

- Hamida Banu Begum, Humayun's other powerful wife and Akbar's mother, was buried here too, making this space a shelter full of Mughal memories.

- The site became a point of refuge during the 1857 Uprising, the last Mughal emperor Bahadur Shah Zafar hid here before surrendering.

- Over 150 Mughal royals rest here, proof that women's patronage created a dynasty of beauty.

NORTH GATE

HUMAYUN TOMB

SOUTH GATE

WEST GATE

GATE

NORTH GATE OF ARAB KI SERAI

AFSAR WALA TOMB

BU HALIMA TOMB & GARDEN

MAIN GATE

ISA KHAN TOMB

QUICK TRAVEL TIPS:

- Best time: early morning or golden-hour evenings
- Opens: Sunrise – 6:30 PM (night visits too)
- Stay hydrated; it's a lot of walking
- Stop by Isa Khan's Tomb—older than Humayun's!
- Picnic vibes? Head to Sunder Nursery next door
- Comfy kicks are a must—steps, lawns & long paths

A Note on Sources

This book draws upon the accounts of several European travellers—Italian, French and English—who visited the Mughal court and wrote about their experiences during the Mughal reign. These include chroniclers such as Niccolao Manucci, François Bernier, Jean-Baptiste Tavernier, and others whose writings offer rare glimpses into the world behind the imperial walls.

Because official Mughal records and court chronicles remain largely silent on women, these foreign observations become vital in reconstructing the lives of the empire's begums and princesses. Yet, it is important to acknowledge that such accounts were often shaped by hearsay, court gossip, or the travellers' own cultural biases. Their descriptions may, at times, appear exaggerated or romanticized.

Even so, when multiple sources mention the same incidents or details, a kernel of truth tends to emerge. This book builds on those convergences, balancing fact with interpretation to recreate a possible portrait of the remarkable women who shaped the Mughal world.

Introduction

Are you a 'badass' woman? And if you are a guy reading this, *do you know a badass woman?*

My dear readers, who have picked this book from the store shelves because of its cover or its name, I want to tell you a story—a handful of stories. They are neither fabricated nor fictionalized, nor was ChatGPT commanded to write viral material. No, these are actual stories of women in history who lived before the internet, before there was TikTok and before marketing brands were selling you stuff in the name of women's empowerment. This is a slice of history that was forgotten and lost in time. The women in these stories were just like us—mothers, sisters, daughters and wives. But one thing set them apart: they were badass.

To give you context and background, I conduct heritage walks. I am a common sight in Delhi—much like pigeons—wandering about in walking shoes, armed with a mic and a tab. I am also constantly surrounded by people—no, not by a mob, but by heritage enthusiasts, perhaps people like you, who spare time to learn about history. A city like Delhi, which in today's time is considered unsafe for women, was once built by women. Some 500 years ago, women of the Mughal Empire started adorning the city with monuments. They built gardens, serais, bazaars, stepwells, mosques and havelis, and patronized Sufi dargahs. The women patronizing and imprinting the cityscape with these public buildings and other constructions were royal princesses, begums, noblewomen and even, at times, courtesans. Why did they build these structures? Who gave them money to fund these buildings? And who were these women? Do people still remember them? Are these structures still there? This book answers all these questions.

Inside the harem

Let us start with the fundamentals: harem/zenana/women's quarter, the innermost sanctuary of a medieval fort or a haveli. This is where the women of the Mughal Empire lived. The Arabic word 'haram' means 'sacred'. The women of the family occupied the domestic space. This meant wives, daughters, aunts, mothers, stepmothers, grandmothers, enslaved people, concubines, servants. The space was restricted not just to women but also to pre-pubescent boys and eunuchs who were considered harmless and provided a sense of security inside the quarters. While the eunuchs acted as spies, confidants and even did surveillance of the zenana, the young boys spent their formative years under the guidance of their mothers, grandmothers and aunts, which shaped their personality.

Women entered the harem through marriage, birth, appointment, and even as gifts. It was a strictly hierarchical structure, where the Padshah Begum, or the dowager empress, reigned supreme.

Interestingly, Mughal women were very good at commerce and had annual incomes to support them. They were funded for their activities through four basic mediums. Firstly, they were gifted a jagir, or a royal land grant, on which the women levied taxes. Secondly, an annual income was set for them, portioned out in monthly sums, helping them to be financially strong. Thirdly, they received gifts during anniversaries, coronations, new year celebrations and other special occasions. They were also given luxurious gifts during events such as hunting expeditions. Fourthly, they ran small businesses with their personal finance teams. Mariam-uz-zamani was one of the earliest women in the Mughal world to be in the shipping trade. She commanded vast ships, such as *Rahimi*, that helped pilgrims to reach Mecca. She was even involved in the sea trade of spices, indigo and textiles. Shah Jahan's daughter, Princess Jahanara, received Surat Port as a gift when she turned thirty. Her ship, *Sahibi*, was one of the most enviable ships on the Red Sea.

The harem spaces were flexible and modest during the rule of Emperor Babur and Emperor Humayun. The wives were mentioned by their names. There was greater mobility within the residential quarters, and women were considered equal halves, worthy partners to share the risky nature of holding a throne. This changed during Emperor Akbar's time. There was peace and stability in his ever-expanding Mughal

Empire. The seventeenth-century historian Inayat Khan in the manuscript *The Shah Jahan Nama* mentions:

> Ever since the reign of the Emperor Akbar, it had been ordained that the names of the inmates of the seraglio should not mentioned in public, but that they should be designated by some epithet, derived either from the place of their birth or the country or city in which they may have first been regarded by the monarch with the eye of affection.

Meet Badass Begums

Mughal women stayed in zenanas under strict confinement. They were financially and artistically independent but their physical movement outside the palace was restricted. Yet, we see examples of brilliance from within those confined spaces. The women selected for this book particularly fall under this category. Some women had privilege but no power; some had privilege and power but no peace; some had no privilege and they had to work hard to rise up the ranks. While most women were seen as power-hungry and ambitious, there were few who managed to gain respect and prestige. Such instances were few and far between.

The book also exclusively selects begums who have contributed to the city of Delhi. There were three basic reasons for it. Firstly, I am very well acquainted with the city. I know the roads like the back of my hand. Secondly, it is amazing how Delhi, which remained a seat of power for a thousand years, was continuously built by women. Yes, the sultans and rulers won the land and the seat. But the very essence of the city was built by women. The culture, the economics, the society were all curated with utmost care. Thirdly, this book finds evidence where we see female power in the city. It focuses on built, tangible heritage. It does not rely simply on literary data, but discovers monuments built by women in the city and creates a roadmap for a feminist lens of reading the city. This is also the reason why strong influential names such as Sultan Razia, Nur Jahan and Hamida Banu Begum are not featured in this book. While all of these women did contribute majorly in the power-building of the empire, we do not find their architecture in the city.

The chapters in the book evaluate the motivations, motives and desires that pushed women to build lasting architecture, what made them badass, and why their contributions mattered. For example, Jahanara Begum used architecture as soft power. She built serais, hammams, mosques and gardens all over the country. Jahanara worked towards community-building, wellness, health and rejuvenation. Her work commandeered a cultural life for the Mughal Empire. Jahanara was instrumental in shaping Delhi as a city. She used spirituality, trade and wellness as ways to strengthen the Mughal Empire beyond wars and tactics. Her privilege could have limited her to an ivory tower but Jahanara chose to use it in a way that mattered. She actively contributed to building Old Delhi, prompted other daughters and wives of Shah Jahan to build architecture and create women-exclusive spaces, and tried to prevent civil war within the Mughal family.

While Jahanara is an example of privilege with power, Begum Zeenat Mahal, also featured in this book, had privilege without power. Zeenat Mahal was the last Mughal empress and she inherited a crumbling empire. She witnessed one of the most momentous events in Indian history, the Revolt of 1857, and instead of being a front-row witness, Zeenat chose to be in the middle of it. She fought tooth and nail to protect the Mughal throne for her son and herself. Her political actions are called 'scheming' by many scholars, and not 'strategic', a more respectful term that would have been given to a ruling male.

A similar conservative outlook was taken by contemporary scholars who called Qudsia Begum terrible names and lamented the idea of Hindustan being ruled by a lowly woman. Qudsia was a former nautch girl who was given the name of 'Udham Bai'. After ruler Muhammad Shah Rangeela's death, Qudsia became de facto ruler for her son and ruled with her ally Javid Khan. It became a sore point for the nobility of the time to pay respects to a woman and to the eunuch Javid Khan. Qudsia had inherited a sinking ship from the previous ruler. There was also a chasm in the Mughal Empire where the aristocracy and nobility were waning and new power blocs were rising. Qudsia was absolutely badass in how she held her ground despite knowing what the public and nobility thought of her, and she ruled like a monarch. Qudsia left her mark by building two prominent structures— the grand Qudsia Bagh which was the last of the Mughal gardens and a mosque near Red Fort, still used by believers. Qudsia is a classic example of how loud, expressive women will never be seen kindly by society.

Another nautch girl who rose up the ranks was Begum Samru, who was a tawaif in Chawri Bazaar. She caught the fancy of Walter Sombre, a European mercenary, and became his wife and travelled with him across the country during his military campaigns. Begum Samru became a silent pillar of strength for Walter Reinhardt Sombre and advised him during his extensive tours. She observed how he strategized, handled military coups, managed high-pressure situations and maintained diplomatic ties with any bidding party. These skills eventually helped Begum Samru after her husband's sudden death. She acted swiftly and managed to get a decree to rule on her husband's behalf with an army of four thousand. Begum Samru used the skills she had learnt from her courtesan days. She was crafty, loyal and pragmatic. She saved Emperor Shah Alam II's life so many times that she was awarded land 500 metres away from Red Fort. Begum Samru ki Haveli is now Asia's largest electrical market. The journey of Begum Samru from a tawaif to one of the richest mercenaries is a truly remarkable tale from history. She was one of the most badass characters in Indian history, with nerves of steel, and it is disappointing how enough hasn't been written on her. Her life story, full of grit and determination, is stuff made for films.

The book focuses on yet another tawaif who is not that well known, except for the architecture she built. Mubarak Begum, wife of Sir David Ochterlony, the British resident to the Mughal court in Delhi. Mubarak was a tawaif who fell in love with a man much older than her. She was a Muslim and she ensured that her children too were raised under the doctrines of Islam. We find references where both natives and the British resented her. For a woman, it is a sort of achievement when you truly rile up several sections of society. She was not liked for her influence on her husband and how she insisted on being addressed with honorifics. After her husband's death, she built a mosque under her name. The mosque soon came to be known as 'whore's mosque' by the public who wanted to defame her. Mubarak Begum remained unbothered and even played a role during the Revolt of 1857. The mosque still stands in Lal Kuan Bazaar, very close to Lal Kuan Haveli of Begum Zeenat Mahal. Her story is a perfect example of how women are shamed if they do not follow the prototype of being a dutiful daughter or a wife.

We have discussed women with privilege and women without privilege, but then there was another set of women who had privilege but were omitted, replaced and overlooked. The famous example of such a forgotten woman is Roshanara Begum. She was the younger daughter of Shah Jahan and practically became the kingmaker. Roshanara grew up under the shadow of her sister Jahanara Begum, who was more beautiful, more creative, more intelligent and definitely more liked by the emperor and her brothers. Roshanara was opportunistic, bitter and vengeful. She supported her younger brother Aurangzeb in the power struggle within the Mughal Empire. She aided him by providing information, became a spy in the royal palace and also supported him financially. When Aurangzeb came to power she became the Padshah Begum, and replaced Jahanara Begum, who left on a self-imposed exile with her father. Roshanara was an impulsive, spontaneous, passionate person and her decisions often caused distress and trouble to her brother. She had several affairs, which Aurangzeb chose to overlook. Yet, Roshanara was never given the freedom to stay separately outside the Mughal palace. Despite enormous privilege, Roshanara faced problems like any other woman at that time in society—her freedom was curtailed, she never married and she had to always work within certain limits. Roshanara eventually retired from courtly life and built a garden for herself, away from the walled city. Roshanara Bagh remains a famous Municipal Corporation of Delhi (MCD) park in the northern part of the city, though very few realize the remarkable, adventurous life of the woman who is buried there.

Another such ignored and overlooked woman in Mughal history was Hajji Begum. While Mughal chronicles are full of love stories between Humayun and Hamida, they discount the other woman in Humayun's life, who perhaps shaped the architectural legacy of the Mughal Empire—Bega Begum or 'Hajji Begum', the first wife of Emperor Humayun. History has certainly disappointed us when it comes to Bega Begum. Her trials and triumphs are not recorded, and she remains a footnote, a passing remark in the important Mughal chronicles. Yet, many travellers have mentioned Bega Begum and her contribution in building the most iconic building of India—Humayun's Tomb. Her anecdotes have been mentioned by Humayun's sister, Gulbadan Begum, that truly shows her free spirit and taste for adventure. Her chapter in this book is full of surprises and gives us a cue on how women rebelled within the walls of patriarchy.

Other such little-known characters in Mughal history are the wives of Shah Jahan who were not Mumtaz Mahal. It was truly hard to find enough source material to write about Fatehpuri Begum and Akbarabadi Begum. While the mosque built by Fatehpuri Begum remains and is, in fact, one of the most important monuments in the city, the mosque constructed by Akbarabadi Begum was razed to the ground post 1857. The other wives of Shah Jahan have been overshadowed in history by the grand love story of Shah Jahan and Mumtaz. The glory of Taj Mahal dwarfs these women, who too witnessed momentous events in history, and who managed to escape the suffocating shadow of the seventh wonder and leave a mark of their own. Old Delhi is peppered with monuments made by these women, who commissioned mosques, bazaars and serais to consolidate the cultural fabric of the city.

The two chapters which are unique to this book are about Akbar's wet nurse, Maham Anga, and the daughters of Aurangzeb. Both Akbar and Aurangzeb have been extensively written about, and both present two extreme ends of the spectrum. It is interesting how the women around them shaped their policies, influenced their decisions and enriched their reign. Maham Anga was a strong influence on Akbar and shaped his formative years. She is one of the earliest examples of strong women in the Mughal imperial family. She built a madrassa and a mosque opposite Purana Qila in Delhi. The madrassa is no longer there but the mosque remains. It is one of the most stunning mosques you could visit. Maham Anga could give a masterclass in using symbolism as a way to project power, especially in an age where symbolic protocol meant everything. The chapter focuses on the matriarch of Mughal royalty and her role in shaping able rulers. On the other hand, we see Zinat-un-Nissa and Zeb-un-Nissa, the two famous daughters of Aurangzeb. Their chapter takes a unique angle of reading history under Aurangzeb's rule. It is not through the optics of politics and propaganda but through the acts of women under his reign. One of his daughters questioned his authority, and dared to rebel against his principles and act against his wishes.

Inspiration behind *Badass Begums*

Badass Begums was only a floating idea until a boy asked me a question in one of my heritage walks. I was conducting a heritage walk in Chawri Bazaar and talking about the tawaifs of Shahjahanabad. The participants and I had just visited Mubarak Begum Masjid. The masjid is close to Chawri Bazaar and holds a special place in the walk since it had been defamed by the public and called 'Randi ka Masjid' (a whore's mosque).[1] After I had finished explaining its history, a boy asked me, 'Why did women only build serais, gardens and mosques? Didn't they build any palaces in the city?' Now, that was indeed an interesting question. Why didn't they?

'Women always had to negotiate for their freedom. It had to be bargained for. A woman knew she would get permission to build public structures for the community. But it was hard to get sanction to build a palace,' I told him.

'So why build anything at all?' asked the boy.

'If not, the women knew they would be erased from history books. Their names would be changed, or worse, completely removed. And it would be hard to write the history of these women when you would need to search for them in the silences, between lines. That is why these women built architecture that would survive time, dynasties and powerful monarchs. They built them for future generations, because people remember history. And look, they have been successful. We are talking about these women today in these walks, because I see a plaque that reads "Mubarak Begum Masjid". Isn't that great?'

And that is how *Badass Begums* was born. Out of a conversation.

The idea took the form of a heritage walk where we explored architecture built by women in Old Delhi. Several walks were conducted over the years and people absolutely loved them. I also saw that most of the time it was women who were on this walk. The ratio generally used to be 1:9. And I did not mind, as long as I could empower my girls in the city. The walk, however, was limited in its scope. It only catered to the city of Delhi. But what about so many other enthusiasts who love history and love feminism? It was also hard to physically cover every area built by women in the city. Most of the time it did not make for a good walking route. All these factors led to this book, which you are holding now. The book has been the culmination of the hard work and research of many years. Through it I want to start a discussion on women's history and their contributions, even if the sources are scant.

Why write a book on Badass Begums?

Though books on famous women from history abound, I feel, in many of them the research falls short on one thing—exploring how these women wanted to be remembered. The biographers create the character sketches using secondary sources and traveller accounts, but do these assist in giving a voice to the women? This book turns the narrative on its head and explores women through their creations, and not the other way around. It first picks architecture built by women in the city of Delhi and then starts the hunting party to find these women in the historical archives.

Architecture here is used as a language of communication. The women wanted to be remembered in a certain way. They chose the language of remembrance by picking the stones, the tiles, the layout and choosing the very purpose of the building itself. Some women commissioned mosques and built structures inside dargahs. They commanded piety and spiritual authority by associating themselves with divinity. Some women built gardens and spaces of entertainment to create places of well-being and cultural life, where poets met, scholars held discussions and families gathered. Other women built serais and bazaars, and actively facilitated commerce in the empire. Many of them built grand tombs and havelis as places of retreat, and as ultimate symbols of power and prestige. *Badass Begums* evaluates women through their commissioned architecture and reworks a new language of writing history.

Challenges while writing this book

One of the biggest challenges while writing the book was the scarcity of resources. History has disappointed women. The names of many of the women featured in this book were changed in the sources and archival documents; there was little to no information about their lives before they got married. Instances of accounts that tell us about how they felt, how they looked and who they actually were are rare. Yet, with the help of traveller accounts, unusual primary sources and the architecture they commissioned, we have been able to do justice to these women and their stories.

The other challenge was how to make these women likeable and agreeable to the larger audience. After a few chapters, I realized the activity was futile. It is best to represent these women as they were—deeply flawed, ambitious, cunning, power-hungry, blinded by maternal love and of dubious character. And that's what makes them human and relatable. Women with such character traits have been villainized and their reputation has been sullied. However, the truth is, when a man uses the same tactics in history, he is called a visionary; he is called indomitable and courageous. *Badass Begums* doesn't attempt to give moral sanction to the actions of the women featured within it. It embraces them with all their flaws.

How to read this book?

The book can be read any way you want. You will not miss the plot if you start in the middle, or from the end like a rockstar, or the very beginning like a no-nonsense person who means business. Each chapter of the book is independent and features different Badass Begums from different eras and historical epochs. The chapters talk about three things: the woman herself, the architecture she built and the present condition of those buildings. It explores how these women wanted to be remembered and how they are remembered in the present time. The book focuses on ten such women who contributed to the city's fabric through their commissioned works. The chapters include maps and images to give you context of the places, and how they looked before and after. So, even if you have not visited Delhi, do not worry. I will hold your hand through the chapters and help you envision an unseen world.

So, my dear readers, if you are considering buying this book, or have fortunately bought this book, I welcome you inside the world of Badass Begums.

1

The Woman Who Built Chandni Chowk

Jahanara Begum

On a foggy December morning in 2023, I hailed a rickshaw from Sunehri Masjid, Daryaganj.

'How much to Town Hall? Ghanta Ghar?' I asked the question for the hundredth time this year.

'*Sau rupay*, Rs 100!' the paan-chewing bhaiya responded without hesitation. Bargaining was pointless; I had lost this delicate negotiation dance too many times. I climbed onto the rickshaw which started out slow, ignoring traffic rules, as it pedalled diagonally into the cloth market near Jama Masjid's Gate No. 3. From the main lane of Chawri Bazaar, the rickshaw took a right towards Nai Sadak, where most shops were yet to open. Only the vendors selling hot paranthas, with dollops of chutney and pickle, were busy serving daily-wage labourers. On the pavement, thick, milky tea was being brewed—an energizing treat for itinerant traders. Soon, a yellow building came into view. The rickshaw crossed the straight road of Nai Sadak and reached a chowk. This chowk opened on three sides: Nai Sadak to the south, Fatehpuri Masjid to the west and Lal Mandir to the east. The north side of the chowk was blocked by a gigantic yellow building, which had narrow gullies on both sides.

I stepped onto the empty chowk and crossed the street to the pavement outside the yellow building, where local vendors have created a mini market alongside the main bazaar. Radhe Golgappe Wallah stood next to Pyarelal, who sold bhelpuri; Manohar Lal sold chole kulche; and Asaf Miyan has been selling birdseed for the past thirty-five years on the pavement.

A lady in a burqa made her way and opened the creaky gate of Town Hall and scattered birdseed on its barren courtyard. Within seconds, hundreds of pigeons came flocking. It is a daily business of this place to sell birdseed to several residents of Old Delhi who believe offering food to birds is a noble habit. Sadly, the statue of Arya Samaj leader Swami Shraddhanand in front of the Town Hall courtyard would feel otherwise. Several pigeons have shat on it and sat on its shoulders, making the features of the black stone statue unrecognizable. I looked at Town Hall: broken windows, some hanging on their hinges and ready to fall, the white trim of the two-storey building blackening with age. I took out my phone and studied an old painting of the same building on my screen, realizing how much had changed.

'Everything you built is now just a memory. Where are you, Begum Jahanara?' I murmured to no one in particular.

In 1614, in the dusty, sacred town of Ajmer, the cry of a newborn broke the silence in the chamber. Prince Shah Jahan's child was born to his wife Mumtaz Mahal (then known as Anjuman Begum).[1] Though they had previously lost a daughter, Hur-un-Nissa Begum, fate allowed this newborn to live, and the family rejoiced at the survival of their child.[2]

Throughout Jahanara's life, her father Shah Jahan favoured her over his other children, an indulgence that could've gone horribly wrong. But in this case, it didn't. Instead, it helped nurture Jahanara into one of the most influential ladies of the Mughal Empire and the architect of Old Delhi.

In the early years, Jahanara was entrusted to Sati-un-Nissa Khanam, sister of the poet laureate of Jahangir's court, Talib Amuli.[3] Sati-un-Nissa, celebrated for her mastery over not only the Quran and Persian literature, but also over household management, medicine and social etiquette, proved to be an ideal mentor for the cherished royal daughter. It was customary in the Mughal court to provide comprehensive education to princesses—ranging from literature and painting to polo, chess and hunting. Royal women also had unfettered access to the Kitab Khana (Akbar's library in Agra Fort), brimming with texts on religion, astronomy, grammar and language, penned in Persian, Turkish and various Indian dialects. In such a nurturing environment, Jahanara's intellect and creativity flourished.

In February 1628, Shah Jahan finally ascended the throne and gave his beloved daughter a gift of one lakh asharfi (gold coins) and four lakh rupees, along with an annual income of six lakh rupees—half in cash and half via jagir.[4] But in June 1631, tragedy struck. Mumtaz died from complications during the birth of her fourteenth child, plunging the royal household into deep sorrow. Jahanara, who was just seventeen, was suddenly saddled with the weight of responsibilities.[5] As the eldest daughter, she had little time to mourn. Not only did she have to look after her siblings— including a newborn sister—but she also had to tend to her grief-stricken father, who had effectively withdrawn from courtly life. Despite the presence of other senior women in the zenana, Jahanara emerged as the empire's First Lady.[6] Shah Jahan divided Mumtaz Mahal's vast estate among his children, granting Jahanara half of the ten million rupees and the royal seal. Her allowance rose from six to ten lakhs, and she became the first Mughal daughter to be named Padshah Begum (empress)—a title typically reserved for an emperor's wife or mother. Shah Jahan also bestowed upon her the epithet 'Sahibat al-Zamani' (Lady of the Age), cementing her role as the foremost woman of the empire. This was extremely rare in Mughal India. Royal women had influence, yes, but official titles like this were given to very few.

Imagine being seventeen, and waking up one morning to find that you now have to navigate not only the management of an entire zenana (often comprising hundreds of women) but also courtly politics. Jahanara had to learn quickly—especially when it came to the nuanced art of negotiations to maintain peace and harmony in the palace. Being the eldest, Jahanara had several siblings who looked up to her, and now considered her as their mother. Yet, by the end of the year, she had successfully managed to bring her father out of mourning and also planned a lavish wedding for her brother, Dara Shikoh. Jahanara silently steered the Mughal Empire through a perilous time. But this wasn't the end to her story. Jahanara had a grand vision for the empire's capital.

And there I was, standing at the doorstep of one of her marvels.

The making of Chandni Chowk—where the world met

Commissioned by Jahanara in 1650, Town Hall (as it is known today) was first known as 'Begum ki Serai'. That Shah Jahan personally visited the serai and oversaw the work his daughter had done, underscores both its significance and Jahanara's standing in the imperial family. This two-storey serai covered approximately 1,674 square feet and contained ninety rooms, each adorned with exquisite frescoes.[7] Entering from the Chandni Chowk side, visitors were greeted by a spacious courtyard, complete with a large pool, greenery and a network of water channels. A mosque occupied one corner, while a balcony on the upper level afforded a superb view of Chandni Chowk.

The ground level featured arcaded rooms along with shops offering crockery, toys, bangles and clothing. Tall bastions flanked each side and the entire structure gleamed in white limestone. Two entrances welcomed visitors: one facing Chandni Chowk's main thoroughfare and another leading to a garden called 'Begum ka Bagh'. Jahanara found inspiration for this design in a comparable serai in Isfahan, Iran. In 1658, the French traveller François Bernier, who visited the Mughal Empire, praised the serai in his accounts:

> The other edifice in Dehly to which I would draw your attention is what they call the Karuansara of the Princess, because it was built by the celebrated Begum-Saheb, Chah-Jehan's eldest daughter, of whom I have so often spoken in my history of the late war. Not only this Princess, but all the Omrahs who wished to gain the favour of the old Monarch, embellished the new city at their own expense. The Karuansara is in the form of a large square with arcades, like our Place Royale, except that the arches are separated from each other by partitions, and have small chambers at their inner extremities. Above the arcades runs a gallery all around the building, into which open the same number of chambers as there are below. This place is the rendezvous of the rich Persian, Uzbek, and other foreign merchants, who in general may be accommodated with empty chambers, in which they remain with perfect security, the gate being closed at night. If in Paris we had a score of similar structures,

distributed in different parts of the city, strangers on their first arrival would be less embarrassed than at present to find a safe and reasonable lodging. They might remain in them a few days until they had seen their acquaintance and looked out at leisure for more convenient apartments. Such places would become warehouses for all kinds of merchandise, and the general resort of foreign merchants.[8]

Begum ki Serai was far from an ordinary travellers' inn; it functioned more like a luxurious medieval hotel. The seventeenth-century Italian traveller Niccolao Manucci observed:

This is the most beautiful sarae in Hindustan, with upper chambers adorned with many paintings, and it has a lovely garden in which are ornamental reservoirs. In this sarae there put up none but Mogul and Persian merchants. The king went to view the work that had been done for his beloved Begum Saheb, and he praised her energy and liberality.[9]

Adjacent to the caravanserai, Jahanara constructed one of the city's largest hammams (public baths), measuring roughly 180 feet by 60 feet, complete with multiple rooms and porticos. It served two key purposes: providing bathing facilities for travellers residing in the serai and supporting pilgrims visiting Fatehpuri Masjid, at the end of the street, who traditionally performed ablutions before entering. Beside the hammam stood an octagonal pool, once shimmering under the moonlight—chandni reflecting softly in its waters—which gave the street its iconic name: Chandni Chowk.

It might be hard to picture now, but this part of Shahjahanabad was once the glittering crossroads of the world. Turbaned merchants from Bukhara, jewel traders from Yemen and Ottoman envoys adorned in silk brushed past each other under the same archways. The air was heavy with the scent of rosewater, while the streets echoed with chatter in Persian, Arabic, Uzbek, French and Hindavi. And water fountains, pools and canals were the soul of the city. Today's parched Delhi would barely recognize its watery past. As the nineteenth-century historian Sir Sayyed Ahmad Khan recounts:

Chandni Chowk [or the Moonlit Square, so called because of its beauty when seen on moonlit nights] lies beyond the platform that houses the police station [Kotwali Chabutra].[10] It is a 480-goz bazaar, with a 100-goz square [chowk] that has a square tank [hauz] in the centre. It is the 100-goz square that is called Chandni Chowk. It is beyond my ability to describe its beauty and attraction. The evenings are magical here with the youth, princes and nobles coming for an evening stroll and entertainment. Very attractively built shops line both sides of the square, selling all kinds of wares. There is nothing in the world that is not sold here.[11]

Merchants travelled vast distances to bring their goods to Chandni Chowk. Traders from Turkey, Zanzibar, Syria,

Yemen, Arabia, Iraq, Khurasan, China and Tibet set up shop alongside Europeans from England and Holland. Their wares turned the market into a treasure trove: rubies from Badakhshan gleamed alongside pearls from Oman, while fresh fruits from Kashmir and Central Asia added splashes of vibrant colour. Weapons, fine cloth, perfumes, elephants, horses, camels, exotic birds, water pipes and delicate sweets filled the air with a symphony of sights, scents and sounds.

Even the East India Company merchants found their place here, offering tapestries, wool and broadcloth to the discerning nobility. The streets were alive with the sounds of haggling, the aroma of sweets and spices, and the colourful sights of dancers and storytellers. The bazaar, however, was more than just a place of trade. It was alive with energy and entertainment. Boys and girls danced in front of shops to the rhythm of passing crowds, their movements a joyful distraction. Storytellers sat cross-legged on carpets, weaving tales of fasting and hardship during Ramadan or recounting the tragic saga of Husayn during Muharram, their voices drawing listeners into distant worlds.

The shops, small and neatly partitioned, were tucked under arcades. Thin walls separated one establishment from the next, and behind each shop, a door opened to a compact warehouse where merchants stored their surplus goods. Above these warehouses, the shopkeepers, along with their families and servants, lived in modest quarters, creating a lively blend of commerce and domesticity. The kahwakhanas of Chandni Chowk, which were spread across the city, were not merely coffee shops; they were vibrant hubs of intellectual exchange, cultural interaction and poetic expression. These establishments, scattered across the bustling lanes of Shahjahanabad, offered steaming cups of aromatic qahwa—strong, spiced coffee often infused with cardamom. The warm, inviting atmosphere made the kahwakhanas a favourite gathering place for scholars, poets, merchants and nobles alike. Inside them, the air buzzed with animated discussions. Scholars debated philosophy, ethics and politics, while poets recited their latest ghazals and sought critique from their peers. The walls often bore calligraphic verses from Persian and Urdu poetry, lending an artistic touch to the ambience. These coffee houses became informal academies, where ideas flowed as freely as the coffee, shaping the intellectual and cultural fabric of the city. The clientele of the kahwakhanas was as diverse as the streets of Chandni Chowk itself. Merchants paused between transactions to exchange news from distant lands, while travellers shared tales of their journeys. Courtiers and nobles occasionally graced these establishments, drawn by the charm of lively conversations.

On many evenings, musicians would join in, filling the space with the soulful strains of the sitar or the rhythmic beats of the tabla, creating an atmosphere that blurred the lines between the mundane and the sublime. For poets, the kahwakhanas were especially significant. It was here that they tested their verses before an audience that was both critical and appreciative. The gatherings often turned into impromptu mushairas (poetry recitals), where the brilliance of

Mir, Sauda or Ghalib might have lit up the night. The debates and discussions in these spaces inspired some of the greatest works in Urdu and Persian literature.

Jahanara collaborated with Mughal officer Ali Vardi Khan, in charge of drainage and irrigation, to channel the Yamuna River into the heart of the city. This waterway, known as Faiz Nahr or the 'Victorious Stream', entered through Kabuli Gate, one of the thirteen gates of Shahjahanabad's fortified walls.[12] From there, it flowed through Chandni Chowk, creating a shimmering canal that mirrored the moonlight at night, lending the street its poetic name. Lined with lush trees, the canal cooled the air and enhanced the bazaar's beauty, eventually terminating at a tank near Fatehpuri Masjid, as part of a sophisticated irrigation system.

Stretching some 1,520 yards and containing 1,560 shops, Chandni Chowk served as the city's vibrant commercial heart.[13] It connected the Lahori Gate of the Red Fort to the Lahori Gate of the city walls, effectively functioning as a central axis of Shahjahanabad, much like Rajpath in New Delhi. Chandni Chowk was divided into distinct bazaars, each specializing in unique goods.

Unfortunately, the hammam, the octagonal pool, the water channel and the serai are all gone. The pool which once caught moonlight in its ripples was cemented over by the British post 1857. The hammam? Broken and discarded brick by brick by the British who wanted to erase any living memory of the Mughals. The serai, once a rest stop, was also removed and redesigned. Delhi lost more than just buildings—it lost the sound of splashing water, the swirl of silk robes, the scent of rosewater, and the daily theatre of travellers and traders in the global city. What is left is just a shadow—but our walk through old Shahjahanabad isn't over yet. There is still some magic left in these streets.

Begum ka Bagh: Creating spaces for women

Leaving Town Hall, I proceed straight, then turn right along a broad lane lined with fabric and suit shops. A short distance ahead rises a tall mosque with freshly painted red minarets, while the Town Hall's imposing facade remains to my right. Eventually, I reach a towering iron gate, beyond which a wide courtyard stretches before the Town Hall. Two security guards sit on chairs, soaking up the weak winter sun. Further on, I spot a public clock atop the Town Hall—its hands immobile, permanently stuck at one o'clock. The grimy, broken glass obscures the numbers. A portico stands in front of the building, once no doubt used by horse-drawn carriages. Off to one side of the courtyard, near a small garden gate, sits a fountain painted red, white and blue. This is the Town Hall's front approach.

One gate of the Town Hall courtyard leads into Mahatma Gandhi Park, formerly known as Begum ka Bagh or Sahiba Abad ka Bagh. The garden was unlike anything anyone had ever seen before. Imagine a space where women could freely talk, move and relax—a safe public space in the world of men. Such reserved spaces still do not exist in the urban landscape.

Begum ka Bagh was once the town's principal attraction; it spanned a rectangular area of roughly 50 acres—some 3,000-feet long and 700-feet wide. In earlier times, Faiz Nahr flowed in from the Kabuli Gate and wound through this garden towards the Red Fort.[14] Possessing a refined aesthetic eye like her grandfather, Jahanara personally chose her gardeners and maintained multiple gardens: three in Kashmir (Bagh-i Aishabad, Bagh-i Nur Afshan, Bagh-i Safa), others in Ambala and Surat, plus another in Bachchol. She also received gardens as royal gifts, such as Bagh-i Safa in Kashmir and Bagh-i Jahanara in Agra, the latter originally her mother's.[15]

At its prime, Begum ka Bagh was the 'OG hangout spot' for ladies. Imagine strolling through rows of jamun, mango, orange, neem and lemon trees, with the sweet smell of jasmine in the air.

White marble baradaris (twelve-pillared pavilions) graced both sides to provide space for musicians to perform and were also an ideal backdrop for a leisurely afternoon. Women cooled off in the gentle mist thrown by the marble fountains.

Whereas noblemen roamed the streets of Chandni Chowk—itself Jahanara's design—Begum ka Bagh provided a rare public space where women could shed their purdah and find recreation. Men—irrespective of rank or order—were not allowed in this exclusive female space. The garden had swings with silk ropes and sandalwood planks, suspended from mango trees, where women often gathered to sing monsoon songs. Jahanara's commitment to female agency is evident in her annual 'Pankho ka Mela', which loosely translates as 'festival of fans', held here. Women entrepreneurs sold an assortment of goods—vibrant toys, glossy bangles, embroidered garments, polished utensils and mouth-watering treats—while poetry recitals, musical shows and charitable events further enlivened the occasion.

One of Chandni Chowk's juiciest bit of gossip involved a bold (or possibly, very foolish) young man who just had to know what magic lay behind the walls of Begum ka Bagh. Tempted by sounds of laughter and music, and the scent of jasmine, he snuck inside, only to be immediately caught by one of Jahanara's fierce attendants and dragged straight to the princess. Now, most people would have been terrified, facing the wrath of a Mughal royal. But not this guy. With nothing to lose, he launched into a flowery verse praising the garden and its legendary mistress. Jahanara, equal parts amused and impressed, let him go with a royal smirk and a wave of her hand!

Never one to play nice with the patriarchy and social injustices that came disguised as 'religious reforms', Jahanara had her own way of shutting down nonsense—especially when it came wrapped in moral policing. Niccolao Manucci gives us a delicious anecdote from 1666: An uptight, influential mullah persuaded Aurangzeb to prohibit women from wearing tight trousers, insisting on looser ones instead. The same rule also aimed to ban women from drinking or consuming opium, nutmeg, bhang and other intoxicants.

When Jahanara heard of this sartorial and social clampdown, she didn't write a polite letter or send a polite envoy—she threw a party. She invited the wives of the empire's most respected qazis and clerics over, poured them wine, and made sure the tight trousers worn by the women at the party were visible.[16]

So, when Aurangzeb showed up to deliver the moral lecture, Jahanara calmly ushered him inside the purdah. There they were—tipsy, tangled in their trousers, mid-giggle. She looked him straight in the eye and asked: 'If this is divine law, why couldn't your scholars enforce it in their own homes?' Aurangzeb, caught off-guard and outplayed, quietly scrapped the entire order.[17]

Let's get one thing straight—Jahanara was a strategist. She didn't just build pretty buildings—she had a motive and a goal behind these constructions. Her caravanserai was not just a pit stop for tired travellers; it was a tool for soft power, diplomacy and empire-building.

Jahanara's 'matronage' was part of her *healing architecture*, such as gardens, baths, serais—her architecture didn't just serve state and trade, but nourished the body and soul. She balanced the line between pragmatic and wellness architecture so well. The bustling Chandni Chowk imagery I painted earlier—merchants from Zanzibar, England, Tibet; weapons, perfumes, elephants—shows how globalized Shahjahanabad was, and Jahanara was the heart of this new change. In a heavily gendered empire, these structures, by virtue of their scale, public visibility and accessibility, became a medium to reclaim space. Architecture was used as a vehicle for reputation-building. The fact that Jahanara chose to invest in a serai—a space that facilitated travel, trade and cultural exchange—speaks of her active participation in the commercial and political lifeblood of the empire. These structures were not just ornamental, they were economic arteries.

Determined to secure a lasting place in the public mind, she commissioned a number of buildings and garden complexes, overseeing a total of twenty-one structures across Kashmir, Agra and Delhi. Sadly, the tumult of 1857 largely expunged her legacy from collective memory, leaving her name preserved mostly in Mughal records and travellers' accounts.

Stepping into the park from the fountain gate, I notice a blue-painted water channel bisecting the grounds. This is not the original channel constructed by Jahanara. Following it leads to a statue of Mahatma Gandhi at the park's centre—now called Mahatma Gandhi Park, open equally to men and women. Gandhi's brown figure stands poised with his walking stick, an eternal paradox of motion frozen in bronze. Gone are the fruit-bearing trees of old. They have been now replaced by the ordinary aesthetic of a typical public garden.

While the park's original dimensions remained intact, its perimeter walls were refashioned with imposing new gates. The nahr (channel) and a selection of trees were retained to foster a pleasant promenade. Of the two baradaris, one was converted into a library, the other into a menagerie, popular with city folk, though access to the space was restricted. Two wells likewise survived to aid with irrigation.[18]

Further modern touches introduced lawns, strawberry patches, potted plants and curving pathways—replacing the straight khiyabans (avenues)—illuminated by newly installed lamps. A cricket pitch was laid, complemented by two tennis courts, christened the 'Aitchison Tennis Courts' after Lieutenant Governor C.U. Aitchison of Punjab. A large nursery stocked with exotic flora and ornamental decorations lent additional charm. In the absence of an imposing ruin, two Mughal-era relics—a marble basin and an elephant sculpture—were initially displayed but later removed and relocated to the Red Fort.[19]

An elaborate bandstand became another attraction in the garden, hosting regular performances by military ensembles. Nearby stood the neo-classical nineteenth-century British Town Hall, on its own lush island and linked to the garden by a direct walkway flanked by fountains, palm trees and flower beds, leading visitors towards the bandstand.

Even before the more modern changes, in 1902, a road was constructed to connect the Old Delhi railway station and Chandni Chowk, slicing through the garden for convenience. Named 'Clarke Road' after Commissioner R. Clarke, it included a decorative wrought-iron gateway—Clarke Gate—which opened the garden to broader public use.[20]

Renamed 'Queen's Garden', the green expanse was hailed as a 'Jewel in the Crown'—a prototype of modern urban parks, aiming to promote visitors' physical, moral and intellectual wellness. Multiple factors shaped its redesign, including municipal ownership, its location near British quarters inside the walled city and the availability of ample space. Unlike a funerary garden, this site lent itself to more radical changes. After 1857, the British were keen to present themselves as custodians of India's architectural heritage, a stance that further guided the park's makeover.

Interestingly, the transformation of both the bagh and the serai began even before 1857, though it truly gained momentum by 1860. After the Uprising, many Mughal structures were levelled—an effort by the British to erase memories of the old regime and assert their own authority. In the process, Jahanara's serai was fully demolished and replaced by a Victorian Edwardian edifice known as the Lawrence Institute. It took five years to finish and was named after John Lawrence, the lieutenant governor of Punjab. Inside, one could find a literary society, a chamber of commerce and even a small museum. In 1866, the Municipal Corporation took over and renamed it Town Hall. From 1866 until 2019, this building served as the Municipal Corporation of Delhi (MCD) office, after which the office moved to the towering Shyama Prasad Mukherjee Civic Centre. Sadly, any clear sign of Jahanara's Mughal heritage vanished beneath this new European-style facade. Two stone elephants, originally adorning the Delhi Gate of the Red Fort, were reassembled from over a hundred fragments unearthed in 1863, then placed outside the Town Hall for a while—only to be removed and discarded later.

The bagh, too, eventually fell into disrepair, its once-gushing water channels silting up and its plumbing failing. The baradaris were dismantled, and overall care for the park's greenery dwindled. The bagh's eastern portion was gifted to the eighteenth-century mercenary Begum Samru by Akbar Shah II.[21] A statue of Queen Victoria later graced the middle of the park, prompting folks to call it 'Queen Victoria Park'. After Independence, her statue was moved to the Delhi College of Art, replaced by one of Mahatma Gandhi, which still stands there today.[22] To appreciate the park's former vastness, imagine strolling from National Club all the way to Lajpat Rai Market—a solid twenty-minute walk. That entire span was once Begum ka Bagh.

Rather than attempt the long, winding walk just yet, I head back to the Town Hall along the main road. Nearby lies a vacant square, known simply as 'Chowk area', where the octagonal pool and hammam once stood. Curious, I ask a rickshaw driver, '*Ghanta Ghar kahan hai* (Where's the Clock Tower)?', to which he responds, '*Wahan par hota tha, ab kuch nahin hai* (It used to be there, now there's nothing).' Standing in that empty space, I can only imagine the layers of sand and history covering the long-lost pool and hammam beneath my feet.

My strolls around Old Delhi left me eager to learn more about Begum Jahanara: what drove her to build so extensively here, how she financed these grand projects and just how involved she was in their design. From my university books, I already knew that Jahanara became Padshah Begum after her mother's passing, but there was so much more to uncover about the intellect and artistry behind this remarkable woman.

One pivotal venture, undertaken in her role as Padshah Begum, involved arranging the wedding of her brother, Prince Dara Shikoh, with Nadira Begum. The lavish ceremony cost an astonishing Rs 32 lakh. In the grand scheme of Mughal court life, the successful orchestration of this wedding cemented Jahanara's influence. Over the following two decades, she provided steadfast counsel to her father and Dara Shikoh on matters of state, governance and diplomacy—all from behind the diaphanous curtains of the zenana. Nobles, kings and visiting ambassadors regularly sought Jahanara's mediation, convinced that her single word of recommendation could alter a petitioner's destiny. By most accounts, Jahanara was fabulously wealthy—perhaps the richest woman in India at the time. The Venetian traveller Niccolao Manucci estimated her annual income at three million rupees.[23]

In addition, at the age of thirty, her father gave her the prosperous city of Surat.[24] She also owned a vessel called the *Sahibi*, which regularly sailed to Mecca, carrying pilgrims and distributing rice to those in need. Jahanara cultivated trade ties with both the English and the Dutch, fostering a highly lucrative business. Manucci also noted her remarkable power and esteem at court.[25] When she 'leaves her palace to go to court, she proceeds in great pomp, with much cavalry and infantry and many eunuchs ... surround her closely, push on one side everyone they find in front of them shouting out, pushing and assaulting everyone without the least respect of persons.'[26]

Jahanara also held the prestigious right to bestow khilats (robes of honour) upon foreign envoys and notable court figures. Through cash allowances, land grants and tax revenues, princesses like Jahanara commanded institutionalized financial power. The scale of her wealth directly translated into her ability to move freely between Delhi, Agra, Kashmir and Ajmer; fund monument construction across regions; and commission public structures rather than purely private tombs and palaces. Unlike many queens and princesses globally, who were confined to their court or city, Jahanara's wealth made her a pan-imperial patron.

Jahanara's pivot to Sufism

Sufism inspired Jahanara to transcend the confines of her gender and imperial duties, and engage in charitable acts and architectural projects that reflected her devotion. Between 1640 and 1650, Jahanara undertook an ambitious range of projects, completing nineteen imperial constructions which included bathhouses, bazaars and gardens in Agra, Delhi, Ajmer and Kashmir. Among her notable projects was the Mulla Shah Mosque and Khanaqah Complex in Srinagar, which she commissioned in 1650. The Khanaqah Complex not only demonstrated her architectural vision but also her alignment with Sufi principles of community and devotion.

Her deep involvement in Sufism is a major thread in her life. Through her, the Mughal court's engagement with

Sufism stayed alive even as Aurangzeb's reign became more orthodox. Her connection to spiritual giants Mian Mir and Mulla Shah made her a respected figure in religious circles, too. Her nineteen projects post Sufism (bathhouses, bazaars, gardens) show that architecture for her was not just to create a legacy but was also about ethical responsibility: serving the community, promoting public health, facilitating commerce, creating spaces of peace. Architecture, for her, was a form of Sufi practice. In her writing, especially the *Sahibiyya*, she's very aware of being trapped by her imperial role. She talks about being lost (this despite being a princess and a Padshah Begum), burdened by imperial expectations—which is very rare and so very fresh to read! How often do you find royals this honest? So, when she found the Qadiriyya Sufi order, it gave her freedom, identity and purpose outside the courtly cage. She was no longer just 'Shah Jahan's daughter'; she was a spiritual authority, too.

Jahanara was not trying to rebel against the Timurid order, rather, she was trying to embody it; she was redefining what empire could mean. Timurid and Mughal ideals greatly valued mysticism, beauty and public welfare.

Her steadfast Sufi connection also clarifies why—and where—she chose to be buried.

On a quest to find her final resting place, I visited Nizamuddin Dargah in Delhi. This area can be chaotic and impoverished, populated by the homeless and an occasional con artist. If you're new to it, it's wise to bring someone experienced to navigate the winding alleys. Over many heritage visits, I've memorized the way. Roses and attar fragrance hang heavy in the air, courtesy of shops selling floral offerings for the saint's shrine. It is around a fifteen-minute walk from the Nizamuddin police station to the inner main shrine. Stepping inside the shrine, I headed for the marble enclosure near the Jamaat Khana, which has only one entranceway that can be entered through a very narrow passageway. For many years now, authorities have dumped debris there making it impossible to enter. This place is in a sad state of neglect; a marble slab has fallen on the main sarcophagus. Here lies Princess Jahanara.

From 1658, when court politics intensified, Jahanara chose to remain with her father, Shah Jahan, who was imprisoned by Aurangzeb in Agra Fort, caring for him until his death eight years later.[27] Despite several invitations from Aurangzeb, Jahanara only returned to Delhi after her father's death. Jahanara's choice to be imprisoned with her father for eight years shows steadfastness but also immense personal agency. She could have lived freely in wealth under Aurangzeb, but she chose loyalty over comfort. This shows a kind of political and moral defiance—she didn't endorse Aurangzeb's usurpation even after he won. Jahanara made hard political and emotional choices at a huge personal cost.

Aurangzeb welcomed her warmly, reinstating her as Padshah Begum, removing their younger sister Roshanara Begum. Jahanara was given one of the spacious mansions of

Ali Vardi Khan near the banks of the Yamuna in Kashmiri Gate.[28] In 1671, following Roshanara's death, Jahanara grew keenly aware of her own mortality and resolved to plan her resting place.[29] She selected the Nizamuddin Dargah of the Chishti order, a revered site in Delhi, perfectly aligned with her Sufi devotion. Unlike the grand mausolea of her parents, she chose a modest resting place. A simple marble enclosure containing three cenotaphs: hers at the centre, flanked by those of Mirza Nilli, son of Emperor Shah Alam II, on the right, and Jamal-un-Nissa, daughter of Emperor Akbar II, on the left.

Jahanara's grave is distinctive for its hollowed top, originally intended to hold soil and grass, in a nod to her ascetic ideals—today, it brims with rose petals as a mark of reverence.[30] Revered by many as 'Faqirah'(female Sufi saint), Jahanara is said to bestow healing upon those with mental afflictions, leading families to bring affected women here in search of a cure. The scene can become unsettling at times, particularly when some of the women attempt to escape, adding a mystical dimension to the place.

The plaque above Jahanara's cenotaph begins with the name of Allah, 'Hayyul Al Qayyum (He is the Living, the Sustaining)', and the last four lines of the inscription read: *'The mortal simplistic Princess Jahanara, Disciple of the Khwaja Moin-ud-Din Chishti, Daughter of Shah Jahan the Conqueror, May Allah illuminate his proof.*[31] This inscription, written in 1681, links her directly to her Sufi devotion, her royal lineage, and her legacy as a powerful spiritual and imperial figure.

The tomb itself is enclosed by four marble walls, each about 16 feet by 12 feet wide and more than 8 feet high. The walls are decorated with three panels each, except for the wall containing the door, which has only two panels, with the door occupying the central position. The walls are adorned with intricate marble latticework, and the top of the enclosure is decorated with a perforated marble balustrade, though only a fragment of this ornament remains today. The four corners of the enclosure were originally crowned with small marble minarets, but only two have survived.

Jahanara's grave is placed in the centre of the enclosure, and at its head is a narrow slab of marble, standing about 6-feet high. The inscription on the headstone is inlaid with black marble letters and carries a verse that is believed to have been written by Jahanara herself. The verse reads:

Let nothing but the green grass conceal my grave. The grass is the best covering for the tombs of the poor in spirit; the humble, the transitory Jahanara, the disciple of the holy men of Chishti; the daughter of the Emperor Shah Jahan; may God illuminate his intentions.

Aurangzeb, deeply moved by her death, adhered to religious guidelines by keeping two-thirds of her estate and allowing the remaining third to fund her intended charities.[32] Manucci writes that she distributed the bulk of her jewels among her nieces, with Jahanzeb Begum (Dara Shikoh's daughter, whom Jahanara raised) inheriting the largest portion.[33]

Jahanara died much as she had lived: on her own terms—choosing her resting place and directing her wealth's final destiny. Though Delhi might have largely forgotten her, a handful of us still honour her memory as a beacon of inspiration. Jahanara breaks the stereotype about royal women in the history. She wasn't just sitting in the background, trapped in the harem—she was leading Sufi orders, building mosques, writing books, mediating political conflicts and advising emperors. Her life shows that even within rigid systems women carved out agency and shaped major events.

Knowing about Jahanara helps us reclaim these lost legacies and understand that power in history often looked very different when it came through women's hands. Yes, Jahanara had immense privilege. That doesn't make her irrelevant but an important case study on how even women with advantages had to navigate deeply patriarchal systems to leave a lasting impact. Even with her status, Jahanara constantly had to legitimize her authority through religion, charity and strategic alliances. In fact, instead of withdrawing into luxury, she invested in public works, supported Sufi causes and pushed for peace during the civil war. Jahanara used her privilege as a tool for doing something meaningful, for doing lasting work, giving us an understanding that can help us think more critically about power, gender and agency today.

According to Niccolao Manucci, a seventeenth-century Italian traveller who spent decades in Mughal India and recorded his experiences in *Storia do Mogor*, Jahanara Begum, the eldest daughter of Shah Jahan, was one of the richest women of her time!

Manucci wrote that she owned several villages, including Achchol, Farjahara, Safapur, Doraha, Medina and Panipat, earning a staggering ten million dams (copper coins) from Panipat alone. He even claimed that the village of Doraha was granted to her just to maintain her gardens, and the revenue from Surat, one of the empire's biggest trading ports, was allotted solely for her betel expenses!

Of course, Manucci was an outsider observing the Mughal court, and his accounts often mixed fact with fascination. Still, his descriptions offer a rare glimpse into how awe-inspiring Jahanara's wealth and influence appeared to those who witnessed her era.

2

The Power Broker

Zeenat Mahal

I am with an *Indian Express* journalist who wants to explore Khari Baoli, Delhi's largest spice market. Our walk has almost ended, and they want to be dropped off at Chawri Bazaar metro station. Before I finish the walk, I take them to Harnarains, the oldest pickle shop in Delhi. Founded by Lala Harnarain in 1808, the shop offers an astonishing range of pickles—lime, mango, green chilli, lemon, mixed pickle, garlic, gooseberry, carrot, cauliflower, and more. They also sell sherbet, murabba, chutneys, syrups, gulkand, papad, and even ingredients for making Christmas cake. Serving everyone from Mahatma Gandhi to the Nehru family, Harnarains is now a permanent vendor for Rashtrapati Bhawan events.

After buying a few items, we head back to the main road. At the T-junction on our left sits Gole Di Hatti—established in 1954 and famed for its spicy, delicious kulhad palak chawal. We turn right, passing Fatehpuri Masjid and Chaina

Ram (my stomach rumbles at the thought of chole bhature, but I'm on assignment). Then, from Chaina Ram, we take another right and enter Galli Badiyan.

It's a short walk. At the end of the street, we see fruit and vegetable vendors sitting on the floor, framed by the backdrop of a forgotten haveli with bright blue doors and ornate windows. We turn left into Galli Lal Kuan, bustling with Sunday activity: vendors hawking shiny but flimsy utensils and cheap plastic goods. E-rickshaws whiz past, horns blaring, forcing us to pause every few steps. Suddenly, I stop in my tracks. 'Do you see this? The two balconies?' I ask Abhinav, the journalist who has been blindly following me.

'The red ones?'

'Yes, the red ones. This is the haveli of the last Mughal Empress, Zeenat Mahal!' I tell him excitedly.

'But the hoarding says it's a school. Look! Zeenat Mahal Govt Sarvodaya Girls Senior School.'

'Yes, you're correct. That's because the haveli has been turned into a school.' I sigh impatiently. I always get worked up when I see important heritage structures in a lousy condition. 'Let's go somewhere quiet and talk about this,' I tell him firmly, ignoring my growling stomach.

In the twilight of the Mughal Empire, amid the decaying grandeur of Delhi's Red Fort, a young woman stepped into history. She was eighteen, sharp-eyed and unexpectedly powerful.

Zeenat Mahal was born to be empress. She had no royal lineage, no divine claim to a throne, and yet, by the time the empire collapsed in fire and fury in 1857, hers would be the most talked-about name in the city's crumbling havelis and crowded bazaars. A queen adored and feared, her rise would contrast with the unravelling of the empire itself.

Married at a young age to the ageing Bahadur Shah Zafar—last of the Mughals, the poet-king clinging to the ghost of a former empire—Zeenat Mahal was not content to remain in the shadows of the zenana. Where others saw a dying court and a powerless ruler, she saw opportunity.

And she took it.

She would rule over the harem and the emperor's heart, and make decisions that would ripple through the court like wildfire. Her ambition stirred gossip. Her defiance drew scorn. And her name would eventually be entangled in one of the empire's darkest scandals: betrayal, bloodshed and murder.

But before all that—before the revolt, before the fall of Delhi, before the exile and ruin—there was a girl in Lal Kuan. A girl who captivated an emperor and bent a fading dynasty around her will.

In 1840, Zeenat Mahal, daughter of the aristocrat Nawab Ahmad Quli Khan, married Bahadur Shah Zafar. She was barely nineteen. He was sixty-four.[1]

On the day of their wedding, the emperor gave her the title 'Zeenat Mahal'. Her birth name remains lost in history. Contemporary Urdu newspapers noted that she received a personal allowance of Rs 500 per month and an alimony of Rs

7 lakh.[2] Gossip swirled around the court, suggesting that the emperor had been enchanted by her tomboyish appearance and manner.

This was just juicy gossip, about his preferences—rumours that his father, Emperor Akbar Shah II, had once doubted his son's interest in women altogether.[3] Such assumptions proved false. Zafar not only had a large harem, but he also married several women before Zeenat, and four more after her. In all, he fathered thirty-one daughters and sixteen sons.[4]

But none held his heart quite like Zeenat.

Although she tolerated the emperor's many concubines, Zeenat Mahal drew the line at rivals who posed a threat to her political standing. Her chief adversary was Taj Mahal Begum—once the emperor's favourite and credited with helping him ascend the throne. Taj's fall from grace was swift. Shortly after Zeenat entered the imperial household, she ensured Taj was imprisoned—allegedly for an affair with Zafar's nephew, Mirza Karman.[5] But the message was clear: this was Zeenat's court now.

Inside Zeenat Mahal's haveli

Bahadur Shah was utterly besotted. He abandoned royal duties for long stretches, choosing instead to lounge at her newly constructed mansion in Lal Kuan—a scandalous move that made headlines. The Persian newspaper, *Khulasa-e Akhbar*, reported in its edition of 20 April 1849:

> Rumors are rife of the emperor spending as many as twelve days and nights at the haveli of Zeenat Mahal in

Lal Kuan … The Begum spent Rs 1000 a day on this count; what a wonder that one should spend this sum in a day for having invited the emperor! The sweeper at the haveli has lodged a report with the police that the emperor of Delhi has been missing, spending 12 days away with Begum Zeenat Mahal. A humorist made fun of the emperor 'living like a common man', setting aside the norms of royalty?[6]

The gossip wasn't entirely unfair. Zeenat Mahal wielded enormous influence over the emperor's daily life. Some historians interpret this as evidence of genuine love; others see it as a shrewd manipulation of the weak and aging monarch by an ambitious young woman. Either way, the marriage unsettled many in the court. The balance of power had shifted.

The Zeenat Mahal haveli became a symbol of this shift. It wasn't just a royal gift—it was a declaration. The emperor, who should have been the central figure in the court, now revolved around his queen. Some scholars argue that Zeenat herself commissioned and designed the mansion; others believe Zafar built it for her in 1846. Till the 1970s, there was a Persian plaque; engraved on it were the following words:

Kardaye Zafar Zeenat Mahal taamir-e-qasr bi badal
Shud bar majal saal banaye khanah-e-Zeenat Mahal[7]

[The work of Zafar, an unmatched edifice, Zeenat Mahal.

This year commenced, the construction of a house for Zeenat Mahal.]

While it is possible that Zafar commissioned the building, the style and grandeur of the building was absolutely Zeenat Mahal. The interior of the Zeenat Mahal haveli was a world unto itself—a lush, secluded sanctuary, nestled within the chaos of dusty nineteenth-century Delhi. Visitors entered through a red sandstone gateway into a courtyard framed by carved rooms and supported by slender arches. A marble fountain in the middle courtyard sang a quiet watery lullaby, cooling the air and easing the senses. Shade-giving trees lined the inner pavilions. The arches opened to daalans (hallways) and dar daalans (inner hallways). Sunlight filtered softly through the filigree jaali windows and silk drapes decorated the sandstone pillars. Khus mats hung from each of the arches which were sprinkled with water every few hours, releasing the earthy smell associated with Delhi summers. The brocade curtains were scented with jasmine and rosewater. Hookahs stood ready in the corners of the room where eunuchs and servants exchanged gossip and banter that filled the haveli. Silver trays of sherbet and dried fruits made slow rounds, as Zeenat lounged on low seating with plush cushions and engaged in meetings with her trusted counsel. Her appearance beyond the haveli was no less theatrical. Chronicler R.V. Smith recounts how her procession was led by the rhythmic beats of naqqarwallahs (drum beaters), earning her the title of 'Danka Begum' by the locals.[8] As per contemporary historian Zahir Dehlvi, Bahadur Shah Zafar's royal carriage was drawn by sixteen horses, but hers followed close behind, pulled by eight—an exceptional privilege for a queen consort in the frugal Mughal court of the nineteenth century.[9]

Beneath all this finery lay the haveli's secret—cool tehekhanas (dungeons), Delhi's underground network of secret tunnels. Two tunnels were said to have extended from the haveli: one leading to the Red Fort, the other to the Ajmeri Gate. In times of British surveillance, such secret passageways offered swift, discreet movement—escape routes for confidential meetings far from watchful eyes.

Though her private quarters were steeped in luxury and indulgence, Zeenat's ambition was anything but passive. Her marriage to Bahadur Shah Zafar marked not only a turning point for her personal life but also a shift in the imperial balance. Soon after their union, Zeenat Mahal gave birth to a son, Jawan Bakht, a child who would become the centre of all her aspirations. Her goal was clear—she was determined to secure the Mughal throne for him, regardless of the established succession lines that had long been acknowledged by the British.

Zeenat plots for Jawan Bakht's future

Zeenat Mahal's shrewd political acumen and strategic manoeuvring came to the forefront following the death of Bahadur Shah Zafar's eldest surviving son, Mirza Dara Bakht, in 1849. While the British naturally expected Zafar's next son, the accomplished poet, calligrapher and historian Mirza Fakhruddin (Mirza Fakhru), to step into the role of heir apparent, Zeenat Mahal had other plans. Her ambition to secure the throne for her son, Mirza Jawan Bakht, then only an eight-year-old boy, became the focal point of court politics.

Leveraging her influence over Zafar, she orchestrated an effort to bypass the candidate preferred by the British. With her sharp intellect and unwavering resolve, she framed Jawan Bakht's candidacy as legitimate and ideal. Zafar, under her sway, echoed her sentiments in his correspondence with British authorities. In a letter to the lieutenant governor, he elaborated on why Jawan Bakht should succeed him:

> Among my other sons, no one appears to me so fit for the office as Mirza Jawan Bakht, who I am glad to say is endowed with natural good propensities. He has not as yet attained the age of maturity and has not been allowed to mix with people who are not upright. Besides, he is from my lawful wife, who is of very high family, Nawab Zinat Mahal ... Under these circumstances, therefore, he is most fit for the high office of Heir Apparent and he always remains under my eyes, and devotes all his time to learning in different branches of education. I feel satisfied that he will never do anything contrary to my wishes.[10]

Ironically, Zafar's stance contradicted the very principle of primogeniture that once allowed him to succeed against his father Akbar Shah II's objections.

In 1852, Delhi was bedecked like a bride. Zeenat Mahal had decided to get her son married, and she was not sparing any expense to make it the grandest event of the century. It was after a very long time that the city saw the famed

Mughal splendour and luxury once again. Zeenat wanted to present this wedding as the launchpad for Jawan Bakht as the heir apparent to the glorious Mughal throne. Zeenat Mahal spared no expense, echoing Mughal precedents like Princess Jahanara's orchestration of Dara Shikoh's marriage to consolidate her own power. Imperial women have always used weddings to assert their influence and be more visible to the public. Zahir Dehlvi, in *Dastaan-i Ghadar*, writes about the wedding: 'Such beauty and magnificence had never been seen before … At least not in my lifetime. It was a celebration I shall never forget.'[11]

Jawan Bakht—then only eleven—wed Nawab Shah Zamani Begum, his mother's niece, in a lavish ceremony. Interestingly, the wedding turned into a battle of wits between famous nineteenth-century poet Mirza Ghalib and his arch-rival Zauq. Zeenat Mahal had requested Ghalib to write a 'sehra', a poem sung in honour of the groom, Jawan Bakht. Mirza Ghalib did write the sehra but also used it as an opportunity to take a dig at both Emperor Bahadur Shah Zafar and his imperial court poet Zauq. When Zauq, after a brief illness, returned to the court, he read the poem and was absolutely furious Mirza Ghalib was advised by his friends to write a letter of apology to both the emperor and the court poet. Mirza Ghalib grudgingly agreed, knowing his head was at stake![12]

As Zafar aged, he grew painfully aware of his financial strains, even pleading with the East India Company for a monthly stipend for Zeenat Mahal and Jawan Bakht—requests the British denied. Reports from the year 1852 show that even before the wedding, Zeenat had been consistently asking the government to increase their allowance and fund the royal wedding! After the wedding, Zafar had to write a letter to the governor-general asking for the allocation of a sum of Rs 3322 for Zeenat Mahal and Rs 2077 for Prince Jawan Bakht. He also requested a grant of four villages to the Begum. The letter also asked for the payment of the debt incurred on the wedding.[13] These repeated appeals came from Zafar's acute awareness of his precarious health and the immediate need to protect his family. To ensure that no harm would come to Jawan Bakht and Zeenat Mahal, the British governor-general himself conveyed such a reassurance in a letter dated 10 June 1852.[14]

Zeenat hits back: The Great Rebellion of 1857

In 1856, just a year before the rebellion broke out, the death of Mirza Fakhruddin presented Zeenat Mahal with a fresh opportunity to advance her son Mirza Jawan Bakht's claim to the throne. However, the British once again overlooked her ambitions, naming the next surviving son, Mohammad Quraish, as the successor. Yet, Zeenat Mahal was not one to surrender her cause easily. At her haveli, she held court with her trusted advisers, weaving intricate plans and conspiracies to achieve her objective. Her determination to secure the throne for her son was matched by her apparent willingness to take drastic measures. Historical accounts suggest that her pursuit of power might have been ruthless. Mysterious deaths of those supporting Mirza Fakhru—among them prominent British official, Sir Thomas Metcalfe—sparked scandal, and it was widely suspected that Zeenat Mahal played a role in them.[15] Strikingly, within a year, several key figures who stood in the way of her son's nomination met untimely and mysterious deaths. These included Sir H.M. Elliot, the British agent in Delhi (1823–1826); James Thomason, the lieutenant governor of the North-West Province; and Sir Thomas Metcalfe. Even Mirza Fakhruddin's own death was shrouded in suspicion.[16]

The British attributed these sudden deaths to the use of 'vegetable poisons', which were allegedly prepared in a way that left no trace—a technique reportedly mastered by the renowned hakeems, or native physicians, of the time.[17] While concrete evidence remains elusive, these events have fuelled speculation about the extent of Zeenat Mahal's determination and the lengths she might have gone to secure her son's future. Zeenat was not a passive queen—she was a ruthless political player trying to secure a future for her son at any cost.

Things between Zafar and Zeenat turned sour when the Rebellion of 1857 broke out. The last straw was when a cannonball hit Red Fort—Zeenat decided to move out of the palace. She was furious that Zafar supported the sepoys and emotionally distanced herself from him. She had only one determined goal in her mind. No matter what, she wanted Jawan Bakht to come out as a winner. If the rebels won and the Mughal Empire was restored with full autonomy, she wanted enough control over her husband to influence him to declare Jawan Bakht as his heir. If the rebels failed, she wanted the British to nominate Jawan Bakht to take over the throne. A mother's love often blinds her towards everything that goes around her. Zeenat Mahal's fierce protective instinct towards her child, and her zeal to come out victorious, made her fight all the opposing forces. As a royal woman, it was not easy for her to get her way against the British, especially when Zafar was weak and inefficient. Yet, Zeenat formed a strong council of allies, built a safe haveli for herself away from the Red Fort and orchestrated the circumstances around her.

Zeenat Mahal was a clever, intelligent woman who knew that the chances of native sepoys winning the war against the British were bleak. From the onset, as the Mughal princes jumped without a parachute into the power battle between the sepoys and East India Company, Zeenat Mahal and her son chose to side with the British. By 1857, rifts between Zeenat Mahal and Zafar became public. From her Lal Kuan haveli, she held meetings aimed at furthering Jawan Bakht's claim to the throne. Zeenat Mahal, along with her son and council, shifted permanently to her haveli at Lal Kuan, where they wrote a series of letters to the officers of East India Company, assuring them that they supported the British cause.

Five days after the war broke out, the sepoys learnt about the pro-British faction of Zeenat Mahal and her council. It became evident that Hakim Ahsanullah, Zeenat Mahal and Ilahi Baksh were conspiring with the British.[18] During the revolt, rumours had already started that the Begum had secretly negotiated with the British. The deal was that she would help them, as long as they agreed to recognize her son's claim to the throne. This angered the rebel soldiers, who claimed to have proof of these talks. They tried to storm her haveli, but the strong wooden gates held them back. Journalists from the time, such as Munshi Muhammad Baqar and others, accused Zeenat Mahal of being pro-British. The sepoys were so angry with her that they threatened to depose her and replace her with Taj Mahal Begum.

Unlike the traditionalists in court who underestimated the British, Zeenat knew the Mughal Empire's days were numbered. She tried to secure alliances, protect her son's future, and even negotiate with the British—all while other royal members remained frozen with nostalgia and pride. She was a deeply logical and practical person. Zeenat Mahal actively negotiated with British intelligence via the British cavalry leader William Hodson's spy, Maulvi Rajab Ali. She hoped to secure protection for herself, Mirza Quli Khan, her father, and Mirza Jawan Bakht—but not the king's other sons. Even when Hodson explained that the Mughal dynasty would not be restored, she still negotiated hard to protect her son and father, and not necessarily their wider family. In fact, according to Matilda Saunders, Zeenat Mahal was thrilled that the elder princes were killed, seeing it as an opportunity for her son to inherit the throne. This epitomizes the desperation and broken alliances at the final collapse of the Mughal Empire.[19]

Farewell, Zeenat: Departure from Delhi

On 19 September 1857, General Bakht Khan, leader of the native revolutionary forces, met with Emperor Zafar at the Red Fort to discuss the crumbling security situation. He urged the emperor to leave Delhi for his own safety. But in a turn of events, the emperor calmly replied that he planned to move that very night from his official residence to Humayun's Tomb, where Bakht Khan could meet him the next day.

Mirza Ilahi Baksh, a member of the royal family whose daughter was married to Emperor Bahadur Shah's son Mirza Fakhru, who died shortly before 1857, was instrumental in the British winning the war and capturing the royal family. Throughout the Revolt, he passed important, confidential information about the movements and schemes of the sepoys and the Mughal family to the British. Upon hearing Zafar's decision to flee, Mirza Ilahi Baksh acted quickly. He sent this information to Hodson through Maulvi Rajab Ali. The message revealed that General Bakht Khan had already left Delhi, leaving the emperor vulnerable and without allies at Humayun's Tomb. Realizing the opportunity, Hodson swiftly set out for the tomb. After two tense hours of negotiation, the emperor, along with Zeenat Mahal and their young son, Jawan Bakht, surrendered.[20]

Hodson paraded them by palanquin through Chandni Chowk to the Red Fort, ultimately imprisoning them in Zeenat Mahal's own Lal Kuan haveli. Deemed a threat, Zeenat and the emperor were exiled to Rangoon; only fifteen out of thirty-one family members made the journey.

It is interesting to note that despite the fact that Zeenat Mahal was instrumental in the British winning the war and her constant communication with company officials, she was still exiled with her husband. The British knew that Zeenat had the courage and the wit to steer public emotions in her favour. If she was allowed to live in Delhi, she would be seen as the representative of the Mughal Empire and the British would never achieve what they had set their mind towards—the complete wipeout of the Mughal name and presence from India. Zeenat Mahal's exile was equally important and necessary towards ensuring peace in the city and removing any threat of rebellion.

Zeenat Mahal wasn't just a queen because of her marriage to Bahadur Shah Zafar—she was out there making the big calls in the empire's final days. While most royal women lived behind purdah, Zeenat Mahal actively involved herself in state affairs, often manipulating court politics to secure the throne for her son. Sure, people gossiped about her court intrigues, favouritism, lavish spending habits—but guess what? The same 'sins' by male courtiers were forgiven and shrugged off. Zeenat refused to don the act of humility and 'graceful suffering' expected of queens. She chose power over likability.

Honestly, she is the most strategic force I've come across in the stories of the crumbling dynasty. Even with the British breathing down Delhi's neck and the Mughal court falling apart from within, she never backed off. She wasn't afraid to go head-to-head with British officers, negotiate, and even spy to gather information. After the 1857 revolt, when most royals fled and surrendered, she stayed with Zafar till the bitter end. And even after defeat, exile and humiliation, she carried herself with dignity in Rangoon—never begging for mercy or giving the British the satisfaction of seeing her broken.

Through several jailers who were in charge of Zeenat Mahal and Zafar, it is known that she mourned the loss of her jewellery and treasures, which she insisted did not belong to the Mughal Empire but were her personal possessions kept in her Lal Kuan haveli. The Mughal royal family quickly fell apart after the death of Bahadur Shah Zafar in Rangoon in 1862. Zeenat Mahal lived alone in a frugal, minimal way, a far cry from her lavish lifestyle with the powerful support of her group of allies in Lal Kuan, Delhi.[21] At the end of her life, she became addicted to opium. She even applied to return to India, a request which was declined by the British.[22]

Zeenat Mahal passed away in 1882, two decades after her husband. By the time of her death, the exact location of Bahadur Shah Zafar's grave had been forgotten and could not be found, so she was buried near a tree that was vaguely remembered to be close to his resting place. In 1903, a group of visitors from India came to pay their respects at Zafar's burial site in Rangoon, but found only unmarked graves, though some local guides pointed to the 'withered lotus tree' as a reference. In 1905, Muslims in Rangoon protested, demanding that Zafar's grave be properly marked. After initial resistance from the Viceroy in Calcutta, mounting pressure from a series of newspaper articles supporting respect and dignity be bestowed to the Mughal ruler, the British authorities finally agreed in 1907 to erect a simple engraved stone slab that read, 'Bahadur Shah, ex-King of Delhi. Died at Rangoon November 7th 1862 and was buried near this spot'. A railing was also placed around the site. Later that year, a memorial stone for Zeenat Mahal was added nearby.[23]

The story of Zeenat Mahal shows that privilege doesn't guarantee power—you have to fight for it. She operated in a world where even royal women were expected to stay silent. Yet, she broke barriers, inserted herself into political arenas reserved for men and refused to go down quietly, even as the Mughal Empire collapsed. Her story isn't just about royalty—it's about resistance, resilience and refusing to fade into the background when the world turns against you. For decades, historians painted her as a schemer or villainess, blaming her for Zafar's downfall. But dig deeper and you see a woman who was fighting a lost battle, but who refused to stop swinging. Many historical accounts show a particular contempt reserved for Zeenat; male courtiers who were equally scheming were not painted with the same brush. Her villainization in history says more about gender politics than her actions. It is important to know about Zeenat Mahal not because of her privilege, but because of how she fought against history's tide when all that privilege meant nothing anymore. She is not your textbook fairytale queen—she was a real woman, who made mistakes, miscalculated alliances and fuelled resentments. And that's exactly what made her real and compelling.

As I finished my story of Zeenat Begum, Abhinav and I sat silently. We had consumed endless cups of tea, and the crumbs of samosas were scattered on the table. I dusted them off and reclined further into my chair. I was too tired from the strain of telling the entire story. The narration had left a dull ache in my throat. Abhinav started drumming his fingers on the table and pressed his lips together. He spoke abruptly,

'Can we go inside the haveli? When did it turn into a school?' Clearing my throat, I felt compelled to finish the narrative of the Lal Kuan haveli, even if its owner was long gone.

After 1857, the British seized all property belonging to the royal family. Zeenat Mahal's haveli was handed over to Maharaja Narendra Singh, the ruler of Patiala, in recognition of his support in suppressing the revolt. The freedom fighter and Gandhian Brij Kishan Chandiwala wrote of Lal Kuan haveli in his book:

> Further down, one reaches Lal Kuan Bazaar, the haveli here of the Patiala royal family was actually the gateway of Zeenat Mahal. It is not much to look at from the outside, but it has some magnificent mahalsara inside. A two-storey house on the edge of the road is known as Zeenat Mahal's rooms. It belonged to the wife of Bahadur Shah and was constructed in 1846 AD. After the Revolt, it was offered as a reward to the Maharaja of Patiala for helping the British.[24]

For many decades, the haveli remained in the possession of the Patiala family. During World War II, the British administration repurposed it, turning it into a food ration office. Later, it was converted into a government school.[25]

Elderly locals recall how makeshift tents were erected in the haveli's garden to accommodate the overflow of students from the main building. Over time, the haveli stood quietly, bearing witness to the changes around it. In 1905, a tram line was laid right outside its gates. By the early 1950s, electric bulbs replaced the old kerosene lamps along the street leading to it.[26]

For the Patiala royal family, the haveli, once a symbol of grandeur, had become a burden. Years of neglect took its toll, and the building was eventually declared unsafe. In 1974, the government acquired the property, demolished the main structure, and built a girls' school in its place.[27] Though the school still carries the name 'Zeenat Mahal', it's a stark contrast from the past. Today, none of the children who study there know the history of the woman after whom the school is named. When I first visited this haveli five years ago, standing near the entrance gate was impossible. There was trash everywhere and bags with food waste were disposed of carelessly near the gate. The stench from the rotting food and the hovering mosquitoes made it impossible to linger there. A dhobi had set up shop near the entrance. It is hard to imagine that this was once one of the poshest areas of Shahjahanabad.

Pavan K. Varma writes in his highly resourceful book *Havelis of Chandni Chowk*:

Mr. Abdul Rauf, a teacher occupying the main section of the haveli on the Lal Kuan side, lacks the proper documentation to claim his property rights. The area has also been illegally occupied by some washermen and other unsavoury individuals despite it being the school's property. One of these residents keeps a fierce dog, often let loose to intimidate schoolgirls and anyone attempting to photograph the mansion. According to Kaleemuddin, a senior resident of Farash Khana near the haveli, multiple complaints to the authorities have gone unanswered. Kaleemuddin recalls that the basic structure of the haveli was intact until the late 1950s, with the grand gateway opening into a courtyard surrounded by rooms supported by intricately carved Kota stone pillars and red sandstone arches. Chitra Gupta, the school's current principal, shared that workers discovered one of the haveli's old tunnels during the construction of the school's assembly platform. However, it was promptly sealed off.[28]

The erstwhile Zeenat Mahal haveli is now Sarvodaya Kanya Vidyalaya, with over 1,100 students, and stands as one of the largest Urdu-medium schools in Delhi. It occupies a rent-free building, featuring eleven classrooms dedicated to instruction. Despite lacking a playground, the school boasts of a library with an impressive collection of 8,366 books. This girls' school has been a true blessing for nearby residents, bringing education right to their doorstep. It is the only educational institution in the area, and all its students are known for their brilliance, consistently graduating with exceptional results. In just five years, the school has transformed from one of the city's worst-performing institutions to one of the best. It has become a beacon of hope and a remarkable success story for government schools, showing that with determination and support, even the most challenging circumstances can lead to incredible achievements.[29]

Abhinav and I settled our bill and walked back. It's hard to imagine these cramped lanes once hosted regal processions of elephants and horses. Today, only the two red sandstone jharokas and a grand but hidden gateway survive as witnesses to its past. A cluster of girls in bright red uniform streams out, chatting happily. We chose not to disturb their privacy, realizing the interior no longer reflects its original grandeur.

I took a picture of the board hanging crookedly from the Mughal gateway which read 'Govt. Sarvodaya Kanya Vidyalaya, Zeenat Mahal, Lal Kuan', and asked a student, 'Do you know who Zeenat Mahal is?' She merely shrugged and grinned. I watched her back as she disappeared into the crowd of Lal Kuan. There are no longer any drums beating in the bazaar, nor a parade of elephants will ever enter the streets. The blood of rebels has dried and disappeared on this road. Zeenat Mahal is no longer a name whispered in the nearby havelis. Her mansion stands more than 150 years later, a silent reminder of a woman who knew how to fight the endgame.

The Royal Museums of Greenwich recently acquired a miniature painting of Zeenat Mahal that was supposed to have been painted during her wedding to Bahadur Shah Zafar. Rivers Francis Grindall, a senior administrator of East India Company, was originally in possession of the miniature. The piece was passed on to the descendants of the Grindall family, who sold it in the auction.

3

The OG Queen of Strategy, Sass and Survival

Begum Samru

I have been in the heritage business for the past seven years and one of my most popular walks is the 'Havelis of Chandni Chowk'. The walk explores Shahjahanabad's lesser-known havelis and the stories of its forgotten residents. Often, people assume that the havelis they visit on this walk will be in grand condition, with lavish European furniture, Persian carpets, rich upholsteries, fireplaces and shiny chandeliers. But, in reality, most havelis in Old Delhi have been converted into warehouses for surplus goods or are encroached on by tenants lacking proper documents. A few, like Chunamal ki Haveli, still house legal owners.

One such haveli is Begum Samru ki Haveli, hidden away in Delhi's largest electrical market.[1] The walk starts early in the morning to avoid traffic and crowds, beginning at the Lal Qila metro station (Gate no. 1). From there, we head straight and turn right at the McDonald's. Till the 1980s, there used to be a single-screen cinema here, where the McDonald's now stands, known as Kumar Cinema, which opened in 1930s. It then changed its name to Abhishek Cinema, but it closed in 2017. People no longer remember a time when long queues of moviegoers to watch blockbusters would extend till Chandni Chowk road.

Just besides the McDonald's is an entrance to a market with a sign that reads 'Delhi Electrical Traders Association 1503 Electrical Market, Bhagirath Palace'. All the shops are shut, since it is early and a Sunday. The lane is quite broad, but is littered with trash, making it especially treacherous in the rain. By mid-afternoon, a famous chaat wallah known as '7 Matko ki Chaat' sets up his stall, featuring seven clay pots for papdi, yoghurt, chutneys and fillings. His papdi chaat and bhalle papdi chaat draw crowds of tourists and locals alike. After around 200 metres, the lane splits. We take the left and walk another 150 metres; on the right is a gate—our entrance point.

'Look up,' I say to the group.

A Greco-Roman facade with white and yellow pillars towers overhead. A plaque reads 'Lloyds Bank'. To go inside, we follow a pair of spiral staircases, though they're partly hidden and littered with rubbish. Ascending them leads to a long corridor divided by a blue gate. Past the gate, we gather near a makeshift tea stall featuring images of Lord Shiva and Parvati on its temporary walls. A Central Bank sign hangs on the wall to the right, but its door is locked behind a shutter. Beyond that, the corridor darkens and narrows, lined with closed shops. The ceiling reveals exposed brick, while tall Ionic pillars—yellowed in places—rise along one side of the corridor. Palladian arches lend a European touch.

'Any guesses where we are?' I ask.

'I want to say it's a bank—Central Bank of India or Lloyd's Bank,' a participant guesses.

'Which bank was started 150 years ago?'

'Llyod's Bank …'

'And before that?'

'Someone's house?'

'Yes, it was Begum Samru's haveli. Just 900 metres from Red Fort.'

'Who was Begum Samru?'

I pause for a moment. There are so many fascinating aspects to this Begum's story. I need to gather my thoughts before I begin.

'She's been called many things—Zeb-un-Nissa, Joanna, the Begum of Sardhana—but history remembers her simply as Begum Samru. It's not even her name, technically. The title "Samru" was a local twist on her husband's name—Walter Reinhardt Sombre. And yet, this mispronounced moniker would outlive them all, becoming synonymous with rebellion, wealth, politics, and one hell of a legacy. And this is her story.'

In the 1760s, approximately 80 kilometres from Delhi, lay a small qasba (hamlet) named Kutana, predominantly inhabited by Muslim families. Life in Kutana was defined by its traditions, customs, and a tight-knit community, but it was also a place where the lines of social hierarchy were clearly drawn. This was a time when the Mughal Empire was in decline, and regional powers were vying for control. The hamlet's tranquillity was shattered when a young concubine[2] and her daughter were disgracefully expelled from their home, setting them on a path of hardship and resilience. The haveli from which they were ousted belonged to a Sayyid of Arabian descent, Asad Khan—a nobleman of great influence who had taken the young concubine under his wing, offering her a life of relative comfort in an era when women's fates were precariously tied to the men. However, Asad Khan's sudden demise left a vacuum of power and protection. His stepson, eager to assert his authority, swiftly removed his father's mistress and her young daughter from the haveli. Together, the women decided to journey to Shahjahanabad, the Mughal capital, known for its opportunities and refuge for those in need.[3]

The journey to Shahjahanabad was long and arduous, filled with uncertainty and peril. The mother–daughter duo travelled by tonga, enduring ten days of an exhausting journey, with soot and dirt clinging to their skin, hair and clothes. Despite their bedraggled appearances, the beauty of both mother and daughter was evident. Upon reaching Shahjahanabad, they found themselves at Kashmiri Gate, one of the thirteen gates of the walled city. The sprawling serai at Kashmiri Gate provided a temporary refuge for weary travellers. And it proved to be a haven for the young concubine and her daughter to rest and regroup before facing the challenges ahead. The young courtesan, familiar with the city's rhythms, believed that her daughter could find refuge and a future in one of the kothas (bordellos) where she had once lived. These kothas were centres of cultural and artistic training, where young girls were taught the refined arts of singing, dancing and acting to become renowned tawaifs.[4] As they made their way through the bustling streets of Shahjahanabad, the mother–daughter duo reached the grand Jama Masjid, the largest mosque in the city. Exhausted, the mother collapsed from fever and the daughter cried out for assistance. A passing palanquin halted, and a compassionate and prominent tawaif (courtesan) took pity on the young girl named Farzana (while also noting her beauty), and decided to raise her at her kotha in Chawri Bazaar.[5]

This moment marked the beginning of Begum Samru's transformation from a helpless girl into a celebrated tawaif.

Under the guidance of her new mentor, Khanum Jan, Farzana was introduced to the world of music, dance and poetry. The tawaif culture in Shahjahanabad's Chawri Bazaar was one of sophistication and elegance, where courtesans were not only entertainers but also patrons of the arts and influential figures in society. Farzana's training was rigorous, demanding dedication and discipline. She learned to sing with melodious grace, to dance with mesmerizing fluidity and to recite poetry with heartfelt emotion. As she honed her skills, she also learned the art of conversation and the nuances of social etiquette. The kotha became her sanctuary, where she could cultivate her talents and refine her abilities. Her mentor, a seasoned tawaif, provided guidance and support, nurturing Farzana's growth as an artist and individual.

The years passed. Begum Samru, who had blossomed into a beautiful and accomplished courtesan, grew up in the isolation of the Chawri Bazaar kotha, her world confined to its ornate walls and dance, music and poetry lessons. The kind-hearted chaudhrayan (matriarch), Khanum Jan, would occasionally take her out for shopping trips, providing her a rare glimpse into the bustling life outside. They would visit Chandni Chowk, buying essentials like tobacco, betel nut and the delectable pishta halwa. With her silk brocade bag and jingling copper coins, Begum Samru relished these outings despite the warnings about lascivious men who might prey on her blooming beauty. She often gazed at the imposing Lal Qila from the top of Jama Masjid, wondering about the mysteries within its red walls.

One evening, a foreign visitor entered the kotha. The sight of European mercenaries, traders and soldiers was not uncommon in the kotha, as they often sought companionship or contacts. However, this tall, imposing figure struck terror as he surveyed the room with a commanding presence. Khanum Jan, understanding the importance of every patron, regardless of reputation, instructed Begum Samru to perform a mujra (dance performance) for the visitor. General Walter Reinhardt, known as 'Samru' by the locals, had a reputation of heroism and monstrosity.[6] He had massacred British soldiers and carried a hefty bounty on his head. Yet, he commanded thousands of soldiers, making him a formidable figure. After the mujra, Samru left abruptly, only to return the next day, pressing gold coins into Begum Samru's hands. He then sought a private meeting with Khanum Jan, sealing Begum Samru's fate without her knowledge. Hours later, she found herself in a tonga with this stranger who spoke Urdu with a heavy accent and a smattering of Persian. Confusion and fear churned within her, but she accepted her qismat (fate), resigning herself to the unknown future ahead.[7]

As the tonga carried them away from the familiar streets of Shahjahanabad, Begum Samru's thoughts drifted back to the kotha, the only home she had known. The lessons, performances, camaraderie with other girls, and Khanum Jan's protective guidance now seemed like a distant dream. She looked at the foreigner beside her, trying to read his intentions. Samru, sensing her unease, attempted to converse with her, but the language barrier and his gruff manner only added to her apprehension.

Days turned into weeks as they travelled to Samru's territory. Begum Samru observed the changing landscapes, from the bustling city streets to the quiet, rural expanses. Samru's soldiers treated her with curiosity and respect, aware of their leader's stern commands. Begum Samru, though fearful, maintained her poise, drawing on the inner strength that had seen her through countless challenges. Upon reaching their destination, she was introduced to a new life. Samru's household blended European and Indian influences, reflecting his mercenary lifestyle and diverse associations. She was provided with fine clothes, jewellery and a comfortable living space. However, the underlying tension of her situation never left her. She was now part of Samru's world and had to navigate it carefully.

Despite his fearsome reputation, Samru showed Begum Samru his softer side. He appreciated her talents and encouraged her to continue practising music and dance. Begum Samru, in turn, used her skills to win over the household, earning the respect and admiration of those around her. Slowly, she began to understand Samru's complexities. War and survival shaped him, yet he found solace in her presence.

Samru already had another tawaif, Barra Bibi, literally meaning elder begum, who was plagued by melancholia.[8] After Begum Samru entered the harem, Barra Bibi quietly made space for her. It was unclear whether Samru sought companionship or a more colourful harem life, but Begum Samru provided both skilfully.

In the 1770s, the now fifty-year-old Samru joined the services of Najaf Khan, the wazir of Mughal Emperor Shah Alam II. He was given the job to hold off the Sikhs, against which he would get the fertile lands of Sonipat and Panipat.[9] Begum Samru, who was twenty-five years of age now, was a fair, plump, bright-eyed, witty woman who managed her husband's diplomatic affairs from behind the zenana. In his diary, Anglo-Indian military adventurer and soldier Colonel James Skinner (1778–1841) wrote that her talents and sound judgement became so valuable to Reinhardt to gain great ascendancy over him.[10] Samru's request to the Mughal emperor for jaidad (property) of Sardhana with revenue of 6 lakh in 1774 came directly from Begum Samru pulling the strings.[11] Sardhana was the most prized region of the doab; it was also the region which held Begum Samru's childhood place of birth Qatana Qasba. While Walter Samru's interest was to use the territory to pay his troops, perhaps Begum Samru wanted to re-visit the area of her childhood humiliation in a new light and with a new sense of power. The couple did get their desired land but their plans came to a shrieking halt.

Begum Samru takes over the reins

In 1778, Walter Samru died, leaving Begum Samru to face her childhood again when her mother was unceremoniously kicked from the house by the stepson.[12] Begum Samru, however, was made of tougher stuff and she would not let Sardhana slip away from her fingers. Begum Samru's chapter in Indian history could have ended here had she not used her silken moves to acquire the doab region under her influence. She pushed away the claims of her stepson Zafayrab Khan and paid the soldiers from the vast sum her late mercenary husband had collected. Her years on the battlefield with the troops ensured support and loyalty from them. She prepared the ground by talking to men with power and influence in the court. She knew nobody would support a feeble-minded son of a concubine for a lucrative area such as the doab.[13]

In an unprecedented turn of history, Begum Samru was given the land and the troops to rule. The emperor's sanad (ordinance) gave her legitimacy and power, making her status legal and unquestionable.

She was considered a firm and just ruler. She dealt directly with subedars (mid-level junior officers) and jagirdars (senior officers granted land rights) who controlled the other ranks. Three years after her husband's death, Begum Samru converted to Christianity and was baptized under the name Joanna at Agra on 7 May 1781.[14] The conversion seems odd, given Walter Sombre was not seen as a religious man. Did she convert to assert her legitimacy as the successor to her husband? Or were her motives to create an affiliation with her European troops? Or did she anticipate the rise of British power? Whatever her motives, her conversion did not catch the attention of the ruling circle. Her outward appearance and her habits remained utterly indigenous. Her history of being a concubine was being erased over time.

Begum Samru was in charge of five battalions, a tract of land that fetched Rs 10 lakh per annum and forty pieces of cannon; she also oversaw the welfare of people and the administration of her jagir.[15] This was a considerable achievement for a single woman who was once a courtesan. A famous story is often told about Begum Samru and how she suppressed insubordination. Once, when Begum Samru was in her camp in Agra, she received information about losing valuable property. Two slave girls were considered culprits for this theft. After receiving evidence and a full report on this matter, Begum Samru commanded that the slave girls be flogged until they were senseless. They were then thrown in a pit and buried alive. Some legends further add that the Begum placed her cot above the pit and smoked her hookah there. The incident was received with chilling silence from the battalions, and nobody dared to speak against her ever again.[16] A direct account comes of this incident by Sir W. H. Sleeman:

> I am satisfied that the Begum believed them guilty and that the punishment, horrible as it was, was merited. It certainly had the desired effect. My object has been to ascertain the truth in this case, state it, and not eulogise or defend the old Begam.[17]

Begum Samru's real military strength and negotiation skills were finally tested in 1788. Mughal Emperor Shah Alam II faced a grievous peril and a problem. The Afghan Rohilla chief Ghulam Qadir attacked Red Fort and occupied it for two and a half months. He plundered the city and ransacked the Red Fort, looking for hidden treasures and riches. Ghulam Qadir even set up his camp within the fort, installing himself in the quarters reserved for the Amir-ul-Umara.

Emperor Shah Alam II, now desperate, sought the help of Begum Samru, who immediately hastened to Delhi with her army. Her arrival with four battalions and eighty-four guns, commanded by experienced foreign officers, gave her strong leverage in negotiations. The incident has been mentioned in *Ibratnamah*:

> Being frightened at her hostile attitude, the artful Ruhela one day went to her camp, situated outside the Delhi fort, accompanied by only two servants. He called her his sister, and tried to make friends with her.

She, however, knew his reputation for cunning and deception, and therefore outwardly promised to join him with her troops—four paltans of sepoys trained for battle with 85 guns—after he had crossed over to the other side of the Jamuna. Falling into her trap he did so, when she guarded the ferry by means of one paltan of her sepoys and some guns to prevent his return! Thus the Emperor was saved.[18]

Emperor Shah Alam II was relieved and bestowed her with a new name—Farzanad-e-Azizi, 'the beloved daughter' (simply known as Farzana), and Zeb-un-Nissa, 'ornament among women'. She was also awarded a huge piece of land just 500 metres from Red Fort, Delhi.[19] The land was part of Begum ka Bagh, built by Princess Jahanara Begum in the seventeenth century. Begum Samru decided to use the garden and constructed a palatial white building made in the Greco-Roman style on this land. This is the same haveli that we visited with the heritage walk participants, where paan stains cover the white walls and trash litter the once majestic staircase. The haveli is now known as Bhagirath Place; it is attached to the larger part of the market with shops spread out in the lanes. Bhagirath Market is one of the largest electrical wholesale markets in Asia.

After reinstating Shah Alam II to the throne, Begum Samru became an indispensable part of the Mughal royal family. She was welcomed every time she made a visit to Delhi and shared a warm relationship with the emperor and his wife.

One valuable foreign account, the journal of Mrs A. Deane, tells precisely what happened inside the Mughal palace when Begum Samru visited.

The dowager queen embraced Begum Samru after she performed the taslim thrice. Afterwards, two senior ladies led Mrs A. Deane and Begum Samru to Diwan-i-Khaas, where the emperor greeted them warmly, talked to Begum Samru freely, and treated her with great courtesy. Mrs Deane recounts that Emperor Akbar Shah II looked very handsome and was very tall even though his long black beard mostly hid his face! The meeting between Begum Samru, Emperor Akbar Shah II and Empress Mumtaz Mahal, Mrs Deane recounts in her diary, was of great historical importance and set the course for Mughal history. The emperor addressed the empress as 'Jahangir ki maa', the mother of the notorious Mughal prince Mirza Jahangir, who was initially supposed to acquire the Mughal throne. Empress Mumtaz Mahal wanted Begum Samru to use her influence to restore Mirza Jahangir's royal favour with the British, allowing him to succeed the throne. This was virtually impossible as the British had a very low opinion of the alcoholic prince, who spent his time in acts of hedonism and revelry, and had little to no political tact.[20]

The party starter

Not everyone was kind to Begum Samru; she was known as the 'witch of Sardhana' by her competitors.[21] But she was the most sought-after mercenary who was scheming and bloodthirsty. She was both admired and notorious in British circles. In English circles, it was known that Begum Samru maintained her Muslim looks and mannerisms. She, however, modified it to function better in society. Lord Lake, a British governor-general appointed in 1790, was a frequent guest of Begum Samru in her Delhi residence.[22] They used to sit down between twenty and thirty guests, and have dinner. When the ladies from the party retired to another room, Begum Samru would remain seated, smoking hookah with other gentlemen, and she made it a point never to leave the pipe half-smoked. While the other women consumed coffee in the drawing room, Begum Samru discussed politics with the men. Mrs Deane had written in admiration about her wide range of skills that gained the respect of everyone who knew her:

> This woman has an uncommon share of natural abilities, with a strength of mind rarely met with, particularly in a female. The natives say that she was born a politician, has allies everywhere, and friends nowhere.[23]

Mrs Deane also gives us details of Begum Samru's banquet in Sardhana, complete with a nautch performance:

> At the Begam Samru's palace we found thirty persons of rank assembled and a splendid banquet in the European style. This ended she arose and threw over the shoulders of each of the ladies a wreath of flowers formed of a tuberose plant united by narrow gold ribbon. No sooner was she re-seated than strains of soft music were heard and two folding doors of the saloon flew open as if by enchantment discovering a number of young girls in the

attitude of dancing a ballet or as it is here termed a notch. It appeared to me however little more than a display of attitudes indeed their feet and ancles were 50 shackled by a large gold ring of more than an inch in thickness and bells strung round another that springing off the ground must have been impracticable their dancing consisted in jingling these bells in unison with the notes of the musical instruments which were played by men educated for that purpose. To this music they give effect by appropriate motions of hands, arms and person not forgetting that more expressive vehicle of the sentiments, the eyes. Their movements were by no means devoid of grace, particularly when accompanied by the voice.[24]

Once a tawaif herself, Begum Samru, through her sheer wit and strength, managed to rise above the rank and twist the arm of fate to write her own destiny. Did she have the same thoughts while sitting on the chair and smoking her hookah, in the large room of that palace? Did she tremble at the thought about how different her life could have been if she had succumbed to the same life of helplessness like her mother—after Walter Sombre's death, had she not been brave and courageous? How did such a woman who made even her fate shiver look?

Several portraits of Begum Samru from her old age give us an idea. She was petite in height, fair in complexion and had beautiful hazel eyes. The famous German painter Johann Zoffany described Begum Samru as a 'perfect model'.[25] In the later years of her life, she got used to giving portraits of herself by Jivanram and other artists as a form of forging diplomatic relations.[26] Many foreign accounts remark that Begum Samru always carried a hookah with herself, perhaps a habit from her courtesan days. Unlike her contemporaries, Begum always wore a turban and never dressed herself with ornaments. Her hair was parted from the front and smoothened back with rose oil and braided behind, a hairstyle which was common in eighteenth-century India. Mrs Deane has left us a pen portrait of Begum Samru:

> Her features are still handsome, although she is now advanced in years. She is a small woman, delicately formed, with beautiful hazel eyes, a nose somewhat inclined to the aquiline, a complexion very little darker than an Italian, with the finest turned hand and arm I ever beheld. Zophany, the painter, when he saw her, pronounced it a perfect model. She is universally attentive and polite. A graceful dignity accompanies her most trivial actions, she can be even fascinating, when she has any point to carry.[27]

Begum Samru was known to host several parties in her later years; she was sixty when she started hosting these parties in her Delhi haveli. The first visitor to the haveli was the Mughal emperor, who had bestowed her the land. Even though Begum Samru moved to Sardhana, her attachment to and love for Delhi were unparalleled. The people were joyous when Governor Hastings repaired the sixteenth-century Mughal water channel constructed by Jahanara Begum. Once again, the water of the Yamuna rippled in the canal. People offered rose petals and garlanded each other with joy. Begum Samru also became part of the celebrations and patronized spectacular fireworks displays.[28]

Nowhere else in India was a Christian mercenary who was once a Muslim tawaif. She was shrouded in mystery, and her courage was historic. Begum Samru's legendary hospitality attracted military troops, Europeans and diplomats alike. According to Lieutenant Thomas Bacon, Begum Samru threw a three-day Christmas festival with a High Mass followed by a nautch performance and fireworks. Nautch performances had become an indispensable part of festivities and were considered natural even for Christmas celebrations.

Unbothered and unmatched—the Begum's final years

In 1820, Begum Samru was seventy years old and no longer the beauty she was renowned for. She had shared her distress with British officials about the welfare of people who were dependent on her after her death. Begum Samru had acquired great wealth through excellent management and survived the Mughal Empire's *gardi ka waqt* (the tumultuous eighteenth and nineteenth centuries). She had, however, become a legend that the British no longer entertained. When the resident of Delhi held a great banquet with over a hundred dancers gracing the occasion, Begum Samru was not invited.[29] There was animosity and miscommunication from both sides. Thomas Bacon narrates an incident:

On her excursions to Delhi during the latter part of her life she did not pay the usual tribute of homage to the Resident, of a visit which as the representative of the British Government he had a right to expect from all persons of inferior rank. The vanity of the official was wounded. He went to the length of reporting the matter to the authorities.[30]

She was also not on the best terms with the Mughal emperor who succeeded Emperor Shah Alam II, Emperor Akbar Shah. In 1834, a misunderstanding arose between Begum Samru and the emperor on a point of etiquette. Bacon has written in his book:

Akbar Shah being pre-eminent by birth the pure stock of the ancient Mughal dynasty and being upon his own ground in the city of Delhi insisted upon receiving homage from all of an inferior degree who met him and the proud Begam although not one of his subjects was compelled to have her elephant kneel down to the Emperor when passing him. This her vanity would not brook, and having been more than once compelled against her will thus to do reverence to a higher prince, she had for several years refrained from visiting Delhi.[31]

By her last years, Begum Samru had stopped visiting Delhi altogether; her eighty-eight-year-old body could not take the strain of travel and she now sought the companionship of dear ones. Even if her body failed her, her mental prowess remained intact. A French traveller, Victor Jacquemont, as late as in December 1830 notes:

> She is, in fine, a sort of walking mummy, who still looks after all her affairs herself, listens to two or three secretaries at once, and at the same time dictates to as many others.[32]

Begum Samru, without a direct heir, wrote her will and gave her everything to her stepson David Sombre. Her inheritance was assessed at approximately 55.5 million gold marks in 1923 and 18 billion Deutsch marks in 1953.[33] Her vast inheritance is still disputed to this day.

'So that's Begum Samru,' I conclude, as the group marvels at how a once-courtesan rose to power and built this palace. Yet, her story doesn't explain how the mansion became 'Bhagirath Palace', stuffed with electrical and surgical shops.

Questions arise: 'Why all these shops? Why the "Lloyds Bank" sign?'

I smile. 'It's a tale spanning a hundred years,' I reply.

Begum Samru's connection with European culture came through her marriage to the European mercenary, Walter Reinhardt Sombre, a man of mixed European and Indian heritage. After his death, she inherited his military estate, and her close associations with European military officers and diplomats influenced her architectural ambitions. This led to the commissioning of palaces and mansions in European styles, notably in Sardhana, Meerut and Chandni Chowk. Her mansion in Chandni Chowk, known as Begum Samru ki Haveli, was among the earliest to incorporate Greek pillars and European architectural styles in Delhi. The palace was a grand four-storey mansion built on a high plinth with spacious halls and verandas, embodying the elegance and aesthetics of European architecture. There is also a belief that there is a hidden tunnel that connects Begum Samru ki Kothi to Red Fort. Begum Samru's strong political alliances and military support for the Mughal Empire, particularly during moments of crisis, ensured her prominence, making it plausible that she would have constructed such a tunnel connecting her residence to Red Fort, a strategic choice given her military role and frequent interaction with Mughal leaders.

A painting of Begum Samru's haveli, dated 1843, is part of the album 'Reminiscences of Imperial Delhi', commissioned by Sir Thomas Metcalfe, the governor-general's agent at the Mughal court. This artwork provides a detailed depiction of the haveli's north and south views. Remarkably, the southern side of the mansion still stands, preserved in much of its original form.

After her death, the haveli changed hands: her stepson sold it in 1847, and it became the Delhi Bank.[34] During the 1857 revolt, the bank's manager, a Mr Beresford, was murdered, and the building was heavily damaged. Rebuilt as Lloyds Bank, it later passed to Munshi Shiv Narain in 1922, then to Lala Bhagirath Mal in 1940.[35] He renamed it 'Bhagirath Palace' but seldom lived there, renting it out for weddings and social events, keeping its legacy alive amidst its many transformations. He, instead, moved into a twenty-five-room outhouse in the adjacent gardens, known as Bagh Begum Samru.[36] Today, the name, colloquially shortened to 'Bhagirath Place', endures—most locals forget its origin as Begum Samru ki Kothi and all they remember is Lala Bhagirath, whose name is proudly written on the market's entrance gate.

As we finish our walk, the group, busy taking pictures, marvels that a courtesan-turned-mercenary once owned this building. Weeks later, I return with my team to interview shopkeepers. Many have never heard of Begum Samru, guessing it's 'Nur Jahan's palace' or a 'British-era building'. A couple do know the name but think she might have been Shah Jahan's wife.

I wanted to get some fascinating insight into what the shopkeepers thought about this heritage structure and whom they thought it belonged to. I have always valued bazaar gossip as much as literary and archaeological sources. If dealt with care and caution, oral stories help us understand how the community views history.

My first stop was at the Central Bank of India to gather information. I wanted to know if the clerks there knew they were working inside a 200-year-old haveli. When I went inside, I tried to talk to a few clerks, but they shrugged me away and said they were not the right people to ask these questions. Outside the bank was a shop, and I thought it might be best if shopkeepers were approached instead. The first person I interviewed was Mohan Lal, who had worked there for twenty-five years. When I asked him if he knew the history of the building, he said, '*Arre, bahut purani hain yeh building. Mughlo ke time pe banayi gayi thi! Shayad Shah Jahan ne banayi thi yeh Nur Jahan ke liye* (It is a very old building constructed during Mughal times. I think Shah Jahan made it for Nur Jahan).' I did not correct him but recorded his information in voice notes. I went deeper into the haveli and stopped at another shop, and approached its shopkeeper; his name was Ram Lakhan. I asked him if he had seen the building change over the years. He simply said, '*Yeh building vaisi ki vaisi hain. Bahut purani hain bas yeh pata hain hume. Shayad 1930 mein banni thi* (This building hasn't changed at all over time. I only know it is a very old building. Maybe it was built in 1930).' As I walked, I also saw a tea-shop guy. When I asked him if he knew about this building he said, '*Yeh jagah Angrezo ke zamane ki hain* (This place is from British time).' There was also a kind shopkeeper named Deepak Kumar who sells surgical goods. He told me the building is now known as 'Central Bank building' or 'AC market'. Interestingly, there was one shopkeeper who had the name right. His name was Mohit Sharma, and he said, '*Yeh Begum Samru ki Haveli hain* (This is Begum Samru's Haveli).' When I asked him who she might be, he said, '*Shayad Shah Jahan ki biwi hogi?* (Maybe she is Shah Jahan's wife).'

This is precisely when the incident happened.

A short, bald man came shouting. He was livid. He introduced himself as the general community chairperson of the building. A crowd gathered around us. He asked me if I had permission to ask the shopkeepers questions. I tried to calmly explain to him about the book I was writing and the questions I was asking. His face became redder as I spoke.

'You cannot do this,' he said. 'You come to my office right now, and then we will see what we can do about you.'

I was not going to the office of a stranger whose designation and personality seemed dodgy. I understood he was anxious and paranoid because all the shopkeepers here had no land permits or proper legal paperwork to open a shop in the building. This is a typical case in Old Delhi, where heritage properties are encroached on. He feared I was writing a newspaper article on the state of Begum Samru ki Haveli and bringing the government's attention to it. The shopkeepers would be turned to the streets if the government decides to preserve the building. While I understood the delicate situation, what rattled me was the force with which local politics works in Old Delhi. A crowd of men had gathered around me. They all seemed hostile, and instead of explaining their situation or making a polite request, they verbally attacked me. When I asked them if they could show me their legal papers to stay in this building, the man started yelling louder, insisting I come to his office. I decided to turn around and make an exit from the building.

As I reached the last step of the staircase, I saw a black signboard with the history of Begum Samru ki Haveli written on it. There were pigeon dropping stains on the signboard, and the words had become faint. I quietly left. All that remains in the name of conservation and her legacy is this signboard. It is not enough and it can never help in saving the history of women's participation in the politics of India. This chapter is a plea of urgency and desperation to preserve the history and legacy of these fearless women.

In the Netflix drama series *Beecham House* (2019) by Gurinder Chadha, actress Lara Dutta plays the role of Begum Samru. She is shown counselling Mughal Emperor Shah Alam II (played by Roshan Seth) inside the Red Fort.

4

The De Facto Empress of Hindustan

Qudsia Begum

Just beyond the borders of Shahjahanabad, near Delhi's well-known North Campus area, lies the historic neighbourhood of Civil Lines. During the British era, this area earned the name 'White Town' as it was designated exclusively for British and European residents. Neighbourhoods like Civil Lines were established in many Indian cities after the Revolt of 1857, driven by a perceived need to physically separate the native populations from the European communities. Today, Civil Lines remains one of the most prestigious areas in Delhi, home to a few colleges of Delhi University, various government buildings, the historic Maidens Hotel (1903) and lush, tree-lined streets.

One summer, many years ago, while strolling around the area, I happened to come by Qudsia Bagh, tucked away neatly in a corner of Civil Lines. And since then it has become a place I often return to.

As you enter the complex, you'll see the Jumna Lodge Masonic Centre and Jumna Lodge Charitable Society to your right—an allopathic and dental clinic. This colonial structure once served as horse stables under Mughal rule. Locally called 'Jumana Hall', it currently houses a dispensary. From here, continue straight and take a right towards the majestic Mughal-arched gateway known as Hathi Darwaza. That day, I decided to sit for a while, watching the setting sun cast its glow upon the gate. Joggers streamed by on the path, and the nearby children's park teemed with energetic kids running, playing and laughing, a sweetly chaotic scene.

Although it is now just another MCD park, Qudsia Bagh was once a lavish riverfront garden with a palace, mosque and pleasure pavilions exclusively for Qudsia Begum and her Mughal entourage. Laid out by the remarkable Qudsia Begum in 1748 CE (1162 AD), it was a jewel along the Yamuna near Kashmiri Gate, featuring a sprawling palace embodying Mughal grandeur.[1] The story of Qudsia Bagh seems straight out of a medieval fairytale. A courtesan becomes the queen of India and rules Hindustan for many years. Seems like the plot of a historical fiction book, right?

But that's what happened.[2]

The story begins 300 years ago, when Udham Bai, a courtesan known for her unparalleled skills in singing and dancing, was born on the cold night of 21 January. The young girl had no inkling of the grand destiny that awaited her. Her life began on a trajectory much like most courtesans of her time. She was part of the kotha system, where she honed the art of seduction, mastering the delicate balance between allure and grace. Singing, dancing and cultivating a refined intellect, Udham Bai transformed herself into a woman of conditioned class, capable of easing the hearts and minds of her suitors and patrons.

But fate, ever unpredictable, had more in store for her. One day, everything changed when she managed to secure an audience with none other than the ruler of Hindustan, the illustrious Emperor Muhammad Shah, the successor to the great Timurid line. Khadija Khanam, the daughter of the influential Amir Khan in the court of Muhammad Shah, played the role of fate's hand, introducing Udham Bai to the emperor.

Udham Bai knew that this was her one and only chance to change the course of her life, and she seized the opportunity with both hands. When she performed before Muhammad Shah, it was not merely a dance or a song; it was a manifestation of her deepest aspirations and her burning desire to rise above the life that had been thrust upon her. She danced and performed with a passion and grace that no courtesan had ever displayed before, each movement and note calculated to ensnare the emperor's ever-frivolous heart. The court, enraptured by her beauty and talent, watched as she skilfully captured the attention of the ruler, drawing him into her world of art and enchantment.

Her life could have followed the predictable path of any other courtesan acquired by a Mughal ruler—a brief existence as a new, shiny toy that graces the harem for a few months or years, before being cast aside in favour of a fresher face. However, Udham Bai was no ordinary courtesan. Through a combination of charm, intelligence and an unyielding spirit, she won not only Muhammad Shah's heart but also his respect and admiration. Her ambition was not limited to becoming just another consort in the harem; she aspired to something far greater. In a twist of fate that defied the norms of her time, she achieved the impossible. Udham Bai rose through the ranks and became the queen of Muhammad Shah's harem, securing a position of influence and power that few could have imagined for a woman of her origins.

But this is only the beginning of Udham Bai's remarkable story. Her life truly began after she ascended to the role of queen. Upon securing her position, she was bestowed with grand titles, marking her transformation from a courtesan to a figure of significant power in the Mughal Empire. Among these titles was 'Qudsia Begum', a special designation given to her by Muhammad Shah himself. She was also referred to as Bai-jiu Sahiba, Nawab Qudsia, Sahiba-uz-Zamani, Sahibjiu Sahiba, Hazrat and Qibla-i Alam, each title reinforcing her elevated status within the royal household.[3] She was officially recognized as important to the Mughal royal family. In fact, the titles proved that she was important not just to the emperor but also to the future of the Mughal court.

Despite these honours, historian Jadunath Sarkar critically views Qudsia's role in Mughal history, describing her character in rather unflattering terms. He suggests that Qudsia was acutely aware of her precarious position within the Mughal harem. Unlike the other wives and princesses, who were born into noble families with royal lineage, Qudsia came from a humble background. This lack of noble blood and royal heritage made her insecure about her status in the imperial household, where lineage was often as important as power. Her insecurity was particularly evident in her interactions with the two former Begums of Muhammad Shah, whom she did not regard kindly. The first, Badshah Begum, better known as Mariam-uz-Zamani, was the chief queen of Muhammad Shah. The second queen was Sahiba Mahal, the daughter of a high-ranking Mughal noble, Sayyid Salabat Khan Zulfiqar Jang.[4]

If you are a woman who has been criticized for being 'too loud' or 'too ambitious', you will relate to Qudsia Begum. In a world where Mughal women were supposed to operate behind the veil, Qudsia was out there—front and centre. She engaged in the political and social dynamics of the court with a boldness that challenged and defied the traditions of her time.

In the Persian book *Tarikh-i Ahmad Shahi,* author Mahmud al-Husayni writes:

Daily the high officers used to go and sit down at her porch (deorhi) and she used to hold discussions with them from behind a screen (through the medium of eunuchs); all petitions (mutālib) of the realm and closed envelopes that were sent into the harem were read out to her and she passed orders on them, which were final.[5]

The author of the book further writes: 'O God! That the affairs of Hindustan should be conducted by a woman so foolish as this!'[6]

I winced when I read Mahmud al-Husayni's words. But Mahmud was a cultural product of his time where it was not common for women to rule, and certainly not low-born women. Qudsia commanded the Mughal Empire and stepped up for her inefficient son while observing purdah. Every time women in history have ruled on behalf of their husbands and sons, they have been villainized, and the story of Qudsia is a perfect example of how men treat women in power.

Qudsia Begum was known not just for her pragmatism, leadership skills but also for her soft, emotional side. The first was her deep, almost instinctive, love for her son. The second was her generous charity. She used her wealth to help the neglected nephews and grandsons of former emperors, who were living in poverty within the Delhi palace. Her kindness also reached many poor people outside the palace, giving them a chance to live with more comfort and dignity. Her cunning, it seems, was only a tool to survive in the ruthless Mughal political world.

Qudsia inherits a sinking ship

Qudsia's life changed when her son was born. From then on, her entire objective and goal was to ensure that he inherited the throne and that she ruled the Mughal Empire indirectly.

Her son, Ahmad Shah Bahadur, was born in the Red Fort on 14 December 1725.[7] He became emperor twenty years later, on 19 April 1748, after the death of his father, Emperor Muhammad Shah.[8] Theirs was a complicated father–son relationship. Ahmad Shah was not his father's favourite and that is reflected in how he was treated by him. In *Tarikh-i Ahmad Shahi*, Mahmud al-Husayni writes:

> The condition of the country after the departure of Nadir Shah was worse than before; the amirs took what they liked. The Emperor spent what remained to him in sports and pastime. He [Muhammad Shah] locked up his son, Ahmad Shah, in one part of the citadel, not wishing him to appear in public. He kept him in the greatest indigence and would not allow him to indulge in the game of chaugan, hunting, shooting, or any royal sports, such as he practised himself.[9]

He adds:

> Ahmad Shah was not a man of great intellect; all the period of his youth till manhood had been spent in the harem, and he had had absolutely no experience whatever of the affairs of a kingdom, or of the cares of government. Besides this, he was surrounded by all kinds of youthful pleasures, which every person, seeing the turn of his mind, was anxious to display before him to entice his fancy. As a natural consequence, he gave himself up

entirely to pastime and sports, and bestowed no thought on the weighty affairs of the kingdom.[10]

After her son's rise to the throne, Qudsia Begum was given the title 'Mumtaz Mahal', marking her high status in the royal court.[11] She was also awarded a mansab, a nominal rank with 50,000 horses—a significant recognition of her influence and importance in the Mughal Empire.[12] This was just the beginning of what was set to come in the following years. Qudsia Begum's engagement in the court increased after Ahmad Shah became ruler. He practically handed over the reins of the empire and trusted her judgement completely.

A famous incident that proves Ahmad's dependence on his mother for judgement in times of crisis has been mentioned by many contemporary chronicles of the time. The story goes that once a group of disgruntled subjects— likely soldiers who hadn't been paid their due salaries— gathered in the empty courtyard in front of the eunuch Nawab Javid Khan's palace. They waited until he emerged to meet the emperor. As soon as he appeared, they surrounded him and voiced their grievances. Despite his attempts to placate them with empty promises and avoid further confrontation, the Nawab was forcefully detained. The crowd held onto his clothes, which were eventually torn to shreds, leaving him in a humiliating state. The soldiers' complaints grew louder each day, and the situation became increasingly dire. Overwhelmed and desperate, the emperor sought help from Qudsia Begum. He confided in her that he was unable to control the soldiers and feared for his reputation. In response to this crisis, Qudsia Begum took decisive action. To address the immediate financial crisis, the emperor had to pledge all the ornaments from his three begums to raise several lakhs of rupees. Despite these efforts, he failed to pay the soldiers their overdue salaries. The lack of pay left the soldiers frustrated, and the absence of effective control over the nobles only exacerbated the crisis, pushing everyone involved to the brink of desperation.[13]

The situation grew so serious that even the royal guards, who had not been paid for over a year and could not get any relief from the emperor or his officials, resorted to a bold protest. In a contemporary Persian source *Tazkira-i Shakir Khan*, written by Shakir, the son of Lutfullah Khan, a scandalous incident has been mentioned:

> They (the angry soldiers) tied up a young ass and a bitch at the palace gate and when the nobles and other courtiers came to attend the darbar, they audaciously urged them, saying, 'First make your bow to these. This one (pointing to the ass) is the Nawab Bahadur, and that (the bitch) is Hazrat Qudsiya, the Queen-mother.!' ... Great God! The people have utterly lost all fear of their sovereign and regard for decency.[14]

You see, Qudsia Begum had inherited a sinking ship. By the time she acquired the throne there was a systematic collapse in the empire—the imperial treasury was empty, the internal and the external revolts were pulling the empire apart—and it had become nearly impossible to stabilize the vast kingdom in those conditions. There was a collapse of faith in the Mughal system.

The reason for this had less to do with Qudsia being a former courtesan, and more to do with her choices impacting royal court and etiquette. One aspect of her influence that particularly outraged public sentiment and diminished the prestige of the Mughal Empire was her close relationship with Javid Khan. This scandal became notorious because Javid Khan, in defiance of longstanding palace rules, would even spend nights in the imperial harem—a breach of decorum that shocked the court and the public alike. Her faith in Javid Khan irritated and rubbed the old aristocracy the wrong way.[15] But Qudsia Begum simply saw him as a strategic and loyal ally. For women of the harem, their eunuchs were the closest confidantes and supporters.

Qudsia Begum vs Everyone Else

The *Tarikh-i Ahmad Shahi* mentions that during a time when soldiers were mutinying because their pay was overdue, and the government couldn't even raise Rs 2 lakh by selling palace treasures, Qudsia Begum made the reckless decision to spend Rs 2 crore on celebrating her birthday on 21 January 1754.[16] This extravagance was seen as a criminal folly, especially since her birthday celebrations were more lavish than those of the emperor himself. Her brother, Man Khan, a wandering figure, who sometimes engaged in the profession of a male dancer behind singing girls, was elevated to the rank of a six-hazari peer, a high position in the Mughal hierarchy, and given the title Mutaqad-ud-daulah Bahadur.[17] This appointment underscores that despite Qudsia Begum's elevated status and the transformation of her own life, the connections to her earlier, less reputable world of entertainment and courtesan culture were still evident in her family's circumstances.

With the new emperor's rise to power, Javid Khan's influence expanded rapidly and dramatically. Upon Ahmad Shah Bahadur's coronation, Javid Khan was immediately promoted to the rank of six-hazari.[18]

The frustration of high-class nobles to take orders from Javid Khan is mentioned by a Delhi historian in a Persian source:

> Never since Timur's time had a eunuch exercised such power in the State; hence the Government became unsettled. The hereditary peers felt humiliated by having to make their petitions through a slave and to pay court to him before any affairs of State could be transacted.[19]

The reaction of the high class towards Qudsia Begum and Javid Khan was a very expected turn of events. When power deviates from traditional sources of legitimacy—such as birth, and the legacy of military and administrative service—it creates a rift between institutional expectations and the new reality. This ultimately sowed a seed of resentment among the established elite. And let's be honest—having to bow down to someone they once dismissed as a slave must have felt like a slap to their pride. The fact that the nobles now had to address their grievances through someone regarded a ghulam (slave) symbolized profound inversion of norms. It was no longer an inconvenience but an attack on their heritage and lineage. There was a growing mutual contempt between the inner circle of Javid Khan and Qudsia Begum, and the aristocracy. As Javid Khan and Qudsia Begum consolidated power by appointing lower-ranked but loyal officials to the royal court, the nobility became more and more agitated. It was a visible cue that the central authority had weakened, and the traditional symbol of powers had begun to erode. However, instead of blaming Qudsia Begum as the reason for this crisis, one needs to analyse if indeed there were any capable Mughal aristocrat of noble birth left in the palace to handle the situation. Qudsia Begum herself was the subject of the growing instability in the empire. She was handling circumstances which were no longer in anyone's control.

Game of Thrones: The Mughal edition

The rise of Javid Khan to power, backed by Qudsia, turned the Mughal court into a hotbed of intrigue and conflict. On 6 September 1752, Safdarjung, the wazir of the Mughal Empire, lured Javid Khan to his residence under the pretence of a breakfast meeting. There, Safdarjung had Javid Khan murdered—his head displayed at the entrance and his body thrown into the Yamuna River. The murder of Javid Khan sent shockwaves through the court. Both the emperor and the queen mother were devastated, with Qudsia Begum even going so far as to dress in white and remove her jewels, as if she were truly a widow.[20] The queen mother, outraged by the assassination of her ally, openly expressed her displeasure, and the emperor, shaken and disillusioned, distanced himself from Safdarjung. After Javid Khan's death, Ahmad Shah largely withdrew from state affairs, leaving Qudsia Begum to handle the government. She became the de facto ruler, managing important decisions and meeting with officials from behind a veil. As Safdarjung's enemy, Qudsia Begum used her new-found power to form a coalition against him, working with allies like Intizam-ud-Daula (the leader of the Turani faction) and Sholapuri Bai to strike back at Safdarjung.[21]

After a series of catastrophic events and a tense confrontation with the emperor, the wazir, Safdarjung, decided to retreat from Delhi to his province of Awadh. His son, Shuja-ud-Daula, later constructed the Safdarjung Tomb, which now stands as a significant landmark in Delhi, a mere ten minutes away from the site where Safdarjung took his final leave of the imperial city.

Interestingly, Qudsia Begum contributed significantly to the famous Shah-e-Mardan Dargah near the Aliganj area, within the vicinity of Safdarjung Tomb. According to historian Rana Safvi, the dargah itself is believed to have been built by Qudsia Begum. In 1724 CE, she acquired a stone bearing the sacred footprints of Hazrat Ali and had it installed inside a marble tank. Later, in 1768 CE, under the supervision of Nawab Javed Khan, she commissioned the construction of a compound wall, assembly hall, *hauz*, and mosque within the complex. The site also came to include the shrine known as

Bibi ki Chakki, which local tradition associates with Fatima, the daughter of Prophet Muhammad (Peace Be Upon Him).

The shrine is very important and sacred for Shia Muslims of the subcontinent. Qudsia, herself a Shia Muslim, thus advanced her profile within the Shia community of Awadh and elsewhere. The shrine is not merely an act of piety. In a period where religious identity boosted political power, an established site linked to the Prophet gave Qudsia a position to strengthen her support and likeability within the Delhi circle as well.

The art of being a little extra

In an interesting article titled 'Udham Bai: Glimpse into the Splendid Life of a Later Mughal Queen', art historian Savita Kumari analyses a painting in which women of the fort entertain Qudsia Begum. The entertainers in the painting are wearing Portuguese costumes. The painting, by Mir Kalan Khan, shows a night scene in the palace balcony. In this scene, the delicate and graceful Qudsia Begum is seated on a throne, leaning comfortably against a plush bolster. Her left hand rests gently on a pillow placed on her lap, while her right hand holds the pipe of a hookah. In front of her, two silver bowls and a paandan are neatly arranged. Standing behind them are four elegantly dressed women, each adding to the richness of the scene.[22]

Kumari has pointed out an intriguing detail about one of the women standing behind Qudsia Begum. The woman holding a fruit basket appears to be more than just an attendant—Kumari suggests she might be a princess. Her distinct appearance, particularly her turban adorned with an aigrette, sets her apart from the others. Kumari argues that this woman could be Hazrat Begum, the beautiful daughter of the late Emperor Muhammad Shah. Here, she is depicted bringing a fruit bowl to Qudsia Begum, her royal stature now overshadowed by the duties of an attendant—a stark reminder of the shifts in power and fortune within the Mughal court. At the top right corner of the painting, two women peer down from a jharoka on the upper floor, observing the performance. Kumari suggests these women might be none other than Mariam-uz-Zamani and Sahiba Mahal, the other two important queens of Muhammad Shah. Through this painting, Qudsia Begum seems to be flaunting her own grandeur, while subtly hinting at the subordinate status of these other royal ladies. The painting was a clear message to the public that the traditional power and the aristocratic power of noble birth—such as the begums and the princesses—have been displaced and overtaken by Qudsia, who was continuously challenging traditional norms of power and class. [23]

Back at Civil Lines, the Hathi Darwaza, which stands on the western side of the garden, is the most prominent surviving feature. It once had two minarets on its flanking pilasters, each topped with clumsy ornaments that resembled flowerpots. Today, the minarets are gone, and the gateway, though still lofty, carries a sense of lost grandeur. On either side of the gateway, there used to be rows of masonry cells that once completely enclosed the garden. These cells are now interrupted in several places, leaving gaps in what was once a continuous wall.

Historian Carr Stephen, in his 1876 book *Archaeology and Monumental Remains of Delhi*, wrote:

> It is not at all unlikely, as related by tradition, that Qudsi Begum took advantage of a garden on the river to improve it and adorn it with palatial buildings and with splendid water works, the foundations of which may yet be seen. Nothing now remains of the palace, if I am to judge from the two sketches of the place that I have seen; the most prominent objects that now belong to Qudsiah Bagh are a gateway, two *baradaris*, three interrupted lines of heavy walls, and a group of deserted shops.[24]

In the northwestern corner, some vats remain, once used to supply water for the garden's fountains, a clue to the intricate waterworks that once made this place lush and vibrant. The eastern side of the garden is now an open space, scattered with ruins of houses and waterworks.

I walk across the gateway and take a sharp left. At the park's centre stands a pavilion, British in style, with stone pillars at the front, a gabled roof and a distinct European staircase—somewhat reminiscent of the twin 'waterfall' staircase at Begum Samru ki haveli in Chandni Chowk.

The pavilion is brick-built, featuring a Bangla-style roof at the back and two Mughal-inspired domes along the wall. Behind the twin stairs is a Shahjahani-style cusped arch, plus another arched entry between the stairways—overall, a fusion of Mughal and British design. Small glass windows and a ventilation window adorn the pavilion's sides, which also has a charming side entrance.

By the nineteenth century, under British rule, many Mughal gardens were repurposed for recreation and picnics, occasionally featuring libraries, circuses and menageries. Today, the British-era bungalow is used by the ASI as a storehouse.

The garden witnessed several grand festivals and durbars that were held in the summer and monsoon season. A rare description of the garden helps us envision how it looked 300 years ago.

The imperial durbar in Qudsia Bagh during the reign of Mughal Emperor Alamgir II has been described in the source *Hadiqat-al-Aqalim* of Murtaza Husayn Bilgrami:

This darbar was arranged in the Qudsiya bagh, where a big tent was raised. The author was present at that time there. The darbar was decorated with fine tents and carpets of different colours. The emperor [Alamgir II] dressed in white garments, sat on the throne. Seven other persons, among the sons and relations of the emperor, were sitting on his left and right side. Besides them, on the right side stood the son of Khan-Dauran, who had succeeded to his father as Bakshi-i Mumali then and Ghaziuddin Khan [wazir], son of Asaf Jah [I], dressed in Aktah-i Jami, the dress which was prohibited in the court up to the reign of Muhmmad Shah, stood on the left of the throne. When the Emperor asked a question, the said noble merely laughed. This behaviour of the noble astonished the author who remembered the court etiquette of Muhammad Shah. On every side the dancing girls, mimics and story-tellers were showing their performances. When the sun was about to set, the darbar was dismissed. At the time of departure, the Emperor regarded the nobles by offering them (betel-leaves) by his own hands.[25]

Today, there are no grand tents, elaborate dance performances or storytellers seen in the garden. Except the gateway and the pavilion, the mosque is the only other significant structure left. Heading northeast, I find a gateway leading into a quaint mosque complex. Near the masjid, a red-lettered sign reads, '*Yeh masjid ka rasta hai, yeh aam rasta nahin hai* (This is the mosque's path, not a public thoroughfare).' The Qudsia Mosque lies in a pretty, small garden. Built in buff sandstone, it features a charming wuzu tank (where Muslims perform ablutions before prayers). It's a three-bay mosque, topped by domes with inverted-lotus designs and a sandstone finial, though the dome's paint has chipped away. The single-aisle interior has an ornate ceiling, prayer mats on the floor and shelves of books in each corner. A clock, fridge, trunk, cupboard and electric cooler also occupy the space. Since the mosque is functional under the Waqf board, visitors must remove their footwear.

Another entrance opens onto the busy Ring Road where the Yamuna once flowed. Across the Ring Road stands Kashmiri Gate, one of the thirteen gates built by Shah Jahan in the seventeenth century. Originally, this mosque served the imperial household relaxing in the Qudsia Bagh palace. Unfortunately, a dirty canal (nala) now runs near the mosque, far removed from the grand water channels once fed by the Yamuna.

In 1857, the once-majestic Qudsia Bagh suffered devastating damage, leaving much of the garden irreparably ruined. The gateway and mosque bore the brunt of the destruction, but the palace was completely obliterated and vanished from sight. Positioned directly across from Kashmiri Gate, a focal point of the 1857 rebellion, Qudsia Bagh became a target for heavy cannon fire, which decimated its buildings. The garden was caught in the direct line of fire from the Indian sepoys stationed at Kashmiri Gate. The British, having captured Qudsia Bagh, used it as a base to attack the sepoys. The thick walls of the garden provided refuge for many British families and soldiers, who mounted cannons on the frontier walls to counter-attack the sepoys. This relentless shelling caused extensive damage to the garden.

During the British Raj, Qudsia Bagh was repurposed as a venue for grand imperial events, reflecting the colonial administration's strategy to blend local heritage with their imperial narrative. In 1903, during the Delhi Durbar held to commemorate the coronation of King Edward VII as Emperor of India, Qudsia Bagh hosted the Delhi Art Exhibition. This grand industrial exhibition was organized under the orders of Lord Curzon, the then governor-general of India, to showcase India's rich crafts and industrial achievements.[26]

A temporary structure was constructed within the garden to house the exhibitions. The facade of this structure was adorned with exquisite tile-work crafted by potters from Lahore, Multan, Halla and Jaipur, highlighting regional craftsmanship. Additionally, frescoes painted by students of the prestigious Mayo School of Industrial Arts in Lahore added an artistic dimension to the exhibition, symbolizing the British Raj's patronage of Indian art and industry.[27] This event exemplified the colonial administration's use of historical spaces like Qudsia Bagh to project their authority while celebrating India's artistic heritage under the imperial framework.

Qudsia Bagh also played a significant role in India's struggle for independence, becoming a witness to a pivotal moment in the freedom movement. On 9 April 1929, a group of revolutionaries gathered in the serene surroundings of Qudsia Bagh. The group shared a simple meal after which an extraordinary act of commitment unfolded.[28] One of the women revolutionaries pricked her finger and applied a tilak of blood to the foreheads of two young revolutionaries, Bhagat Singh and Batukeshwar Dutt, symbolizing their solemn vow for the nation's freedom.

A few hours later, these two revolutionaries carried out their historic act of defiance by throwing bombs in the Central Assembly in Delhi. This act was not intended to harm but to make a powerful statement against British colonial rule and to awaken the masses to the cause of independence. Qudsia Bagh thus stands as a silent witness to this courageous act of resistance, forever etched in the annals of India's fight for freedom.

The most drastic alterations occurred post-Independence. In the 1960s, constructing the Inter-State Bus Terminal (ISBT) devastated the garden's integrity. Large portions of Qudsia Bagh were destroyed to accommodate this significant transportation hub, drastically altering the historic site's layout and character. Urbanization, population growth and prioritizing infrastructure over heritage contributed to its decline.

Today, only fragments of the original garden and some architectural elements, such as the mosque and pavilion, remain as faint reminders of Qudsia Bagh's once magnificent past.

I had thought my tryst with Qudsia Begum had ended with visiting Qudsia Bagh. I never thought I would encounter another of her commissioned works. A year later, while visiting the Red Fort, I stumbled upon another structure commissioned by Qudsia Begum.

Sunheri Masjid is a well-known parking lot in Daryaganj. Anyone visiting Red Fort or Old Delhi parks their car here and then takes a rickshaw to Old Delhi or walks to the Red Fort entry gate. During her son's brief reign, Qudsia Begum, alongside her trusted aide Javid Khan, commissioned this mosque between 1750 and 1751.[29] Situated along the main road, just south of the palace, the mosque's compound is accessed through a beautifully carved red stone gate. Although small and delicate in structure, the mosque is flanked by two towering minarets on either side. The mosque is a quaint place where believers often sit on the compound wall, under the shade of trees. Not many people realize that this mosque was commissioned by a woman. Her name is mentioned in the sandstone slab outside the compound. Pedestrians often take pictures of the mosque and walk by it.

Qudsia Begum remains a fascinating study of reinvention in the twilight of the Mughal Empire. Despite the constraints of the patriarchal and stratified court, she dared to assert her power by directly engaging in the state affairs—displacing established figures like Safdarjung—and by commissioning structures across the city. Born in a humble background, she didn't let the rigid class system of the Mughal court hold her back. She rattled the elites, the gatekeepers of power, and showed them that real strength did not require noble blood. After all, being badass is all about breaking boundaries and owning your unique power.

In the last years of her life, Qudsia Begum and her son, Ahmad Shah, were imprisoned in Salimgarh Fort, under the orders of the new emperor, Alamgir II. They were cruelly blinded by the wazir, Imad-ul-Mulk, and his men. The mother and son duo spent the last days of their lives in prison. Unfortunately, there is no grave in Delhi that can be traced to Qudsia Begum.

5

The Kingmaker

Roshanara Begum

There is a place in Delhi that is a fountain of youth. It has wide boulevards, tall trees, food joints at every corner, red-brick universities, teeming with young and curious students from all over India. This is Delhi University (DU) headquarters—India's largest institution of higher learning, with over seventy-seven colleges affiliated to it. The university was founded in 1922, but some colleges started in the late nineteenth century. Even though the university's colleges are spread all across Delhi, the North Campus is its beating heart and I am a proud alumnus of one of its prime colleges.

The campuses across DU have evolved and grown over time. And, symbiotically, so have the spaces for eating out, recreation and entertainment. The three main areas for food and shopping are Majnu ka Tila, GTB Nagar and Kamla Nagar. All at a comfortable walking distance.

At the roundabout of Kamla Nagar—a popular market with food and shops for students—is the Ram Swarup clock tower, popularly called Ghanta Ghar. This seventy-two-year-old clock tower has a miraculously functional clock and an iron grille surrounding the structure. It is set amid the heavy traffic and the bustling market of Kamla Nagar.[1] The clock tower separates Roshanara Bagh and Guru Hanuman Akhara from Kamla Nagar. Despite its outward appearance, the clock tower is one of the market's most famous landmarks.

In the winter of 2015, I found myself at Manohar Bikaneri, a popular sweet shop that started in 1960, having moved its base from Bikaner to Delhi, tucking into their marvellous seasonal offering—crispy mattar samosa. It pairs wonderfully with kadak chai, which a nearby makeshift shop sells. The shop also provides a comfortable view of the clock tower. After my little snack, I walked down the street to Maharana Pratap Dwar, an unruly pit stop for trams and cable cars. Also, a fifteen-minute walk from Manohar Bikaneri is the legendary Guru Hanuman Akhara, outside Roshanara Park. Started in 1925 by Padma Shri awardee Vijay Pal Yadav, it is one of the oldest extant akharas in Delhi and has produced the strongest and most talented wrestlers. Today, the akhara trains more than 200 wrestlers.

However, on that day, my destination was Roshanara Park, 800 metres from Ghanta Ghar. Punjabi Gate, the original entry gate to the park, was closed, so I took the modern entry gate. There is a relatively small Hanuman mandir just outside the park. A nearby shop sells everyday groceries like biscuits, crisps and chocolates. Locals come by with their dogs, and older residents amble in for a morning walk.

Entering Roshanara Bagh, I walked straight along a paved path until I encountered a Mughal structure standing in the park's centre. On either side, lawns hosted people dozing on benches, youngsters playing cricket and women gathered for conversation. At first glance, it looks like any neighbourhood park—until that Mughal pavilion brings its deeper history into focus. Roshanara Bagh, once a stunning Mughal retreat, is now but an echo of its past.

Founded around 1650 by Roshanara Begum—Emperor Shah Jahan's second daughter—this garden was designed as an escape from the political intrigues of Shahjahanabad. Located about 4.8 kilometres from the walled city, Roshanara's creation embodied the Mughal aesthetic of blending natural and man-made elements into a private sanctuary. Roshanara Bagh was conceived as a leisure garden—a space where nature and architecture coalesced to create a sensory haven. Enclosed within high walls, it offered privacy and seclusion, shielding its patrons from the bustling world outside.

I closed my eyes and imagined walking through the opulent halls of the Mughal zenana, where delicate wisps of rosewater and sandalwood lingered in the air, and the sound of anklets tinkled softly across white marble floors. In one such chamber, carved into the wall, is a tiny piggy bank—its smooth surface polished from years of loving use. Two young princesses, Roshanara and Jahanara, giggle as they take turns dropping gold and silver coins into its narrow slot, their laughter ringing in the Mughal palace.

This is the story of the second princess—the one that history forgot.

Roshanara Begum, whose name means 'adornment in light', was the second surviving daughter of Shah Jahan and Mumtaz Mahal. She was born on 24 August 1617, in Burhanpur, Madhya Pradesh. She was younger than her sister Jahanara, and brother Dara Shikoh, but was older than her other brothers— Aurangzeb, Shah Shuja and Murad Baksh.

Roshanara and Jahanara were raised with the same education and privilege, but anyone at court could tell— Jahanara was the favourite. The relationship the sisters shared was close-knit, but also competitive and layered. Roshanara knew she was always just a step behind when it came to their parents' affection and presence in the public eye. Perhaps that was what shaped her and her motivations. She wasn't content just being the second daughter. And she would do much to change that, going on to play a key role in one of the biggest political power shifts in Mughal history.

When Shah Jahan ascended the throne in 1628, he granted Jahanara an annual allowance of six lakh rupees, while Roshanara received only one lakh.[2] While both women were among the wealthiest in the empire, the difference in their allowance was significant. Like her sister, Roshanara never married. The lack of suitable alliances, combined with a rule from Akbar that discouraged women of the Mughal household from marrying (especially outside the family), meant no man could pose a threat to the throne. Despite this, both sisters were undeniably powerful figures, possessing the finest buildings, jewels and wardrobes the empire had to offer.

While Jahanara was known for her piety and grace, Roshanara's life was far livelier and more expressive. Their relationship, in many ways, can be compared to that of Queen Elizabeth II and her outspoken sister, Princess Margaret. The key difference, however, was that Jahanara was far more subtle in her approach, often relying on the support of powerful men to navigate the court. Roshanara, on the other hand, was more direct, doing little to mask her ambitions or desires. Her straightforwardness often came across as bold and, at times, tactless—an approach that set her apart from her more refined sister.

In his travelogue, François Bernier, seventeenth-century French traveller, describes Roshanara:

> Rauchenara-Begum, the Mogol's young daughter was less beautiful than her sister, neither was she so remarkable for understanding; she was nevertheless possessed of the same vivacity, and equally the votary of pleasure.[3]

Roshanara's resentment towards Jahanara's privileged position in the Mughal court was hard to ignore. Not only was Jahanara their father's favourite, her wealth too was staggering. To add insult to injury, at the age of seventeen, Jahanara was made Padshah Begum, the head of the imperial household. In contrast, Roshanara had to constantly fight for her father's attention and affection, often feeling neglected, overshadowed by Jahanara's status and influence.

As the war of succession unfolded, the sisters' loyalties took opposing sides. Shah Jahan and Jahanara supported Dara Shikoh, who was known for his religious tolerance, cultured nature and his patronage towards the arts, while Roshanara aligned herself with her younger brother, Aurangzeb, whose temperament was in stark contrast to Dara Shikoh's. He was pragmatic, disciplined, a skilled military strategist and a devout, orthodox Muslim.

Roshanara, however, wasn't just a passive observer in the struggle for the throne. Living in the royal harem, she became adept at gathering information from a network of spies. They secretly relayed crucial information to Aurangzeb, helping him in his quest for power. Bernier remarked at Roshanara's cunning:

> She became the ardent partisan of Aureng-Zebe, and made no secret of her enmity to Begum-Saheb and Dara. This might be the reason why she amassed but little wealth, and took but an inconsiderable part in public affairs. Still, as she was an inmate of the Seraglio, and not deficient in artifice, she succeeded in conveying, by means of spies, much valuable intelligence to Aureng-Zebe.[4]

Roshanara did everything she could to assist Aurangzeb in his quest for the throne. She became a key informant, secretly gathering intelligence from the royal courts in Agra and in Delhi, ensuring Aurangzeb was always updated on the moves of their father and Dara Shikoh. One of the most significant episodes, mentioned by the French traveller François Bernier, was her warning Aurangzeb of an *alleged* plot by their father to kill him under the pretense of a meeting. This information, whether grounded in truth or court rumour, allowed Aurangzeb to act swiftly, a debt he would never forget.

Her role in the war of succession went beyond just covert actions; she was a key player in shaping the outcome. As François Bernier noted:

> I have been told that Chah-Jehan did, in fact, send the elephants, with the roupies of gold, to Dara, on the very night of his departure from Dehli, and that it was Rauchenara-Begum who communicated the information to Aureng-Zebe. That Princess also apprised him of the presence of the Tartar women, by whom it was intended he should be assailed when he entered the castle. It is even said that Aureng-Zebe intercepted some letters written by his father to Dara.[5]

Not only did she help to secure her brother's future, Roshanara also positioned herself as a powerful figure in the Mughal court. One foreign account claims that she supported the execution of Dara Shikoh and, in the aftermath, held a grand feast celebrating the triumph of her side, though the veracity of this account is uncertain. After Aurangzeb's victory and the acquisition of the Qila-e-Mubarak fort, Roshanara rose to a powerful position. For her, this was more than just a political move—it was her opportunity to step out from her sister's shadow. For years, Jahanara had held the position of the emperor's favourite and the head of the imperial household. But with Aurangzeb's victory, the tables had turned. Roshanara could finally rise and claim her own space in the imperial structure. As a kingmaker, in her own right, she had successfully navigated the cut-throat politics of the Mughal court, proving that she could wield power just as efficiently as her more celebrated sibling. Roshanara had proven herself indispensable. She wasn't just a witness to Aurangzeb's rise; she was one of its architects.

When Aurangzeb came to power in 1659, he installed Roshanara as Padshah Begum, replacing Jahanara Begum, and also gave her a cash award of five lakh rupees. But perhaps it was never Aurangzeb's decision, because he didn't really have a choice but to install his sister Roshanara as Padshah Begum and keep his promise to her. Jahanara was in voluntary exile with her father, Shah Jahan in Agra Fort, and she refused to come to Delhi.

Soon, Roshanara grew to be her brother's most trusted confidante in court. She didn't just support him emotionally but actively shaped political strategy. Travellers and diplomats quickly realized that if they wanted anything done, or wanted access to trade rights or imperial favours, it was Roshanara they needed to please. In 1668, François Bernier wrote from Surat about how essential it was to win Roshanara's favour: 'Roshan Ara Begum is so much in favour that it would perhaps be better to give her a few presents.'[6]

Seventeenth-century French gem merchant Jean-Baptiste Tavernier also referred to her as the 'Grand Begum', a title that reflected the reverence and authority she commanded. He once gifted Roshanara's eunuch a watch in a jewelled case—a strategic gesture of diplomacy.[7]

Her position in court wasn't symbolic; she wielded real influence. Bernier noted that even Aurangzeb's decision to travel to Kashmir in 1664—while Shah Jahan was still under house arrest—may not have been purely for health reasons. He suggested it was Roshanara's influence that nudged the emperor forward for the journey:

> … this excursion may not rather be attributed to the arts and influence of Rauchenara-Begum, who has been long anxious to inhale a purer air than that of the Seraglio, and to appear in her turn amid a pompous and magnificent army, as her sister Begum-Saheb had done during the reign of Chah-Jehan.[8]

When Roshanara travelled with Aurangzeb on this royal expedition, it was a grand spectacle designed to cement her status at court. Bernier's descriptions paint a vivid picture of the power she commanded:

> [...] you can conceive no exhibition more grand and imposing than when Roshan Ara Begum, mounted on a stupendous Pegu elephant and seated in a Mikdembar (decorated howdah), blazing with gold and azure, is followed by five or six other elephants … nearly as resplendent as her own, and filled with ladies attached to her household. In front of the princess marched the chief eunuchs on horses richly caparisoned, each mounted with a baton of office in his hand. Behind her followed a troupe of female servants, Tartars and Kashmiris, fantastically

attired and riding handsome pad-horses. Immediately behind Roshan Ara's retinue appears a principal lady of the court, mounted and attended much in the manner as the princess. This lady followed by a third, she by fourth, and on, until fifteen or sixteen females of quality pass with a grandeur of appearance ... these distinguished lovely females seated in Mikdembars are thus elevated above the earth like many superior beings borne along through the middle regions of the air.[9]

It was certainly a choreographed image of power—Roshanara, elevated both literally and politically, borne above the ground like a celestial being, impossible to ignore. The message was clear: this was no longer the sidelined younger daughter of Shah Jahan. This was the woman who helped make a king.

But power in the Mughal court was never without scrutiny, especially when it came to women. And Roshanara, for all her political clout, was no exception. Once she had secured her place as Aurangzeb's most trusted advisor, whispers of her private life began to echo more loudly through the zenana walls.

Roshanara, much like her sister Jahanara, had her share of admirers and romantic entanglements—stories that didn't just remain in hushed corners of the harem but spilled into foreign accounts. François Bernier, who had close access to court gossip, doesn't shy away from detailing the scandals. What's striking is not just the nature of these stories, but how differently the two sisters were treated by the emperors they served. Under Shah Jahan's rule, the consequences for romantic indiscretions were severe, even deadly. One brutal incident involving Jahanara's lover is recounted by Bernier with chilling detail:

> Chah-Jehan was apprised of her guilt, and resolved to enter her apartments at an unusual and un-expected hour. The intimation of his approach was too sudden to allow her the choice of more than one place of concealment. The affrighted gallant sought refuge in the capacious cauldron used for the baths. The King's countenance denoted neither surprise nor displeasure; he discoursed with his daughter on ordinary topics, but finished the conversation by observing that the state of her skin indicated a neglect of her customary ablutions, and that it was proper she should bathe. He then commanded the Eunuchs to light a fire under the cauldron, and did not retire until they gave him to understand that his wretched victim was no more.[10]

This wasn't an isolated event. Bernier details two further escapades—one involving a lover hidden in the gardens of the harem, and the other who was caught wandering and excused with little consequence.

> I learnt that Rauchenara-Begum, after having for several days enjoyed the company of one of these young men, whom she kept hidden, committed him to the care of her female attendants, who promised to conduct their charge out of the Seraglio under cover of the night. But

whether they were detected, or only dreaded a discovery, or whatever else was the reason, the women fled, and left the terrified youth to wander alone about the gardens: here he was found, and taken before Aureng-Zebe; who, when he had interrogated him very closely, without being able to draw any other confession of guilt from him than that he had scaled the walls, decided that he should be compelled to leave the seraglio in the same manner. But the eunuchs, it is probable, exceeded their master's instructions, for they threw the culprit from the top of the wall to the bottom. As for the second paramour, the old Portuguese informed me that he too was seen roving about the gardens, and that having told the King he had entered into the seraglio by the regular gate, he was commanded to quit the place through that same gate. Aureng-Zebe determined, however, to inflict a severe and exemplary punishment upon the eunuchs; because it was essential, not only to the honour of his house, but even to his personal safety, that the entrance into the seraglio should be vigilantly guarded.[11]

While the lovers didn't always escape unscathed, Roshanara herself remained largely untouchable. Aurangzeb, though known for his orthodoxy and severity, was oddly more forgiving when it came to Roshanara.

So, what does it tell us?

Roshanara wasn't just serving court politics—she was bending it to suit herself. Her influence was such that even when Aurangzeb, a ruler known for his moral rigidity, caught wind of her affairs, he chose to overlook them. This wasn't leniency; it was respect. Roshanara had become so indispensable that she could walk a line no other woman at court could. She carved her space as the unapologetic political operator who didn't need to pretend.

Despite her power, Roshanara still had to bargain for the kind of personal liberty her brother exercised freely. On one occasion, she asked Aurangzeb to grant her the same palace where Jahanara had once lived—what she really wanted was not just a new address, but the autonomy and indulgence that came with it. She was asking, in effect, for the same space her sister had carved out under Shah Jahan—a space that allowed her privacy, and a certain freedom of movement and choice.

Aurangzeb, who had long learned to mask his calculations behind piety and politeness, denied her request with a velvet-gloved refusal:

Roshanara Begum, my beloved sister! I would gladly grant you what you ask, but my affection for you prevents me from living without your company. It is also customary for the daughters of the emperor not to reside outside their father's palace. My daughters would feel deprived of your presence. Therefore, for many reasons, it is most appropriate that you remain with them and guide them in the ways of royal princesses. Tell me, is there any deficiency in the palace where you currently reside? Or do you feel that the grandeur you enjoy falls short of what your sister, Begum Sahib, experienced? You are well aware

that all the resources and wealth of the Mughal Empire
are at your disposal.[12]

And here is the irony: Aurangzeb, like other emperors before
him, had multiple wives, concubines and the freedom to
engage in relationships as he pleased. Roshanara, on the other
hand—unmarried by design, politically indispensable, rich
beyond imagination—still had to navigate her personal life
like it was a state secret.

For all her political cunning and strategic foresight,
Roshanara's greatest miscalculation may have been that she
believed that Aurangzeb's love for her was unconditional.

In the early years of his reign, she wielded enormous
influence—not just as his sister, but as his most trusted
advisor, his kingmaker. She moved confidently through
the zenana and court, untouchable, despite scandal, even
when whispers of her lovers reached the emperor's ears. He
dismissed the gossip around Roshanara with diplomatic tact,
choosing to protect her rather than punish her. But power in
the Mughal court is as fickle as spring rain.

And it was ambition that eventually triggered Roshanara's
downfall. In 1662 CE, Aurangzeb fell ill. He was delirious with
fever, bleeding heavily and paralysed in speech. It was during
this time that Roshanara made her move.

Assuming the emperor would not survive, she seized the
royal seal and began dispatching letters in support of his nine-
year-old son Azam, whom she hoped to install as a puppet
ruler under regency.[13] She barred access to the emperor's

bedchamber, controlling the flow of information, thus consolidating her power in secret. Manucci writes:

> When the mother of Sultan Mu'azzam learnt this, she said to Roshan Ara Begam that what she was doing was not right ... while the king was still alive and there was hope of his recovery. Having said this, she proceeded to the king's bedside, but Roshan Ara Begam boldly seized her by the hair and ejected her from the royal chamber. The queen, not to afflict her suffering husband, bore it quietly and patiently. ... Roshan Ara Begam was the causer of all this uproar. She allowed no one to see the sick Aurangzeb, except one eunuch belonging to her faction. But Sultan Mu'azzam, who was sixteen years of age, and lived outside the fort, in the mansion of Prince Dara, was afraid that his father was already dead, and that Roshan Ara Begam did not want the news to spread until she had persuaded the Hindu princes to support Prince A'zam Tara ...[14]

What Roshanara did was bold and audacious. It was also a step too far. When Aurangzeb recovered—barely—he was furious. Not just at the political overreach, but at the cruelty Roshanara had shown towards the mother of another of his sons, Mu'azzam.

From that point on, Aurangzeb began to think more highly of his queen. He raised her status and gave her a new title—Nawab Bai Ji, meaning 'Greatest among Women'.

His affection for their son, Sultan Mu'azzam, also deepened. Aurangzeb renamed him Shah Alam, or 'King of the World', a title that reflected both pride and promise.

But not everyone got a share in his growing warmth. Roshanara Begum, once his favourite sister and close confidante, fell from grace. Her actions had angered Aurangzeb, and the bond they once shared started to crack. The love he had for her was no longer the same.

Between 1658–1666, Roshanara was one of the most powerful women in the empire—rich, feared and politically shrewd. But her reign had always been precarious, dependent as it was on Aurangzeb's affection. Once that faltered, her fall was inevitable. When Shah Jahan died in 1666, Aurangzeb reached out to Jahanara, and begged her to come back to Red Fort. He invited her back to the court, and reinstated her as Padshah Begum. With that symbolic gesture, Roshanara was quietly replaced.

I crossed the gate that divides the pavilion from the rest of the park. The sandstone baradari, an exquisite pavilion commissioned by Roshanara Begum, rests serenely within a shallow rectangular hauz, or water tank, once adorned with sparkling fountains. The pavilion is approached by graceful walkways inviting visitors into its tranquil embrace. The hauz, now dry and empty, features intricately carved kangura, or battlement designs, along its edges, evoking a bygone era of elegance. The baradari, constructed in the Shahjahani architectural style, was a masterpiece of interconnected arched spaces and colonnades. It stood in the middle of the tank, accessible via walkways and surrounded by four water channels that followed the charbagh layout—a hallmark of Mughal garden design. Constance Villiers-Stuart, in her 1913 work *Gardens of the Great Mughals*, observed that these channels extended in cardinal directions, connecting the baradari to other pavilions and spaces.[15]

Elevated on a 2.5-metre plinth, the pavilion commands attention with its imposing height. To reach it, one ascends four broad steps, stepping into a world of architectural splendour. A chajja, or parapet, encircles the structure, offering respite from the blazing sun and the monsoon rains. Spanning an area of 65 square feet and rising 21-feet high, the square pavilion boasts of classic Shahjahani architecture, with its signature cusped arches and slender, ornate pillars.[16]

At the heart of the pavilion lies a square chamber, its walls adorned with exquisite jaali work, filtering light and air into the serene space where Roshanara rests. The cenotaph, though missing, once symbolized her resting place, surrounded by an atmosphere of quiet reverence. Her grave, modest yet poignant, is crafted in the same style as her sister Jahanara's, though the cenotaph is conspicuously absent. An empty space marks where it might have stood, pointing towards the burial site beneath. The tomb chamber itself is 10 square feet, with a floor of pristine white marble.[17] Earth surrounds the grave, a humbling contrast to the grandeur of the pavilion. The idea behind both Jahanara's grave and Roshanara's grave was to keep it open to the sky and air, and be buried as humble slaves of God unlike the bewitching grandeur of their parents' graves inside the Taj Mahal.

The cusped arches are painted with vibrant frescoes of cherry trees, pomegranate blossoms and other flowering plants, their natural beauty immortalized in delicate strokes. The cusped Shahjahani arches are supported by bulbous pillars which are typical to the architecture of that time.[18] The central hall connects seamlessly to the four corners of the structure, where staircases ascend to the first floor. These upper rooms, too, are adorned with frescoes, their walls whispering tales of a bygone era. Crowning the pavilion are four elegant turrets, each rising 5–6 feet high, each capped with an intricately carved stone kalash, symbolizing prosperity and completion. The roof, with its stunning symmetry and artistry, stands as a testament to the skill and vision of the artisans who brought Roshanara's dream to life. While Roshanara's elder sister Jahanara Begum was engaged in grand projects like the Begum ki Serai, hammams and Chandni Chowk, Roshanara chose a more modest yet equally elegant creation. Despite its smaller scale, Roshanara Bagh reflected the Mughal Empire's hallmark of refined aesthetic sensibilities, emphasizing leisure, beauty and harmony with nature.

One can imagine the spectacle of Roshanara's elephant procession leaving Delhi Fort—massive elephants draped in gold-embroidered cloth, jingling silver bells echoing through the streets and the princess reclining in a rose-curtained litter. As they neared her tranquil garden, the noise of the capital fell away, replaced by the fragrance of blossoms and the murmur of fountains. It was a graceful escape from courtly heat and chaos into the cool, serene embrace of Roshanara Bagh.

By the eighteenth century, Roshanara Bagh had faded into relative obscurity, a reflection of the political instability of the era. The garden attracted few visitors, including Europeans, resulting in scarce archival records or eyewitness accounts. After the British occupation of Delhi, the garden became part of the Nazul lands—property seized by the British crown. It was handed over to the Delhi Municipality. In 1875, under the direction of Colonel Cracroft, the then commissioner of Delhi, Roshanara Bagh underwent extensive remodelling. During this process, all garden structures—except for the baradari-turned-tomb, the water channel and the eastern gateway—were demolished. The garden was subsequently 'modernized' and transformed into a public park.[19] The Delhi Municipality undertook several initiatives to remodel Roshanara Bagh during the late nineteenth century. A key change was the introduction of expansive lawns that replaced much of the former orchard, with the baradari standing prominently amidst the lush greenery as the garden's main attraction. Both ornamental and fruit trees were planted, the latter aimed at making the garden self-sustaining.

Winding pathways were laid out, dividing the original orchard into sections, allowing visitors to leisurely explore the grounds. Significant work was also done on the large tank in 1884–1885, including desilting, increasing its depth to 15 feet, smoothening and turfing its edges, and enhancing its appeal with the addition of gold and silver fish sourced from the public gardens near the Taj Mahal in Agra.[20] These efforts collectively transformed the historic Mughal garden into a more modern recreational space.

A unique aspect of this complex that secures its place in history is its association with the country's cricketing heritage. The Roshanara Club, once linked to this garden, is believed to date back to 1922, to the British era. This club holds a significant place in cricket history, as it was here that the Board of Control for Cricket in India (BCCI) was established. Additionally, the nation's first cricket pitch was built on the club's grounds, where cricket matches have been played since 1927.[21]

Thus, between 1917 and 1918, one of the most significant changes to Roshanara Bagh took place when a large portion of its lush lawns was transformed into a cricket ground, complete with the construction of a cricket pavilion. The Delhi Municipality praised this development as an 'improvement' and a 'great boon to the cricket-loving public'. Once completed, cricket matches became the garden's primary attraction, overshadowing its historical and cultural significance. The Mughal-era centrepiece, Begum Roshanara's baradari-turned-tomb, was left to languish in obscurity. In 1922, approximately 22 acres of the garden, located to the west of the baradari and beyond the tank, were allocated to the newly established Roshanara Cricket Club.[22] The club, which still exists today, has since replaced the original Mughal garden as a prominent city landmark. The Roshanara Cricket Club, the oldest in the city, continues to be an enduring part of Delhi's heritage. The baradari-turned-tomb also doubled as

(Previous page) **Painting of Princess Jahanara Begum**, aged eighteen, a year after her mother's death.

The painting is attributed to Lalchand made at Agra or Burhanpur, India. Ca. 1632
Source: British Library, Add Or 3129, f.13v.

(Clockwise from above) **Jahanara Begum's caravanserai** that formed the original Chandni Chowk, from Sir Thomas Theophilus Metcalf's 1843 album. The serai featured a vast courtyard with two wells and a mosque, surrounded by a double-storeyed structure with ninety rooms, balconies and corner bastions. This painting depicts the front of the serai that opened to Chandni Chowk. Behind the serai was Begum ka Bagh, exclusive to women. Ca. 1843.
Source: British Library, London, via Wikimedia Commons

The northern wing of Town Hall is framed by **Begum ka Bagh**. Before 1857, Begum ki Serai stood facing this extensive garden, which was carefully designed by Jahanara Begum, with a stream from the Yamuna flowing through it.

After 1857, **Begum ki Serai** was demolished and Lawrence Institute was built. Later, it came to be known as Town Hall. Delhi's famous poet Mirza Ghalib has written about Town Hall in his letters, mentioning how the building was used by rich and influential merchant and trading classes to meet and make decisions for the entire city.

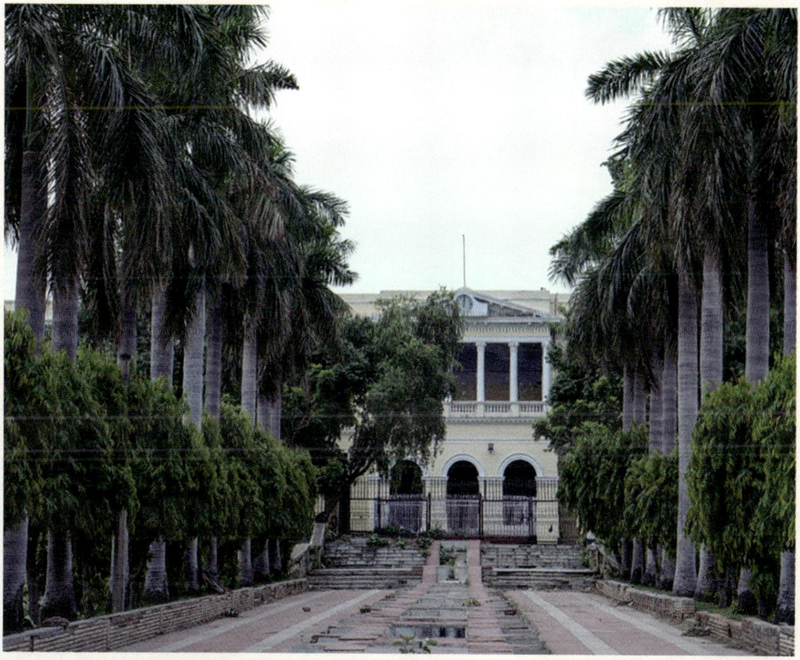

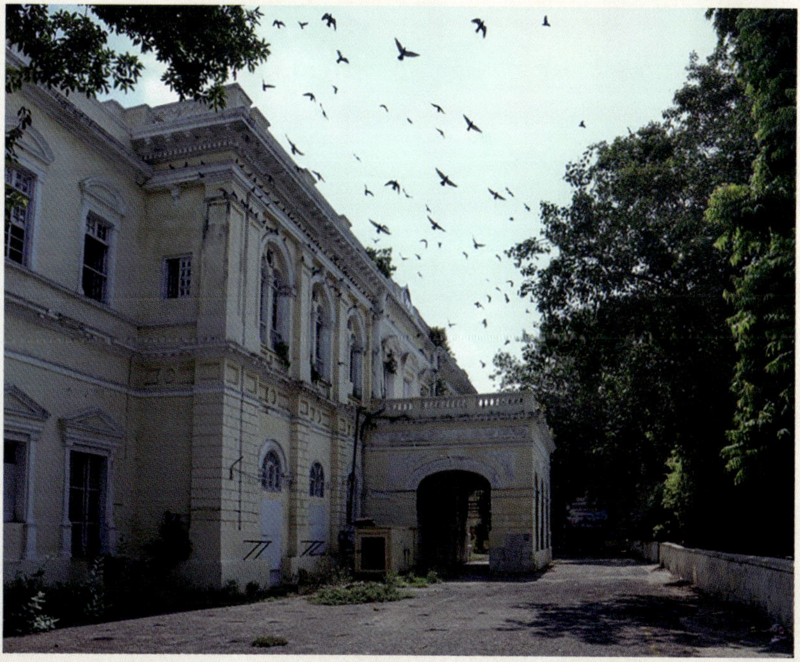

(Clockwise from above) Watercolour on ivory of **Begum Zeenat Mahal**, wife of **Emperor Bahadur Shah Zafar**, one of eleven bust portraits of Mughal ladies and princesses.
Source: Victoria and Albert Museum, London

The house of Zeenat Mahal in Lal Kuan where the British confined Bahadur Shah II. Photograph by Felice Beato, 1858.
Source: The J. Paul Getty Museum, Los Angeles. Partial gift from the Wilson Centre for Photography via Wikimedia Commons

The tombs of Emperor Bahadur Shah Zafar's wife and son, next to where he was presumably buried in Yangon, Myanmar.
Photograph by Emerald Range.
Source: Wikimedia Commons

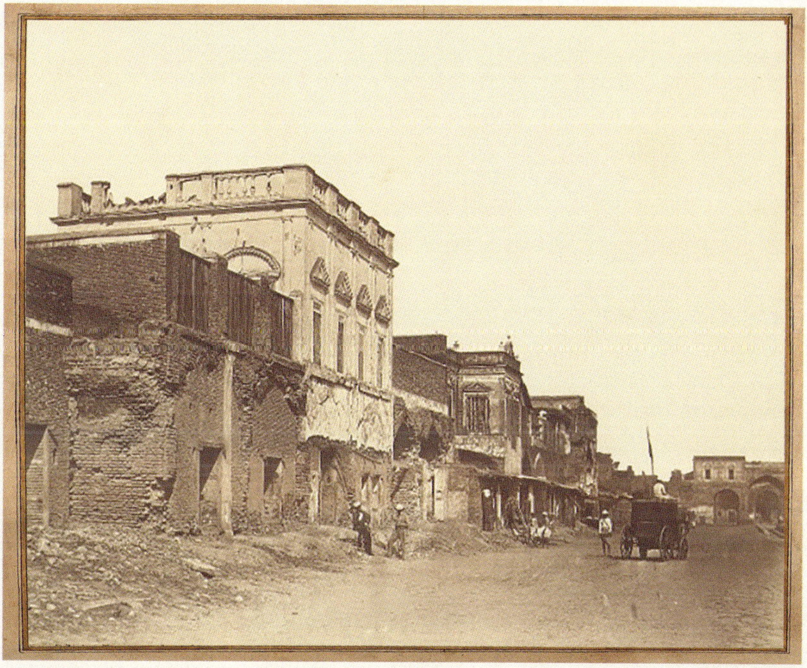

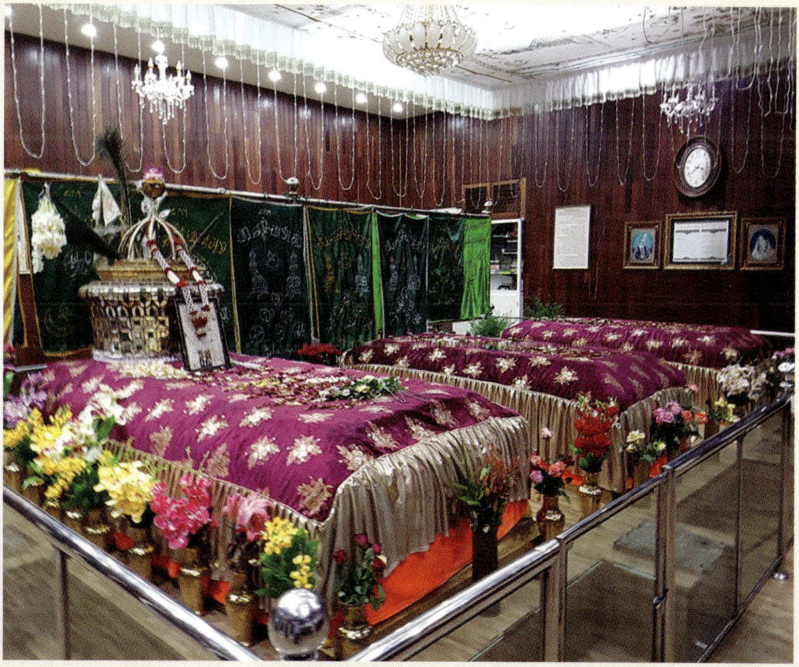

(Above) The once grand front facade of **Zeenat Mahal's** haveli marked by red sandstone jharokhas, a Belgian glass mirror window and delicate sandstone carvings was tall enough for Zeenat Mahal to ride in on an elephant.

(Below) **Begum Samru's haveli is now Bhagirath Place**, Asia's largest electrical market. Sold to Delhi Bank in 1847, it became Lloyds Bank after 1857.

'Begum Samru and Her Household', painting, colours on paper, by
Muhammad A'zam. Delhi, India, 1820–25. This crowded scene shows
the ruler of Sardhana, Begum Samru (1751–1836), and her extensive
household, receiving four guests who are seated in a row in the centre.
Every figure has been named in a small inscription, including the four
visitors (three nawabs and a bakshi, or paymaster), who have been
linked with the Mughal court of Akbar Shah II in Delhi. The Begum's
international household included David Dyce-Samru (sitting on her
right), to whom she would bequeath most of her wealth, and John
Thomas (beside Dyce-Samru), an Irish-Indian officer in her army, who
had been adopted into her court in 1795.

Source: Chester Beatty, Dublin, CC BY- 4.0

(Clockwise from above) The mosque inside **Qudsia Bagh** in Civil Lines.
It once faced Kashmere Gate, one of Shahjahanabad's entry points, and
the Yamuna River. The mosque was damaged during the Revolt of 1857
due to heavy shelling but has since been restored. On Google maps the
mosque is renamed as 'Shahi Masjid' (meaning Royal Mosque).

This is the only remaining gateway inside Qudsia Bagh. Grand and
spacious, the gateway has inner chambers and a staircase leading to
the roof.

The Sunheri Masjid commissioned by **Qudsia Begum**, stands across the
Red Fort parking lot, interestingly called Sunheri Masjid Parking. The
copper plates that gave it the name Sunheri (meaning 'golden') have long
been lost.

The painting by Mir Kalan Khan, 1742, shows **Queen Udham Bai** being entertained by actors in Portuguese costumes and ladies in European attire. Set against the backdrop of the Red Fort with the Yamuna flowing behind, the scene highlights her stature at court. Lesser queens watch the performance from their jharokas, underscoring Udham Bai's authority at the height of her influence over the Mughal throne.

Source: San Diego Museum of Art Edwin Binney 3rd Collection. Accession Number: 1990.383

(Next page) **'The Qudsia Bagh, Delhi: Eastern View'.**
Coloured aquatint by Thomas Daniell, 1795, depicting the palace inside Qudsia Bagh.

Source: Wellcome Collection

NORTH EAST VIEW OF THE COT

PUBLISHED AS THE ACT DIRECTS FOR THOS DAN

ON THE RIVER JUMNA, DELHI.

HISTORIC GALLERY, PALL MALL, MAY 1795.

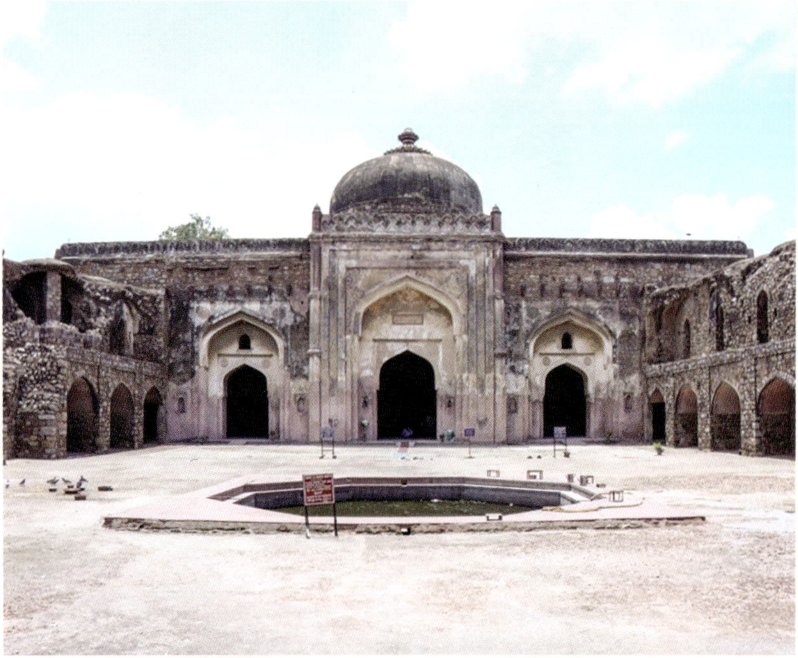

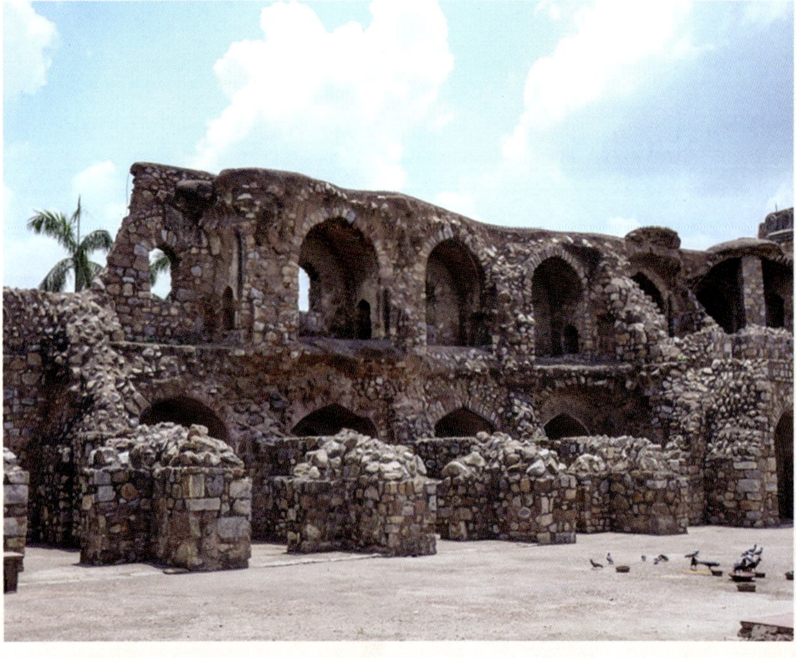

(Above) **'Marriage of Adham Khan' (c. 1590–95)**, from the *Akbarnama*, painted by Sanwala Lal. The scene depicts the wedding ceremony of Adham Khan, son of Maham Anga. Maham Anga, dressed in bright yellow, is shown seated beside the young Emperor Akbar on the throne. Its inclusion in the *Akbarnama* underscores the influence Maham Anga and her family held in Akbar's formative years.
Source: Victoria and Albert Museum, London

(Previous page above) **Khair-ul-Manazil, built by Maham Anga**. The mosque's facade still displays traces of its once-vibrant glazed tiles, though time has worn much of them away over its 500-year history. Locals also believe the mosque is home to djinns, especially after dusk.

(Previous page below) The madrassa within the Khair-ul-Manazil complex. A woman commissioning a madrassa is rare in history. Maham Anga's move was not just pious, but deeply political. Her use of religious patronage to legitimize her power was a masterclass in strategy.

(Above) **'Sir David Ochterlony in Delhi'** (1820s). Watercolour by an anonymous Delhi-style artist. The painting depicts Ochterlony in his residency at the former Dara Shikoh Library (today the Partition Museum), seated in Indian attire and smoking a hookah in the manner of a nawab. The setting blends European elements—such as portraits on the walls and vases—with a distinctly Indo-Mughal ambience. At the centre, a nautch performance unfolds under the watchful eye of an elderly matriarch.

Source: British Library, London

(Previous page from above) **Zeenat-ul-Masjid**, popularly known as Ghata Masjid (meaning 'cloud mosque'), is one of the most beautiful mosques of Shahjahanabad. After the Revolt of 1857, the British used the mosque as a bakery for many years.

Fatehpuri Masjid is second only to Jama Masjid in popularity. Built at the far end of Chandni Chowk, it directly aligns with the Lahori Gate of the Red Fort. The mosque houses a functioning madrassa. Uniquely, the mosque has a single dome instead of the usual three.

The entrance to Fatehpuri Masjid is surrounded by the iconic flavours of Old Delhi. To its left is the legendary sweet shop Chaina Ram. To the right are shops brimming with dry fruits and winter favourites like rabri.

J. V. Schley direx.

'Roshanara Begum' (1746–59). An eighteenth-century European engraving from *Histoire générale des Voyages* (Paris, 1746–59), compiled by Abbé Antoine François Prévost with illustrations by Jacques-Nicolas Bellin. The image reflects how Roshanara Begum, Aurangzeb's sister, was represented in European imagination of Mughal royalty.

Source: Courtesy of Columbia University Libraries, via Wikimedia Commons

a 'refreshment room' for visitors and for tourists who would indeed venture thus far.

Additionally, with the expansion of Delhi's railway network, the Delhi Municipality carved out sections of the garden and handed them over to the railways for operational use. This act further diminished the garden's status as a historic site. Despite all the remodelling, its location, away from the walled city and New Delhi, makes it a better preserved Mughal garden, unlike Begum ka Bagh, built by Jahanara in Chandni Chowk, that has completely disappeared.

Before Independence, this area was home to many soldiers, with horses tethered along the roadsides. Later, Punjabi families who migrated from Pakistan during Partition also settled in this area, adding to its unique history. Roshanara Bagh remains one of the most quaint, beautiful Mughal gardens and, despite losing its regal glory, it is a popular spot for residents who visit to sit under the shadow of Roshanara Begum.

Tragically, in the 1960s, a section of this historic garden was redesigned in the Japanese style, disregarding its original Mughal character and heritage. A Japanese garden design expert, Mr Mori, was invited by the federal government to identify a suitable location in the nation's capital for a Japanese garden. The chosen site was none other than the historic Roshanara Bagh. The proposed plans included constructing a restaurant on an island, along with a pond, waterfalls, brooks, rock formations, shelters and Japanese-style landscaping—entirely altering the character of this Mughal-era site.[23]

Today, Roshanara Bagh bears little resemblance to the splendour of its original days. The garden's layout has been altered significantly, and many of its structures have vanished, leaving only the baradari as a testament to its past glory. The fountains are dry, the water channels are in disrepair and the once-vibrant flora has dwindled. A plaque by the Archaeological Department marks the site, but it lacks maintenance, leaving the garden overlooked amidst the crowded urban sprawl. Roshanara Bagh holds immense potential to be a special attraction in Delhi, showcasing the cultural and architectural brilliance of the Mughal era. With proper restoration and revitalization of its fountains, water channels and gardens, it could reclaim its status as a serene retreat and a testament to Roshanara Begum's legacy.

Roshanara passed away in 1671, aged just fifty-four, during the thirteenth year of Aurangzeb's reign. According to her wishes, she was buried in her beloved garden, beneath the open sky. There is no ornate tombstone, no imperial dome—just a modest grave covered with soil and surrounded by jaali. It is perhaps no coincidence that her final resting place is now considered a spot in Delhi that provides a strange sense of peace. Locals say that fights brought to Roshanara's grave do not last. Couples, friends, siblings, all arrive with anger on their tongues, but after sitting near her tomb, something shifts. Conversations begin. Resentments melt. By the time they leave, their tempers have softened, replaced by quiet understanding.

There is something hauntingly fitting about that. Roshanara herself never found resolution with her family. She was estranged from her father, betrayed her brothers, and was ultimately discarded by the very emperor she had once helped to the throne. Perhaps this is why her tomb draws the broken-hearted and the angry. Perhaps it's because she, more than anyone, understood what it meant to be unheard, unloved and unforgiven. Her story is a stark reminder that power never guarantees peace.

The Roshanara Club in Delhi was a popular hangout for dignitaries like Jawaharlal Nehru, and cricket legends like Lala Amarnath and Mohinder Amarnath. It was also the birthplace of the BCCI! Founded in 1922, this exclusive club saw R.E. Grant Govan, a founding member, become the first president of the BCCI in 1928. The club's cricket facilities were open to non-members for a fee—Rs 11,800 on weekdays and Rs 16,500 on weekends. However, in September 2023, the Delhi Development Authority (DDA) sealed the club, claiming it had illegally occupied land worth thousands of crores for years!

6

The Power behind the Throne

Maham Anga

There are two well-known heritage and cultural sites along Mathura Road—Purana Qila and the National Zoo. In the weekends, they witness a heavy footfall of visitors keen on making a day of it by exploring both locations. Many families head to the National Zoo, bringing excited children, eager to spot elephants, rhinos, bears, lions and tigers. Outside the zoo, near the parking area, several simple food stalls offer quick bites like chole bhature, pav bhaji, samosa chole, Maggi, momos and other snacks. Meanwhile, young couples, photographers and heritage enthusiasts often visit Purana Qila, though most remain unaware of its history. Few realize why Purana Qila—literally 'Old Fort'—carries that name, given that other Delhi forts are actually older.

It's deemed 'old' because it's traditionally identified as Indraprastha, where the Pandava brothers from the Mahabharata once reigned. But most people's curiosity ends there, and the surrounding neighbourhood—rich with

134

hidden heritage—remains overlooked. With this in mind, I set out to map Purana Qila's environs and spotlight the lesser-known heritage sites around it—equally beautiful and deserving of renewed attention.

I parked near the National Zoo and crossed the very busy Mathura Road. It took me a few attempts to successfully navigate across Mathura Road, which is always choked with traffic. At the bustling intersection of Subramanya Bharati Marg and Mathura Road, directly facing the imposing Purana Qila, stands a lesser-known yet historically rich monument—Khair-ul-Manazil (which means 'The Most Auspicious of Houses'). Often mistaken as part of Purana Qila, this grand mosque was built after the fortress, in 1561–1562, by Maham Anga, the formidable and influential wet nurse of Emperor Akbar. The monument was built as a functional mosque and a madrassa where young students could study and learn. The area was known for imparting learning and education. The structure presently only functions as a mosque. As I stood before this overlooked architectural treasure, I felt a profound connection to the layers of history beneath my feet—where once young scholars debated scripture and philosophy, now only whispered prayers remained, echoing through centuries of forgotten knowledge.

Maham Anga was the wife of Nadim Khan Kuka, Humayun's foster brother. Following the political turmoil of the early 1540s, when Humayun was exiled to Persia, Maham Anga's life took a dramatic turn. Her husband left to serve Humayun and Hamida Banu Begum in Persia in 1541, leaving her behind to raise their son, Adham Khan, and care for Hamida's young charge, Akbar, in the secure fortress of Qandhar, Afghanistan.[1] Though Maham Anga was not Akbar's biological mother, she would become his most influential maternal figure. Despite never breastfeeding him, she was the chief wet nurse in charge of a team of eleven women, tending to Akbar's every need and ensuring his well-being.

In the Mughal Empire, wet nurses held significant importance within the royal harem, as they were responsible for the upbringing and care of the emperor's children, especially when political or personal circumstances separated the child from their biological mother. These women, often called 'Anagas', were given high ranks within the harem and were trusted with the nurturing and protection of the royal heirs. Their influence went beyond the mere act of breastfeeding—they were integral to the child's early development and emotional well-being, often acting as surrogate mothers.

These wet nurses, thus, played a crucial role in the royal family. As seen with Akbar, who was separated from his biological mother, Hamida Banu, for several years due to political reasons, these women often raised the royal children. Some of Akbar's foster mothers, such as Jiji Anaga (wife of Shams-ud-din Atka Khan), Fakhr-un-Nissa (wife of Nadim Koka) and Khildar Anaga, were prominent and well-respected figures in the Mughal court.[2]

In many cases, these nurses formed a close bond with the children and could influence them throughout their lives. Their loyalty was highly valued, and many were connected to influential figures in the empire, which enhanced their status. Wet nurses were often married to influential men in the Mughal administration, like Shams-ud-din Atka Khan.[3] They could hold significant sway in the political and social spheres of the empire. Some wet nurses even had the authority to negotiate political matters, as their closeness to the royal family granted them a unique position of power.

Maham Anga's bond with Akbar was a special one. She was his protector in the truest sense. Around 1545 CE, Humayun secured control of Qandhar from his brother Mirza Askari with the support of the Shah of Persia and, five years later, captured Kabul from his other brother Mirza Kamran. According to the *Akbarnama*, when news of Humayun's return from Persia spread, Mirza Kamran insisted that Akbar be sent to him. After much deliberation, Mirza Askari decided to send Akbar to Kabul. Abul Fazl wrote: 'Eventually, Mirza Askari disregarded wise counsel and sent His Majesty Shahanshah Akbar in the depth of winter, through snow and ice, to Kabul.'[4] Along with him were his sister Bakshi Banu Begum, Shamsuddin of Ghaznin (who had received the title of Atka Khan), Maham Anga (the mother of Adham Khan), Jiji Anaga (the mother of Mirza Aziz Kokaltash), and several other servants.

When Akbar was just three years old, his uncle, Kamran Mirza, imprisoned the young prince in Kabul, intending to take control of him. The story goes that when Kamran's forces turned violent, Maham Anga placed herself between the child and the pointed cannons aimed at him, risking her life to save the future emperor.[5] Her heroic act effectively cemented her role as his first guardian and as a power broker in the empire. Her courage sent a clear message: women could step into the fiercest arenas (even battlefields) and shape history. It set the stage for later Mughal 'Badass Begums' like Nur Jahan and Jahanara, who also used their unique positions to protect, advise, and eventually rule.

From nursery to Mughal court

In the following years, Maham Anga's role expanded beyond that of a nurse and protector. Her political acumen and ambition began to shine through. When Humayun reclaimed his throne in India and brought Akbar with him, Maham Anga accompanied them. However, her political journey truly started after Humayun's untimely death in 1556. At just thirteen years of age, Akbar was thrust into the throne of the Mughal Empire, with Maham Anga as a silent force behind him. During this period, her true nature, her hunger for power, began to surface.

When Akbar ascended the throne, Maham Anga who was at the centre of a delicate power struggle. She quickly realized the growing influence of Bairam Khan, Akbar's regent, and sought to limit his control. Abul Fazl writes:

One day in 1557 there was a prolonged contest between two of the royal elephants called Fatuha and Lagna. By chance these two during their fight came near the Khan-Khanan's tent. The crowd of people and the general uproar caused apprehension and annoyance to the Khankhana [Bairam Khan], and he came to suspect that perhaps the thing had occurred at the sublime suggestion (of Akbar). He was confirmed in this suspicion by some strife-mongers. He sent one of his confidential servants to Maham Anaga with this message. 'I am not conscious of having committed any offence in this sphere-circled threshold, and I have not displayed anything except well-wishing respect. Why then have mischief-makers imputed some offence to me, and caused such unkindness as that furious elephants should have been let loose against my tent?' Maham Anaga by soothing expressions quieted his disturbed mind.[6]

What is particularly intriguing here is that Bairam Khan directly sent the message to Maham Anga. This exchange hints at the ongoing political rivalry and tension between them, suggesting deeper conspiracies.

According to *Tarikh-i Alfi*, during the execution of the sixteenth-century military commander Tardi Beg in October–November 1556, Bairam Khan secured Maham Anga's cooperation through bribery.[7] This detail is notably absent in the *Akbarnama*. This omission indicates the constant power struggle between Bairam Khan and Maham Anga, both keenly aware of each other's manoeuvres and political moves. According to the *Akbarnama*, Maham Anga opposed Bairam Khan from the beginning and played a key role in orchestrating his downfall.[8] Politically ambitious and power-hungry, Maham Anga sought to exercise her influence in the administration of the empire from behind Akbar, effectively making him a puppet in her hands. She had always despised Bairam Khan, who was a Shia, unlike Mughals who were Sunni, for his excessive power and dominance in the administration. Akbar's growing discontent with Bairam Khan's high-handed ways gave Maham Anga the perfect opportunity to rise politically. She was biding her time, waiting to avenge Bairam Khan and remove him from power.

This task was not too tricky for Maham Anga, as many of her close relatives already held important and influential positions in Akbar's court. One of her sons, Baqi Muhammad Khan, was the governor of Aligarh; Adham Khan held a high post as well.[9] In 1560, when Akbar went on a hunting expedition from Agra, Maham Anga negotiated with Shihabuddin, the governor of Delhi. She urged Akbar to visit his ailing mother in Delhi, knowing this would allow her to work on the emperor without Bairam Khan's interference.

While Akbar was in Delhi, free from Bairam Khan's influence, Maham Anga and Shihabuddin poisoned Akbar's mind against Bairam Khan. They also told him about their intention to make a pilgrimage to Mecca, as they were tired of Bairam Khan's domineering behaviour. Already weary of Bairam Khan, Akbar was pleased with the idea of parting ways with him and taking control of the administration himself. He publicly announced that he had taken the reins of the empire into his own hands and sent orders to Bairam Khan to go on a pilgrimage to Mecca.

Meanwhile, Maham Anga and Shihabuddin spread the news about Akbar's decision and encouraged others to visit the emperor, promising jagirs and titles to those who came. In response, Bairam Khan sent some messengers to Akbar, but Maham Anga, ever the manipulator, encouraged Akbar to arrest them, claiming they may have evil motives for their visit. The divide between Akbar and Bairam Khan grew wider. Badauni in his *Muntakhab ut' Tawarikh* described the event as follows:

> Close by Sikandrah-rao which is [more than] half-way to Dihll Mahum Ankah represented to His Highness, that the Queen Dowager [Mariyam Makani], who was at Dihll, had fallen suddenly ill, and impressed upon him that he ought to direct his course thither. Shahab-ud-dln Ahmad Khan the Governor of Dihli came to meet the Emperor and they two in concert made mountains of mole-hills, and prejudiced his mind against the Khan Khanan. Eventually she made the following representation: 'When the Khan Khanan learns that the imperial cavalcade is come to Dihll at my instigation, he will be sure to wish to avenge himself, and I have no power to resist him, so it is best that I should receive permission to make a pilgrimage to Mekka.'[10]

Akbar stood at a crossroads. The court was tense. His attendants, already shaken by his unexpected decision to travel without Bairam Khan's consent, now feared his wrath. But there was one person Akbar simply couldn't part with:

Maham Anga. The fear became more palpable, until Akbar finally sent word to Bairam Khan.

In his message, the young emperor tried to ease the tension: 'I've come this far without your leave,' he admitted, 'and my attendants are deeply afraid. I ask you to show them kindness—let them continue in my service without fear clouding their minds.'[11]

The response from Bairam Khan was dignified, but laced with sorrow. 'The emperor's heart has turned away from me,' he wrote. 'So be it—there's no place now for public friendship. But I cannot pretend to be something I'm not. After devoting my entire life to him, how could I stain my honour in my old age? That would be a disgrace I could never live down.'

Akbar knew he had to put an end to Bairam Khan's defiance, and he did. The rebellion was crushed. But the emperor could not forget the years of loyalty, the man who had once been his guardian, his mentor, almost a second father. Bairam Khan was pardoned and granted leave to make a pilgrimage to Mecca. But fate had other plans. On the road to Mecca, in 1561, Bairam Khan was ambushed and murdered.

Maham Anga's family rules Mughal court

This move, carefully orchestrated by Maham Anga, marked a turning point in Akbar's reign. For a brief period, Maham Anga held the reins of power, acting as the de facto ruler of the Mughal Empire. Even though Munim Khan held the official title of vakil (prime minister), Maham Anga managed the empire's affairs. She ensured her son Adham Khan was placed in key positions, cementing her influence over the imperial court. However, her quest for power was not without its challenges. That very year, Maham Anga attempted to install Adham Khan as Akbar's prime minister. But Akbar, now maturing into a more independent ruler, resisted her suggestions. Instead, he appointed Munim Khan to the post, who celebrated the promotion with festivities.[12] Maham Anga, to compete with him, soon arranged the marriage feast for her elder son, Baqi Muhammad Khan, with the sister of Adham Khan's wife.[13] Munim Khan was aware of the rising power of Maham and tried to complain quite a few times against this female interference in administration, but Akbar paid no heed to it. He was too occupied with the pleasures of life.

Yet, she did not relent. Always calculating, Maham Anga used every opportunity to assert herself. Despite being a mother figure and wet nurse to Akbar, she relentlessly strove to control the political landscape. She manoeuvred skilfully, using her network of loyalists within the Mughal court to push her agenda. It was said that though the formal title of vakil was held by Munim Khan, the true power in the administration lay with Maham Anga.

Maham Anga's ambition though was not without consequences. Her methods became more transparent as she grew more assertive in her political dealings. She became known for her 'power behind the throne' approach, often manipulating Akbar to serve her interests. Despite her intelligence and devotion to Akbar, her ambition alienated many courtiers, including Munim Khan, who had grown wary of her interference in state affairs.

The period of Maham Anga's influence is often referred to as the 'petticoat government'. According to Von Noer, her dominance extended from 1550 to 1562 CE, until the death of her son, Adham Khan.[14] The exact nature of her influence remains uncertain, but it is evident that Akbar never fully succumbed to the control of palace women. Thus, the claim that he was under a 'petticoat government' appears exaggerated.[15] As Maham Anga attempted once more to sway Akbar with her persuasive words, the young emperor took subtle steps to distance himself from her grasp. He appointed Pir Muhammad as the governor of Malwa and recalled Adham Khan.[16]

Her blind spot

Despite being shrewd, Maham Anga was blinded by the devoted love she had for her sons—Baqi Muhammad Khan and Adham Khan. She was deeply attached to them and used her power to alleviate their societal status. Baqi Muhammad Khan served the emperor till 1584 and rose to be a chief of 3,000 men. But we know little of his character.[17] However, her younger son became a crucial part of her relationship with Akbar.

Maham Anga doted on and indulged her notorious and hard-to-handle son Adham Khan. One of the ways to show imperial power for women was through arranging festivities and weddings. Maham Anga celebrated the weddings of her sons with grandeur. One notable occasion was the marriage of her younger son, Adham Khan. She arranged a lavish feast for him, inviting Emperor Akbar, who attended the celebration out of his affection for his wet nurse. Akbar's favour towards Maham Anga and her family extended to this event, where he bestowed his blessings upon the marriage of Adham Khan. The marriage was arranged to the daughter of Baqi Khan of Baqlan, who had been the secretary of Emperor Humayun's brother Mirza Hindal for a long time. The marriage feast was a significant event, with Maham Anga ensuring it was a grand affair with much celebration. Abul Fazl notes:

> One of the happy occurrences of this year [1559 CE] was the arranging of the marriage of Adham Khan. The succinct account of this is that the favour of the Shahanshah which was bestowed on the cupola of chastity, Maham Anaga and her children, directed itself towards the marriage of Adham Khan, who was Maham Anaga's younger son, and after inquiry and consideration the daughter of Baqi Khan of Baqlan [Balkh] who for a long time was Mirza Hindal's secretary was betrothed to him. In a short time, preparations for a feast were made and the marriage took place. The lofty disposition of the Shahanshah made this feast the occasion of thousand favours.[18]

Maham Anga played a crucial role in balancing the relationship between Akbar and her sons. In 1560–61, Adham Khan was sent to Malwa, where he defeated ruler Baz Bahadur. But he kept the treasures and dancing girls for himself instead of sending these spoils to Agra as protocol demanded. When Akbar learned of this, he moved to discipline Adham Khan, first sending a messenger to warn Maham Anga. She intervened, convincing Akbar to resolve the situation peacefully. However, during their return journey to Agra, Akbar discovered Adham Khan had hidden two of Baz Bahadur's courtesans. Fearing exposure of her son's treachery, Maham Anga murdered the women, reasoning that 'a severed head makes no sound'.[19]

Despite her interventions, Adham Khan's actions led to his downfall. Consumed by pride and jealousy when Atgah Khan was appointed prime minister on Akbar's recommendation, Adham Khan entered the royal palace with a sword and killed Atgah Khan while he presided over the Diwan.[20] Adham Khan then proceeded to the zenana where Akbar was napping. Hearing the commotion, Akbar confronted him. When Adham Khan justified the murder, claiming the prime minister deserved his fate, Akbar ordered him bound by his feet and hands, and thrown from the palace terrace. When Adham Khan survived the first fall, Akbar ordered him to be thrown down again, this time killing him.[21]

When Maham Anga learned of her son's death, she was devastated. Though ill, maternal love drove her to rise from bed and approach Akbar, hoping for mercy. Upon hearing Akbar's reasoning—'Adham killed our Atgah, and we have killed him'—Maham Anga acknowledged the justice but felt profound sorrow.[22] Though she didn't lament aloud, her grief worsened her illness. Forty days later, she died. Akbar, respecting her long service, shouldered her bier as a final honour, personally escorting her body a short distance. He arranged a grand funeral and built a tomb for her and Adham Khan, known as Bhul-bulaiyan, located north of Qutub Minar in Mehrauli.[23]

Two tall neem trees shade the entrance pavement of Khair-ul-Manazil. Outside, policemen chat lazily as traffic rushes by. But stepping inside the premises, as you face the grand gateway, brings immediate quietude. This impressive arch frames the masjid, with an ASI information board and layout map to the right. Two red sandstone benches flank the gateway. The heavy wooden gate requires strength to move.

The gateway's stunning facade combines red sandstone and quartzite, outlined in white marble. It features an outer gateway adorned with lotus medallions on the pendentives, and the inner entrance to the masjid and madrassa compound similarly decorated. Inside the gateway, four niches (taq/ala) for oil lamps line the walls, with a central opening. A half-dome ceiling enhances the gateway's grandeur.

Entering reveals a vast compound (sehan/angan) with an empty wuzu tank and a central well. The mosque consists of a single-aisle, five-bay structure with a central dome blackened by years of exposure. Double-storeyed colonnades on three sides once housed the madrassa. The lower level featured larger rooms for lectures, while the upper level contained smaller chambers, likely serving as living quarters. Though its academic life has faded, the mosque stands as a testament to its vibrant past.

Maham Anga was not just a political figure but a patron of learning. Well-educated herself, she valued scholarship and established this college in Delhi, known as 'Khair-ul-Manazil' or 'Madrasah-i Begum' according to historian Badauni. Her primary purpose was creating a madrassa for children, reflecting her belief in education's power.[24]

Medieval madrassas taught both religious and secular subjects. Delhi became a prominent learning centre in the thirteenth and fourteenth centuries, especially after Mongol invasions drove scholars from Central Asia to India. These institutions were well-organized, providing lodging and teaching subjects from astronomy and mathematics to philosophy.

Khair-ul-Manazil remains the only surviving madrassa commissioned by a Mughal woman. Why did the most powerful woman at court choose an educational institution rather than a fort or palace? In Islamic tradition, building structures benefiting others—schools, hospitals, wells— constitutes 'sadaqah jariyah' (continuous charity). Each lesson taught earned Maham Anga spiritual merit. It is widely believed Prophet Muhammad (Peace Be Upon Him) said, 'The ink of the scholar is more sacred than the blood of the martyr.' By building a madrassa and mosque, Maham Anga secured both divine favour and a lasting public legacy.

A pivotal moment in Emperor Akbar's life unfolded near this madrassa. In the eighth year of his reign (1564), an assassination attempt occurred as the emperor passed by. The *Tabaqat-i-Akbari* chronicles this incident in detail. The would-be assassin was Koka Fulad, a loyal slave to Sharaf-ud-Din Hussain, who had fled from the Mughal court to Nagaur. Having previously served Sharaf-ud-Din's father, Koka Fulad harboured deep animosity towards Akbar and vigilantly sought an opportunity to strike against him. With unwavering determination, he infiltrated the royal camp and bided his time. His moment came when Akbar, returning from a hunting expedition, rode through Delhi's bustling bazaar near Maham Anga's madrassa. From the madrassa's roof, Koka Fulad shot an arrow at the emperor. By what many considered divine intervention, the arrow merely grazed Akbar's skin, inflicting only a superficial wound. The emperor's attendants responded with swift vengeance. They immediately descended upon the assassin, cutting him down with swords and daggers, ensuring his treachery ended there. Akbar, though injured, eventually recovered and returned to Agra.[25]

Today, the madrassa roof where the assassin stood still remains, overlooking the very road where Akbar rode on that fateful day. Besides the madrassa, there are a few more striking features in the mosque, such as the wuzu tank and the well. In the early twentieth century, Amir Habibullah, a famous politician from Afghanistan, visited Delhi. The Amir, who was later assassinated in Kabul in 1919 amidst political turmoil, had travelled to India for diplomatic talks with the British Viceroy. During his stay, he took the opportunity to explore several medieval monuments, particularly those built by Afghan rulers.[26]

Among the structures that caught his attention were those commissioned by Sher Shah Suri, who had re-established

Afghan rule in India for fifteen years. The Amir visited Khooni Darwaza near Kotla Firoz Shah and Lal Darwaza adjacent to Khair ul-Manazil, both built by Sher Shah Suri. He also paid a visit to the mosque. While visiting the mosque, the Amir noticed the dilapidated condition of the wuzu tank, which provided water for worshippers to perform their ritual purification before prayers. Moved by its state of neglect, he personally financed its restoration.[27]

After crossing the wuzu tank and the well, I reached the part of the courtyard covered with carpets, where I could walk comfortably during the harsh summer. I had to remove my footwear there to walk further inside the mosque. The mosque was a single aisle with five arches, the largest and most prominent being the central arch. The epigraphic inscription above the central arch of Khair-ul-Manazil was a Persian chronogram composed by Maulana Shihabuddin Ahmad Khan, a historian and poet in Emperor Akbar's court. This marble plaque not only commemorated the construction of the building but also served as a tribute to Maham Anga, its patron.[28]

The inscription read:

In the time of Jalal-uddin Muhammad
[Who] is great [Akbar] among the just kings,
Maham Begam, the root of purity,
Laid the foundation [of this house] for good men;
But the building of this gracious house was helped by
Shahab-uddin Ahmed Khan Bazel.
What blessings [there are in] this auspicious building,
That its date is found in the words: Blessed among Houses!

Interestingly, the name 'Khair-ul-Manzil' is a chronogram. In Persian script, the numerical value of the letters adds up to 969 Hijri (1561–62 CE), which marks the year of its construction. This clever use of numerology in epigraphy was common in Mughal inscriptions, blending poetry, history and mathematics into a single artistic expression.

The exterior of the Khair-ul-Manazil mosque is adorned with beautiful glazed tiles, reminiscent of the Chini ka Rouza in Agra, showcasing the intricate artistry of the period. Upon entering, remnants of glazed tile-work can be seen above the mihrab (prayer wall), while the ceiling has been largely exposed, adding charm and a sense of serenity to the mosque. The quiet atmosphere inside stands in stark contrast to the bustling world outside.

Despite its historical significance, the Khair-ul-Manazil mosque operates without electricity and relies on oil lamps to light its interior. However, this traditional approach has led to some concerns about preserving the mosque's heritage. In 1992, ASI proposed a ban on Friday prayers at the mosque due to its fragile condition. The ASI feared that the congregation's presence could damage the structure further. However, a local committee named Masjid Basao, represented by Hafiz Mohammad Irfan Dehlawi, challenged the proposed ban by filing a petition in the Delhi High Court. The court ruled that prayers should continue, though the case remains ongoing. Despite the legal challenges and the mosque's delicate state, locals gather here every Friday for prayers. Since there is no electricity, oil lamps illuminate the mosque. Over time, smoke from the lamps has begun to stain the alcoves inside, leaving dark marks on the walls. The mosque's caretaker remarked on the necessity of lighting: 'There has to be some light when people pray, so what can we do? We cannot install electrical fittings as the ASI will not allow drilling. So, we light lamps instead.'[29]

Although the mosque is a shadow of its former grandeur, it stands at a critical junction. The mosque was built opposite the western gate of Purana Qila, thus asserting its importance and the power of its patron, who had built a structure close to the imperial seat. Several factors led to the construction of Purana Qila and Khair-ul-Manazil on Mathura Road. Firstly, the river Yamuna used to flow in the eastern direction, making it easy to carry heavy stones. Secondly, Mathura Road connected Agra to Delhi; Agra was the seat of power for the Mughals, and constructing a mosque and a madrassa here meant travellers could pay their respects while on their journey. Mathura Road is also part of a more extensive road network, namely the Grand Trunk Road connecting Afghanistan to Bangladesh. Thus, the road was always busy with travellers, pilgrims and tourists. A construction commissioned by a woman meant an immediate status of power and a proclamation of their popularity and wealth.

For a long time, I sat inside the mosque and watched the sun cast shadows on the courtyard. There were the distant sounds of traffic and beside me two men were sitting on the floor, talking to each other. A sweeper cleaned the dust from the courtyard, making a reassuring swooshing sound every time he moved his long broom. I turned to the two men and asked if they had ever felt the presence of djinns in this mosque. I had once read a few newspaper reports about the same and was curious. One of them said he has often felt the djinns talking to him and has felt their presence, while the other said he is yet to find a place where djinns do not reside. I got up and started walking back to the main gate. A crow sat near the well and drank some water. I left the gate open, hoping more pedestrians would notice this Mughal wonder.

In Turki tradition, when a child begins to walk, it's customary for the father, grandfather—or their representative—to take off their turban and playfully strike the child with it, causing them to fall. This ritual is believed to protect the child from the evil eye. When young Akbar took his first steps, Mirza Askari performed this custom at the request of Maham Anga, Akbar's caretaker. He tossed his turban at Akbar, causing him to fall—a moment that Akbar later recalled vividly.

7

The Silent Architect

Bega Begum

I remember standing on the raised walkway of Isa Khan's tomb, the stone beneath my feet still warm from the October sun. It was one of those afternoons when the air smelled faintly of dry leaves and old walls, and the world seemed to hum just below the surface of things.

To my left, a friend was mapping out his future—plans stitched together with ambition and the easy confidence of someone untouched by failure. He spoke of cities he hadn't yet seen and fortunes he hadn't yet earned. I nodded, half-listening.

On my right, a man sat cross-legged before a blank canvas propped against the aged enclosure wall. His brush moved with quiet urgency as he coaxed the shape of an orange-laden tree into existence—its imagined fruit glowing brighter than the afternoon itself.

Just then, the azan unfurled across the complex, a silver thread of sound weaving through the domes and archways.

The muezzin's call didn't just echo; it seemed to settle into the bones of the stone, vibrating faintly underfoot. For a heartbeat, the earth itself felt devout.

I remember saying, almost carelessly, 'We should come here more often.' Of course, we never did. And like so many other well-meant promises, that memory faded—blurring at the edges, swirling into nothing.

Time shifts. I'm here again, but the scene has changed.

A couple walks ahead of me now—bride and groom in rehearsal. They've chosen white, both of them, a small act of defiance against the riot of colour expected in this land. The photographer circles them like a satellite, clicking away. The girl walks in silence, her eyes cast low.

He notices. Of course he does.

'Everything alright?' he asks gently. 'Why so quiet?'

She shrugs, a small, hesitant movement.

'Worried about the photos? Don't be. They've turned out lovely. You look … perfect.' His words reach her, but they don't quite settle.

After a pause, she admits it—softly, almost to herself. 'I'm afraid my lipstick's too dark.'

I don't need to be closer to know what she really means. Her skin is dusky; his is lighter. And in a world still quietly obsessed with fairness, she worries—will the photographs betray her insecurities? Will she look 'too dark' against him?

I've seen this before. The silent, stubborn battle that brown-skinned women wage with their reflections.

He understands. That's the most remarkable thing. He doesn't dismiss her worry; he simply reaches out, squeezes her shoulder, and says, 'You look just fine. And don't forget, the photographer will add all the magic effects.'

That, right there—the instinct to reassure without being asked—is the real measure of a partner, isn't it?

Around us, couples wander between the arches, hands brushing, eyes stealing glances. Caste, religion, backgrounds—all blurred under the generous shade of ancient trees. And really, who can resist this place? With its crumbling walls, lush greens and tombs, it is a lover's paradise.

Humayun's Tomb complex is one of the most visited monuments in Delhi. The tomb has several garden complexes attached together, making it an impressive heritage circuit. The entrance of the tomb complex is from Mathura Road right across the Nizamuddin Dargah. There is generally a long queue outside the ticket counter. I often see vagabonds sitting inside the complex, near the ticket counter, soaking in the sun. Often, several schools with busloads of children come as a part of their heritage course activity to explore the area with their teachers. I see them in their winter clothes, wearing identity cards, excited and relieved to have been taken outside the classroom.

I move past the crowd and start walking towards Isa Khan Tomb. This is the first complex you come across as you enter the Humayun Tomb Complex. The gateway is beautiful and ornate; it frames the tomb in the most pleasing manner. The tomb is set within a sunken garden that makes it a unique structure in Delhi. Isa Khan Niyazi was a nobleman in the court of Afghan ruler Sher Shah Suri—Humayun's nemesis—who helped Islam Suri take the throne in the war of succession, and was given this land near the auspicious Nizamuddin Dargah as a reward. The tomb complex was constructed in 1547–48, approximately twenty years before Humayun's Tomb was built. The tomb was built during the time of Isa Khan himself and is quite similar in architecture to Muhammad Shah's tomb from the Sayyid dynasty inside Lodhi Garden.[1] The garden is divided into two parts by a retaining wall. The sunken garden is the outer circle of the tomb surrounded by an enclosure wall. The wall has 128 iwans (enclosures) where people can find shade from the sun and shelter from the rain. The outer garden once was bursting with orchard trees such as citrus trees of oranges, lemon and even jamun. The enclosure wall has a staircase at intervals that allows you to climb it and walk around the complex, giving you a wonderful view of the tomb. The idea was for the visitors to see the top of the orchard trees as they walked. Sadly, the fruit trees have long gone and the outer garden is now just a lawn area. For many years now, the staircases have been shut off, depriving visitors the joy of enjoying Isa Khan Tomb. The purpose of the sunken garden is to allow water channelled from River Yamuna to flow easily through pipes around the boundary wall and irrigate the trees and plants. During the conservation work of the complex taken up by the Aga Khan Foundation, around 125,000 cubic metres of earth was removed manually to create an original depression of 4 feet below the inner ground. The damaged retaining wall that separated the two gardens was also reconstructed with rubble and masonry to recreate the original Persian garden.[2]

The pathway around the tomb is well made with stones and allows the visitor to walk around the tomb in a circle. A staircase takes you inside the tomb where Isa Khan is buried, with his family. The ceiling of the tomb has been re-done with incised plaster using blue and red colours, giving visitors the experience of the original work. There is also a mosque with a single dome and two chhatris towards the western direction in the complex. Only curious visitors go there, often confused by the purpose of the building. There is also a well outside the mosque that used to supply water to perform wuzu rituals.

The ceiling of the tomb has a large dome with eight chhatris that gives the appearance of chicks and a hen. The chhatris have been decorated with blue tile-work. The finial atop the dome is 2.5 metres high and was recently restored. The central dome had layers of cement that were removed to avoid seepage. The blue tiles of the chhatri were missing, and craftsmen from Uzbekistan were invited to restore the tiles. They worked with local craftsmen for six months to reproduce the original tiles. No doubt that Isa Khan is one of the finest garden tomb complexes in Delhi.

Once you exit from Isa Khan Tomb, you find an enclosure wall that is badly broken from the middle. Under the British Raj, in 1911, the wall was broken down to allow visitors to enter Bu Halima's garden after Isa Khan Tomb.[3] Nobody knows who Bu Halima was and a square tomb burial complex atop Bu Halima's tomb's roof, makes things more puzzling. It is possible that Bu Halima was a wet nurse for one of the Mughal emperors and thus received such an important place near Isa Khan's and Humayun's tombs. The gate to Bu Halima's complex can only be seen from behind, owing to the British Raj who broke the wall to allow the entry of visitors from Isa Khan's Tomb. The front side of the grand gateway to Bu Halima's complex is stunning, with colourful tile-work. Tile-work was a popular art form done around Emperor Akbar's reign. The craft was certainly more expensive than incised plaster but less so than pietra dura and inlay work that his great-grandson Emperor Shah Jahan introduced.

On the right, adjacent to the Bu Halima gateway, is the northern gateway to enter Afsarwala Tomb Complex. As you enter the gateway, you will observe that the octagonal ceiling is open, letting sun enter the gateway. The pathway gives you a sense that you are walking in a dense forest. It leads to the Afsarwala Tomb and a mosque built on a high platform. There is a huge garden that is in front of the two. The octagonal tomb has a drum and a dome mounted on top. The dome with incised plaster was once painted with limestone, but has become dark with time. Once you enter the tomb, there is a marble cenotaph on the ground which mentions the year 1566.

The Afsarwala Tomb was built before Humayun's Tomb was completed.[4] Lot of people assume that the tomb was built for a clerk (afsar) in Humayun's court.[5] Afsar is also a Persian tribal name and people from that tribe were employed in the early Mughal courts. The legend goes that one such person helped Humayun return to India after his exile in 1555. Next to the tomb is a three-bay mosque, with the central projecting arch being the tallest.[6] The inside of the mosque is airy and spacious, with a minbar, indicating it was once used as a congregational mosque. Towards the right side of the mosque is a hammam, a public bathing area which was once used by travellers and pilgrims to do the wuzu rituals before they entered the mosque.

Outside the two structures, there is a platform which is absolutely empty, giving a commanding view of the garden. The platform was used as a sehan, or a congregational area, for pilgrims. A board near the platform clearly instructs visitors to remove their shoes before they enter the mosque. However, I often find rowdy youngsters clicking photos and sitting on the platform with their footwear on, unmindful of the religious sanctity of the place. In the garden, there is a tall semal tree which people often confuse with the parijat plant. The semal, or cotton tree, blooms beautifully in spring with bright red flowers. The huge tree has a sandstone bench under it, an ideal spot to read a book. On this particular visit, I can see a couple sitting on the bench. The girl in burqa is feeding the boy with her hands. The clearly well-prepared home-cooked meal is her way of showing affection and love.

Most visitors, tired or time-pressed, turn left at this point—towards the grand spectacle of Humayun's Tomb. But I choose the path less taken. Straight ahead and then a right, where the air thickens with the heady fragrance of champa trees and the ground feels strangely soft beneath my feet.

The pathway leads to a modest gateway. A narrow staircase descends, the light fades, and suddenly you're in a darkened passage that feels more like a forgotten memory than a historical site.

Arab ki Sarai isn't easy to find. It doesn't announce itself like grand monuments do. Overgrown bushes and stubborn trees keep it hidden, as if the land itself has conspired to guard its secrets.

This eastern gateway—once a stately entrance—now serves a different purpose. It's a shortcut into the polished neighbourhoods of Nizamuddin Colony, where morning joggers trace their circuits and the memory of the serai has been reduced to a backdrop. In the film *Gulmohar*, Manoj Bajpayee jogs through this very passage, though even the camera frame barely glances at the crumbling stones he passes.

But stop a while, and the beauty of the gateway asserts itself.

Blue, green and red tiles still cling to its facade, fragments of what must have once been a vibrant mosaic of Persian craftsmanship. This was no mere resting place. Legend says it was commissioned by Mihr Banu, one of Jahangir's wives, though another story ties it back even further—to Bega Begum herself, the formidable Hajji Begum.[7]

And this is where the story curls back on itself.

They say she built this serai for the 300 Arabs who accompanied her from Mecca—some scholars, some artisans, some ordinary men—brought here to aid in the construction of Humayun's Tomb and to create a community bound by faith and purpose.[8] Another version claims it was meant for Quran reciters, a living chorus of devotion to echo through the stone halls.

But like most things connected to the women of the empire, the purpose of Arab ki Sarai has been softened by time, its narrative blurred by indifference.

Today, the descendants of those early Arab settlers have all but vanished, though a few remain—elderly men, with names heavy with forgotten lineage. According to Sir Syed Ahmad Khan, when he was writing his *Asrar-us-Sabadid* in 1847, a man named Sayyid Mohsin Sargiroh, in his sixties, was said to be one of the last recognized elders of the community.[9]

In its prime, this serai was more than a shelter. It was a node in a vast network of Mughal hospitality—places that welcomed pilgrims and traders alike, offering safety, shade and the promise of a meal after a long, unforgiving road. Trade flourished because of such places. Ideas travelled freely. And here, in this tucked-away corner of Delhi, Bega Begum's vision of care and community took quiet, practical shape.

Even if few now remember her name.

Long before Humayun's Tomb rose against the Delhi skyline, there was a woman who dared to imagine it—Bega Begum. Or, as history would later call her, Hajji Begum.

She wasn't born into obscurity. Her life began in 1511 in the cultural heartland of Khurasan—in modern-day Iran—a region steeped in poetry, medicine and the refined diplomacy of Persian courts. She was the daughter of Yadgar Beg, Humayun's maternal uncle, and from the start, she was raised not just to marry well but to think deeply, lead quietly, and—when the moment came—stand unshaken.[10]

Details of her early years are elusive. Some Persian chronicles suggest she had a regal bearing, tall, with sharp features and kohl-darkened eyes that could hold a room in thrall. The Mughal miniatures that followed painted women like her in a riot of silks—emerald greens, deep ruby reds, and golds bright enough to rival the noonday sun. Was she among them? Perhaps. It's tempting to imagine her moving through the marble halls, her presence both admired and quietly feared.

At sixteen, she married Prince Nasir-ud-Din Muhammad—Humayun himself—in Badakhshan, where he was stationed as viceroy. The wedding, if the scattered accounts are to be believed, was a lavish affair. Tents billowed against the mountain air, musicians played well into the night and gifts arrived from every corner of the empire. But this was no simple union of hearts—it was the forging of a political alliance, and with it, came a destiny far more turbulent than any fortune teller might have dared predict.

Their first child, a son named Shahzada Al-Aman Mirza, died in infancy.[11] A brief, flickering joy extinguished before it could warm the palace walls. Still, Bega Begum's position remained unchallenged—chief consort, first among equals.

And then came the chaos.

In 1539, at the Battle of Chausa, Humayun's fortunes crumbled against the ferocity of Sher Shah Suri. The Mughal army scattered, and in the confusion, Bega Begum was captured.[12]

The chronicles say she was treated with dignity, escorted safely under the watchful eye of Khwas Khan, Sher Shah's general.[13] But how much dignity can there be in captivity? And what weight did those days and nights bear upon a woman who had already buried a child, and now faced the terrifying uncertainty of political disgrace?

It gets darker. Somewhere in the chaos, their last surviving child—a daughter, Aqiqa Sultan Begum—died. She was only eight.[14]

Legend has it that Humayun, stricken with grief and shame, confided to his brother Hindal that he regretted not ending his wife's life himself, fearing she'd suffer dishonour in the enemy's hands.[15] Whether or not those words passed his lips, they reflect the crushing, tangled burden of love, loss and the relentless fear that came with royal life.

But Bega Begum was made of sterner stuff.

When Emperor Humayun fled India after losing his throne, his chief consort, Bega Begum, didn't accompany him into exile in Persia as many later believed. Historical accounts grow hazy about her exact whereabouts during this time. Some suggest she remained in Kabul, waiting for Humayun's return.

Yet it was after his comeback that she emerged as a figure of immense devotion and vision, commissioning Delhi's first grand Mughal tomb, Humayun's Tomb. Perhaps her years of waiting, spent between faith and loss, planted the idea of the magnificent resting place that would later inspire the Taj Mahal.

If exile revealed Bega Begum's fortitude, it was Humayun's affection for another woman that tested her pride.

Hamida Banu Begum was barely fourteen when she captured the emperor's wandering heart. Young, luminous and impossibly graceful, she became the new centre of Humayun's attentions. History is often kind to youthful beauty, and Hamida Banu found her place as the beloved mother of Akbar, the future emperor.

But Bega Begum refused to be written out of our texts. Where a lesser woman might have retreated into the dimly lit corners of the harem, Bega Begum asserted her presence with quiet, measured grace. Gulbadan Begum—Humayun's sister and a rare female chronicler of those times—records an episode that speaks volumes.

One evening, during a royal gathering, Bega Begum approached Humayun directly. Her words, though courtly, carried the unmistakable weight of reproach. 'It has been days since you visited my quarters,' she reminded him, her voice poised and unwavering.

Humayun, ever the philosopher-king with a touch of mischief, suggested she write him a formal petition if she felt neglected.

So, she did. And not just once.

A second letter followed, the ink barely dry on the first, a silent insistence that her worth would not be diminished by time or younger rivals.[16]

This wasn't mere sentiment. It was political acumen cloaked in personal grievance. Bega Begum understood that to be forgotten by the emperor was to lose influence in the court—and she would not have that.

And yet, when Humayun died in 1556, his body barely cold beneath the relentless Delhi sky, Bega Begum was consumed by a different emotion—grief.

While others stumbled through the fog of loss, she made a decision that would etch her name across the ages. She vowed to build a mausoleum for her husband unlike any seen before on Indian soil. Not just a tomb, but a statement. A monument that would speak of loyalty, of grandeur, of an eternal love that outlasted betrayal and exile.

She threw herself into the project with a precision and authority that left no room for doubt.

In 1564, she undertook what was then a perilous and rare journey for women of her standing: the Hajj. But this was no solitary act of faith—it was a display of both spiritual and political power.

Before she left, she arranged every detail for the construction of Humayun's Tomb, leaving behind clear instructions and trusted overseers.[17] While men argued over succession and territory, she ensured her husband's legacy would stand unchallenged—in stone.

She wasn't alone on this bold journey. Her Hajj was no quiet caravan of supplicant women but an imperial procession. Bega Begum was among the first Mughal women to undertake the pilgrimage to Mecca, and her voyage set a precedent that later royal women would follow. A decade later, during Akbar's reign, other women of the court, Gulbadan Begum, Salima Sultan Begum, and a host of noblewomen, embarked on their own celebrated pilgrimage in 1575. Their journey, famously recorded in the *Humayunnama*, carried forward the legacy Bega Begum had begun.[18]

They performed the Hajj three times. On their way back, they stopped at Ajmer to pay homage at the shrine of Khwaja Moinuddin Chishti, the saint of saints, cementing their journey as both a religious pilgrimage and a statement of imperial piety.[19]

Imagine this: royal women crossing the seas, braving unfamiliar lands, commanding entire retinues. These were women who had lived behind intricately carved jaalis—stone screens that filtered their view of the world. And now, they were in the outside world where few women of their stature had dared to walk. It was almost a declaration of independence.

When she returned three years later, in 1567, the outlines of that magnificent vision had begun to rise against the sky. And she remained its vigilant guardian, ensuring every stone, every delicate inlay, reflected not just the memory of Humayun, but her own enduring presence. She took up residence near Humayun's Tomb—overseeing its final completion, managing the daily affairs of the site and continuing her lifelong tradition of charity.[20]

Akbar, the mighty emperor, revered her as more than a stepmother. He called her his second mother, and by many accounts, their bond was closer than that of blood. So deep was his respect that when she passed away in 1582, he personally arranged her funeral rites and accompanied her body to its final resting place—beneath the very structure she had dreamed into existence.[21]

Her death was mourned not just as the passing of an empress, but as the end of an era.

Even the *Akbarnama*—usually more concerned with courtly triumphs and imperial conquests—paused to remember her:

> This lady of the family of dominion was an ocean of goodness, and loved the sovereign from his earliest years. He also was wonderfully attached to her. The ladies of the harem wept and tore their hair on account of a pain for which there was no medicine.[22]

She was buried within Humayun's Tomb, alongside the man she had loved, mourned and immortalized.

But who really built Humayun's Tomb?

Tradition tells us it was Bega Begum, the grieving widow. And yet, in the halls of historical scholarship, you'll hear a persistent whisper: Surely, a woman couldn't have done this alone.

Some historians are blunt in their dismissal. R. Nath, in a rare moment of academic condescension, wrote, 'Can we afford to ascribe this marvelous innovation to an old, mediocre lady of the deceased king's harem? This is impossible …'[23]

It's strange that we can imagine Humayun—dreamy, often indecisive—being remembered for this grand mausoleum, but struggle to accept that his wife, a woman educated in the arts and intellect of Persian culture, could have been its driving force.

The facts, however, refuse to be silenced.

Bega Begum was born and raised in Khurasan, a land that had already perfected the idea of the charbagh—the quadrilateral garden of paradise. She walked the dazzling halls of the Safavid court during her exile with Humayun, where architecture reached sublime heights. She understood proportion, symmetry and the delicate conversation between space and power.

If ever there was a woman equipped to imagine a new kind of monument—one that blended Persian grace with the solid authority of Indian stone—it was her.

And then, there's the architectural evidence itself. Humayun's Tomb doesn't quite fit into the Mughal architectural tradition that Akbar would later establish. His structures leaned heavily on grand fortifications and sandstone extravagance. But this tomb? This is Persian poetry carved in stone. The double dome, the geometrical precision, the lush interplay of water channels and gardens—it all sings of Bega Begum's Persian roots and her memories of the lands she once called home.

This wasn't just a final resting place; it was a vision of paradise—one she had seen, perhaps longed for, and then recreated in memory of a man who had loved her, disappointed her and left her to shape his legacy.

And yet, ask most visitors today who built the tomb, and they'll shrug. Ask historians, and they'll point to Akbar—after all, wasn't he the great builder? The emperor with coffers deep enough to fund dreams carved in marble?

Perhaps. But if we only follow the money, we lose sight of the mind that envisioned the dream in the first place. Isn't it telling that the same history that credits Shah Jahan with the Taj Mahal without hesitation, endlessly debates Bega Begum's role here? When a man commissions a monument, it's seen as an act of power and vision. When a woman does the same, it's often reduced to sentimentality—or worse, it is credited as someone else's idea entirely.

The tomb isn't merely a building—it's a carefully constructed argument, a declaration of how Bega Begum understood love, loyalty and the afterlife.

The charbagh layout isn't a casual choice; it's an architectural rendering of paradise itself, as described in the Quran. Four rivers—of water, milk, honey and wine—meant to nourish the soul eternally. But here's the subtle genius: these aren't metaphorical rivers. The garden is a living system of hydraulics, where water channels criss-cross the grounds, not just to cool the air or please the eye, but to enact a vision of heaven underfoot.

Now, look at the orientation. Unlike later Mughal tombs, where grandeur swells with each successive generation, this tomb holds back ever so slightly. It's monumental, but intimate. The double dome towers above, but step inside, and you find an astonishing restraint. No extravagant pietra dura, no gaudy marble inlays—just clean lines, perfectly proportioned spaces and light filtering through delicately carved jaalis that dapple the floors in patterns as fleeting as breath.

This isn't an emperor's mausoleum, shouting about his glory from the rooftops. This is a wife's final, measured offering—a paradise promised, a memory enshrined.

Even the placement of the tomb tells a story. Set apart from the Yamuna by an open eastern side, it invites the river's breeze to slip through the gardens, carrying with it the scent of water and the murmurs of a city forever on the move. Humayun's body, it is said, was initially interred in Purana Qila.[24] But it was Bega Begum who chose this site for his final rest, a place where earth, water and air conspired to create eternal serenity.

And then there's the architectural silence. Unlike later tombs that proudly advertise their makers—inscriptions, dedicatory plaques, elaborate credits—Humayun's Tomb holds its secrets. There's no bold signature carved into its stones. No official proclamation of the woman who saw it through.

Perhaps that's the most telling sign of all.

Bega Begum didn't need to leave her name etched in stone. She left her vision, which is a more enduring legacy.

But let's examine the timeline of events.

Abd al-Qadir Badauni, the famously cynical court chronicler, records that the tomb was completed around 977 AH, which translates to 1569–70 CE. He even mentions the Persian architect Mirak Mirza Ghiyas, who oversaw the project for nearly a decade. That would mean construction began around 1561 or 1562, barely five years after Humayun's death—right when Bega Begum was still very much in charge of her own destiny.[25]

However, between 1564 and 1567, she was away, performing Hajj. And that gap—those three years—has created a chasm wide enough for generations of historians to cast their doubts through. Could she really have left a project of this magnitude unsupervised? Could she have wielded such control and foresight before setting off on a pilgrimage?

It's a peculiar double standard—when emperors and male patrons leave their projects in the hands of trusted architects and administrators, we call it leadership. Delegation. Vision. But when a woman does the same, her capability becomes suspect.

More troubling still is the archaeological evidence—or rather, its absence. Of the more than 150 gravestones found within the complex, none are dated to before 1570. This gap is often used to suggest that the site wasn't fully operational— or even completed—until Bega Begum had returned and Akbar had taken a more direct role.

But perhaps that's precisely the point. Even if the work slowed in her absence, the vision had already been set. The plans drawn, the artisans hired, the materials sourced. Her absence didn't signal abdication; it reflected a leader confident enough to trust her people and her plan.

This is how I see it—after her return from Hajj, it's well documented that she resumed overseeing of the project actively. She moved to the area surrounding the tomb, managed its daily affairs, and ensured its completion down to the last detail.

And yet, some historians still insist that Akbar—just a boy of thirteen when his father died—was the true mastermind behind the project. That it was his imperial coffers, his political clout, his grand vision that gave rise to the tomb.

There's no denying that Akbar, as emperor, eventually funded much of the project. But to reduce Bega Begum's role to that of a grieving widow who merely signed off on someone else's work is to erase her memory in history.

Stand in the gardens of Humayun's Tomb long enough, and the realization dawns slowly: this tomb is a prototype. For Agra's Taj Mahal.

But where the Taj Mahal is about love and grief and perfection, Humayun's Tomb hums with a quieter, more measured power. It isn't trying to overwhelm you. It's inviting you to linger, to sit, to breathe in the balance between stone and sky.

This is also where the Mughal garden tomb concept took root. Before this, Delhi's monuments leaned heavily on the rugged austerity of the Tughlaqs and Lodis—solid, grim fortresses, more concerned with defence than grace. The idea that a tomb could be a vision of paradise on earth—that death could be greeted with beauty rather than sorrow—was a radical one in India.

But Bega Begum had seen it before. In Persia, in the delicately laid charbagh gardens, in the blue-tiled mosques of Isfahan, in the way architecture wasn't merely built but breathed into the landscape. And so, she created new styles—carved channels with water gurgling through, where symmetry took precedence, and where the dead rested not beneath cold stone but within a carefully tended paradise.

Even the materials spoke of her intent. The red sandstone was a deliberate choice—bold and warm, a contrast to the pale marble that would come later. The double dome—so often celebrated in the Taj Mahal—finds its first expression here. A smaller interior dome ensures harmony and proportion, while the larger outer dome rises high above, a grand gesture visible for miles. This architectural sleight of hand wasn't just about aesthetics; it was about creating a sense of awe without sacrificing human scale.

And then there's the remarkable economy of ornamentation. Where Shah Jahan's later structures would explode with intricate inlays and shimmering semi-precious stones, Bega Begum's vision remained elegantly restrained. Patterns were carved, not encrusted. Light was the primary decoration, streaming through the jaalis and shifting with the hour, creating a living artwork that changed from morning to dusk. This was a reflection of the Sufi ideals that had long infused Mughal thought. Balance, humility and beauty in simplicity.

This was also a statement of power. For Bega Begum, the tomb was more than a monument to her lost husband.

It was a public assertion of her own agency, her cultural sophistication and her ability to shape imperial memory.

By the time I step through the western gateway to leave, the air is thick with the scent of impending rain. A soft drizzle begins. Couples huddle beneath ancient arches, children squeal with delight and run barefoot across the slick stone paths, their laughter bouncing off the tomb's walls.

And standing there—watching the old red sandstone darken with rain—I realize that the Mughal chapter of Delhi might have ended long ago, but its spirit hasn't entirely departed. This place still shelters lovers and wanderers, the lost and the hopeful. Its canopies still offer refuge from the heat, its gardens still promise a moment of quiet in a city that rarely slows down.

Yet, the woman who gave this city its first true vision of paradise remains obscured—her story eroded by time, her name absent from the plaques.

Bega Begum is here, yes—buried quietly alongside the emperor she loved and outlived. But to most visitors, she is no more than a footnote, if that. And that, perhaps, is the greatest injustice. Maybe one day, a conversation will start. A guide will pause before the nameless gravestones in the north-west chamber and say, 'Here lies the woman who imagined all of this.'

During Partition, Humayun's Tomb became a major refugee camp in Delhi, along with Purana Qila and Safdarjung's Tomb. It first sheltered Muslims migrating to Pakistan, and later Hindus and Sikhs arriving from Pakistan. The refugee camps caused significant damage to the gardens, water channels and main structures of Humayun's Tomb. To prevent vandalism, the cenotaphs inside were encased in brick, and the twenty-two marble graves on the first floor were covered in masonry for protection. The camps were active for about five years, leaving lasting impacts on this historic monument.

8

Aurangzeb's Daughters

The Scholar and the Rock

Life in the harem

Mughal princesses, the daughters of the empire, held a unique place in the grand world of the seraglio. Though the birth of a girl in those times was often overshadowed by the arrival of a boy, Mughal emperors cherished their daughters and spared no effort in ensuring they were educated, talented and surrounded by luxury. They were raised in an opulent environment, with access to all the finest things life could offer.

However, starting from Akbar's reign, a curious trend emerged—many Mughal princesses remained unmarried. This has sparked endless debate among historians and writers, including foreign travellers, like Manucci, who blamed Akbar for initiating this practice. But was he truly at fault? Not quite.

Akbar arranged marriages for his sisters and daughters, ensuring they wed suitable men. What he firmly opposed, though, was the idea of marriage between first cousins, a stance that shaped the matrimonial norms of the empire. By the time Shah Jahan ruled, some restrictions on marriages of princesses had crept in. This was likely a strategic move to limit the number of potential claimants to the throne. Yet, Aurangzeb seemed to break the mould, as he allowed some of his daughters and nieces to marry their first cousins, defying this restraint. Despite these marital complexities, Mughal princesses enjoyed immense privileges and affection. Fathers and brothers adored the women of the empire, and this bond often became the stuff of legend. Shah Jahan's deep love for his eldest daughter, Jahanara, is well-documented. Similarly, Aurangzeb held a special place in his heart for his daughter Zeb-un-Nissa—until her growing influence and independence began to clash with his policies, even threatening his reign.

The lifestyle of Mughal princesses in the royal harem was a blend of grandeur, privilege and strict protocols, reflecting the opulence of the empire. Even today, the remnants of their magnificent existence can be seen in the palaces and forts of Delhi, Agra, Fatehpur Sikri and Lahore. The royal women lived in luxurious quarters, referred to as Mahals or Shabistan-i-Iqbal, which were often part of the palace nestled within a larger fort complex. These spaces were exquisitely designed, with intricate details and amenities to provide both comfort and beauty. The Hira Mahal in Delhi's Red Fort, for example, was specifically built for the harem ladies, though it constituted only a small portion of the sprawling complex.

While grand, not every woman in the harem enjoyed individual, spacious residences. According to Abul Fazl, Emperor Akbar once provided separate apartments for his 5,000 women, but this was more an exception than the rule.[1] The harem quarters were more than just living spaces—they were miniature paradises. Nearly every chamber boasted of a reservoir of running water at its doorstep, surrounded by lush gardens, shaded pathways, fountains and cool grottoes offering respite from the blazing sun. Terraces and divans were designed for serene night-time repose. These oases of comfort ensured that even in the scorching summers of the subcontinent, oppressive heat was never an issue within the harem walls. Life within the harem was carefully organized, with a strong hierarchy and numerous roles assigned to its inhabitants. According to the accounts of Manucci, there were around 2,000 women of different backgrounds within the palace, each entrusted with specific duties. These roles ranged from attending to the emperor, his wives, daughters and concubines, to managing household operations. To maintain order, each woman was assigned her own room and matrons were appointed to oversee their activities.[2] Female guards provided security within the enclosure, while eunuchs stationed outside ensured no unauthorized entry. Music and the arts were also integral to harem life, with female superintendents and musicians adding to the cultural richness of the environment. For Mughal princesses, life in the harem meant access to unmatched luxury, but it also came with strict supervision and expectations. Surrounded by beauty and privilege, they grew up in an environment designed to protect and nurture them, preparing them for their roles as cultural patrons, scholars, or, at times, political figures in the vast Mughal Empire.

The royal ladies earned money through several sources—first, through the jagirs that were given to them by the emperor himself; second, through the monthly income that was provided to them from the royal treasury; thirdly, through special events such as birthdays, coronations, new year celebrations, festivals and hunting parties; and lastly, through ships and ports the royal ladies handled. It is thus not surprising that so many serais, mosques, gardens, havelis and community buildings are commissioned by begums. Continuing with my hunt for such spaces, I decided to visit the only surviving structure built by Aurangzeb's daughter Zinat-un-Nissa.

Every time I drove down Raj Ghat Road, a sign pointing to Ghata Masjid always caught my attention, and every time I promised myself that I would visit. But time slid by. One day, I found myself on the same road, and in the spur of the moment, I decided to explore the mosque. I reasoned that I would never do it if I left it for another day.

Finding Ghata Masjid is simple; its tall minarets beckon like hands waving in a crowd. Outside stands a man ironing clothes at a makeshift stall; the backdrop, a striking view of the serene mosque. The mosque's green-and-white entrance reads: 'Way to Zeenat-ul-Masjid urf Ghata Masjid'. Climbing a narrow staircase, I enter a spacious courtyard. Potted plants line the edges, and a low red sandstone parapet barely reaches my knees. Everything is calm, imparting a sense of peace rather than unease. Though the midday June sun blazes outside, the mosque's interior is notably cooler and comfortable.

Ahead lies a compound with several rooms; a second building's interior also comes into sight. Underfoot are large red sandstone slabs, shaped like cusped arches—these are battlements, or 'kangura'. It's unclear why typical wall battlements now lie on the floor, but they seem to have fallen and been reused by those managing the site. The masjid's triple dome—white marble with black lines—rests between two slender minarets, forming a triple-bay structure that welcomes worshippers. While reminiscent of Emperor Shah Jahan's style, subtle elements reflect Aurangzeb's era. Constricted necks and cusped arches on slender piers accentuate the building's height.

A projecting arch marks the mosque's main entry, with its pishtaq (rectangular frame around an arched entryway) framed by slim turrets. Positioned south of the Red Fort (once overlooking the Yamuna), it's elevated on a plinth for added height. I search for the grave of Aurangzeb's second daughter, Zinat-un-Nissa, but it is long gone—the British removed it after the 1857 revolt. Under the Commissariat Department, the mosque was even converted into a bakery for troops. Later British additions further compromised the mosque's original beauty.[3]

Between 1650 and 1857, more than 200 mosques were commissioned in the city,[4] most notably, during the reign of Aurangzeb. Historical accounts paint a picture of an emperor who prioritized the architectural and spiritual upkeep of these sacred spaces above all else. Remarkably, he is said to have repaired more mosques than any of his Mughal predecessors, extending his efforts to include structures originally built by the Tughluq, Lodi and Deccani sultans.[5]

His dedication went beyond mere restoration. Aurangzeb personally ensured that mosques were maintained with utmost care, even in remote areas. On one occasion, he ordered a lamp for a mosque situated in an old outpost, demonstrating his commitment to their upkeep, regardless of location. In another instance, he expressed displeasure to his prime minister, lamenting that the carpets and furnishings of the royal palace were in far better condition than those in the palace's mosque.[6] This attention to detail reflects an emperor deeply invested in aligning his personal devotion with the material and spiritual vitality of the mosques under his domain.

It's easy to picture him as a ruler consumed entirely by duty and faith, but if you look closely, there's another side to the story—one found not in his court records, but in the quiet loyalty of his daughters.

Aurangzeb loved his daughters—of that there is no doubt.

While many scholars view him as a harsh, unforgiving ruler, and others regard him as an upholder of Islam, his daughters offered him unconditional affection. He fathered numerous children, but it was primarily two of his daughters—Zeb-un-Nissa and Zinat-un-Nissa—who became the apples of his eye. While his sons schemed for the throne, his daughters provided solace to their ageing father, absorbing the depth of his paternal devotion.

During his reign, Mughal women asserted their independence and contributed to the cultural landscape of Shahjahanabad. As we have seen earlier, his sisters, Jahanara and Roshanara, were trailblazers in their own right. Similarly, two of his daughters carved out their own paths under his rule. His daughters are often mentioned in official Mughal documents because Aurangzeb gave them many key responsibilities. That does not mean they did not escape his wrath. When the time came, Aurangzeb showed no mercy, even to his own blood.

Aurangzeb had several children and his principal wife, Dilras Banu Begum, gave birth to five children. She was Aurangzeb's chief consort, and was a woman of notable lineage and grace. She was born into the illustrious Safavid dynasty of Persia, a prominent royal family renowned for their cultural and political influence. She was the daughter of Shah Nawaz Khan, whose great-grandfather was a younger son of the Persian King Shah Ismail I Safavi. He served as the viceroy of Gujarat.[7] As Aurangzeb's principal wife, Dilras held a unique position in the Mughal court. Known for her regal demeanour and refined upbringing, she was deeply respected by the emperor and the royal household. Despite Aurangzeb's austere nature, Dilras maintained her dignity and influence, bearing him five children, including their remarkable three daughters—Zeb-un-Nissa, Zinat-un-Nissa and Zubdat-un-Nissa—who stood out for their contributions towards literature, architecture and culture.

I've always found it striking—Aurangzeb ruled with an iron fist, but it was his daughters who quietly softened the sharp edges of his reign. And as we move forward, you'll see how their lives added grace and complexity to his otherwise unyielding legacy.

Born on 15 February 1638, in Daulatabad, Zeb-un-Nissa was Aurangzeb's eldest daughter and an intellectual powerhouse.[8] She had a sharp mind and a love for learning, traits she clearly inherited from her father. Educated by the accomplished Hafiza Mariam, Zeb-un-Nissa memorized the Quran by heart, earning a hefty reward of 30,000 gold coins from her proud dad. She was fluent in Persian and Arabic, with handwriting so elegant it could be a work of art itself.[9] Zeb-un-Nissa was a literary patroness like no other. Her personal library was legendary—larger and better curated than any private collection of the time. Scholars and poets flocked to her, as Aurangzeb wasn't exactly known for his love of poetry. With her support, works like *Zeb-ut-Tafasir*, a famous commentary, came to life, although people mistakenly credited her with writing it.[10] She even dabbled in poetry herself under the pen name Makhfi (The Concealed One), although it's worth noting that others used the same pseudonym, so not all the poems attributed to her are actually hers.[11]

Aurangzeb personally took interest in her education. For Zeb-un-Nissa, poetry wasn't just a pastime—it was a form of self-definition. She wasn't openly defying her father, but by choosing to immerse herself in literature, by nurturing poets and by writing under her pen name, she carved out an intellectual space for herself in a world that sought to limit it. Her ghazals often explored female desire, love and longing, and through use of metaphysical themes, she inserted herself in cultural conversations. Her poems were deeply evocative and sensual. She writes:

> *You with the dark curly hair and the breathtaking eyes,*
> *your inquiring glance that leaves me undone.*
> *Eyes that pierce and then withdraw like a blood-stained*
> *sword,*
> *eyes with dagger lashes!*
> *Zealots, you are mistaken—this is heaven.*[12]

A skilled calligraphist, Zeb-un-Nissa could write in the style of Nastaliq, Shikast and Naskh.[13] This was not just an artistic flex—in the Islamic world, calligraphy was revered as the visual embodiment of the divine and of intellectual refinement. For a Mughal woman to have command over the ink was an extension of legitimacy and respect. She also established a translation department and employed many scholars, unheard of in the Mughal world. Many works were dedicated to her. From her early youth, she wrote verses in Arabic. Once, an Arabian scholar saw her verses and commented: 'Whoever has written this poem is Indian. The verses are clever and wise, but the idiom is Indian, although it is a miracle for a foreigner to know Arabian so well.'[14] By establishing translation bureaus and supporting scholars, Zeb-un-Nissa positioned herself as a cultural conduit. She bridged the gap between the Persian, Arabic and Indian intellectual worlds. She was shaping a distinct Indo-Persian voice.

Apart from intellectual achievements and scholarly pursuits, Zeb-un-Nissa was fond of gardens and she herself laid out a garden near Lahore, which was known as Chau-Burji or Four Towers. Presently, it is only a gateway, covered all over with turquoise, amber and azure tiles. Only three of its four tall minarets remain. She built one more garden in Lahore, known as Nawan Kot Bagh, which was not far away from Chau-Bhurji. These open tree-lined gardens became spaces for discussions, readings and scholarly debates under the shade of fruit trees.

Aurangzeb was a doting father and was, in fact, quite proud of Zeb-un-Nissa's achievements. At three, when she had memorized the Quran, Aurangzeb was overjoyed. He declared a public holiday and held a grand feast, which was belied his austere nature. Aurangzeb sought counsel from her for state affairs and encouraged her education. He also acquiesced to her every whim and wish. After Aurangzeb came to power, he imprisoned his father-in-law, Shah Nawaz Khan, who did not support him in the war of succession.

Displeased by her father's conduct, she fasted for days until Aurangzeb released him. Zeb-un-Nissa thus held control and power over Aurangzeb and his decisions. But the bond between father and daughter broke and, tragically, they could never reconcile.[15]

Zeb-un-Nissa Begum was a supporter of her brother Muhammad Akbar who openly rebelled against their father in 1681. She maintained secret correspondence with Prince Akbar.[16] But his rebellion failed and his camp near Ajmer was seized by the royal army. On 16 January 1681, Zeb-un-Nissa's letters to Prince Akbar were recovered from the camp. Aurangzeb was furious. Her property and annual allowance of four lakh rupees were confiscated. She was imprisoned in the fort of Salimgarh (attached to Red Fort), where she died.[17] Describing the condition of the grief-stricken emperor, Saqi Mustad Khan, the author of *Maasir-i Alamgiri*, writes:

> News came to the Emperor from Delhi that Zebunnisa Begum had died. The Emperor was so saddened by the news that he shed tears but had to resign himself to God's will. Order was sent to Sayyid Amjad Khan, Shaikh 'Ataullah, and Hafiz Khan (Nur Muhammad) to give alms (for the benefit of her soul) and build her tomb at the appointed place, namely the Garden of thousand (Tis Hazari), which was a legacy from Jahanara.[18]

Tragically, her tomb, located in the garden of Tees Hazari near Old Delhi, was demolished to make way for a railway line—an unfortunate end for such a brilliant mind.[19]

Next up was Zinat who was born on 5 October 1643, most likely in Aurangabad.[20] Unlike her older sister, Zeb-un-Nissa, who embraced poetry and the intellectual world, Zinat chose a quieter path. She devoted herself completely to her father, especially during his final years in the Deccan. For twenty-five years, she stood by his side, earning the title of Padshah Begum—a position of real authority in the imperial household.

Known for her piety and generosity, Zinat left behind a legacy that still stands. In 1700, she built the Zinat-un-Nissa Masjid in Delhi, a mosque often called the Kuari Masjid—the Maiden's Mosque. There's a local story that she asked Aurangzeb for her dowry, but instead of marrying, she used it to build the mosque.[21] Whether or not that's entirely true, it's the kind of story that sticks—and tells you something about the woman she was.

Even after Aurangzeb's death, Zinat remained a respected figure, a living reminder of a fading era. She passed away in Delhi on 7 May 1721, and was buried in the mosque she built. That grave, like much else from the Mughal past, didn't escape the disruptions of colonial rule—it was later moved by the British military.

But this is just the outline. Zinat's story runs much deeper than a list of dates and titles. She held things together when everything seemed to fall apart. And we'll return to her soon, when her quiet strength takes centre stage.

Now, about the youngest—Zubdat-un-Nissa. She was born on 2 September 1651, in Multan. Her life took a different course. In 1673, she married her cousin, Sipihr

Shukoh, the son of Dara Shikoh—Aurangzeb's ill-fated brother.[22] Unlike her sisters, she lived a more private life, away from the political and cultural spotlight. But even so, she remained close to the family and part of the inner circle of the empire until the very end. She died in February 1707, just before her father passed away.[23]

Each of these daughters lived differently—but all of them left their mark. Zeb-un-Nissa with her literary brilliance, Zinat-un-Nissa through the mosque that still bears her name and Zubdat-un-Nissa as a keeper of family ties during some of the empire's most fragile years. But their stories didn't end there. One of them took her influence far beyond the palace walls, changing the empire in more practical ways than most remember.

Zinat-un-Nissa wasn't content with palace life. At thirty-seven, she poured her personal wealth into a project that most royals wouldn't have touched—building a network of fourteen caravanserais between Oudh and Bengal. These weren't just brick-and-mortar stops; they were lifelines for traders, pilgrims and weary travellers moving across the empire. Safe, sheltered rest stops on the road weren't a luxury—they were essential for keeping commerce, culture and imperial communication alive. In the era where royal women were expected to remain behind the curtain, Zinat-un-Nissa claimed literal space on the empire's highways, using her influence to solve everyday problems on a massive scale. Like her aunt Jahanara, Zinat-un-Nissa led urban development and welfare projects, and became an active agent of infrastructure.

While a lot has been mentioned already about her Ghata Masjid, what stands out is the legend attached to it. By defying to marry like her sisters, and choosing to use her dowry to build a mosque, Zinat-un-Nissa proclaimed she was person of her own. She rejected domesticity and voted for public life. Even now, in the twenty-first century, there are very few examples of women using their parents' savings to pursue education and a career rather than using it for a big fat Indian wedding. Distribution of alms at her mosque became an everyday affair and not an occasional performance. Her father, Emperor Aurangzeb, took notice and praised her for her innovation and dedication to sadaqah.

One of the most courageous contributions of Zinat's life was perhaps her years in the Deccan. Aurangzeb, apart from his determination to acquire the Mughal throne, had another obsession—to conquer the Deccan. His single-minded pursuit made him and the royal entourage stay in camps, and march from site to site. And one of the most trusted people towards this pursuit was not a son, which one would expect, but his daughter Zinat-un-Nissa. Several incidents from the Deccan years have been mentioned in contemporary sources. For instance, when Prince Muhammad Akbar, brother of Zinat, rebelled against his father in 1681 and tragically failed, Akbar took refuge under the Marathas, the most fatal rival of Aurangzeb. This was not a very prudent move by Akbar, and it further antagonized Aurangzeb who did not flinch from giving the harshest punishment to his blood. Zinat acted deftly, and used her power of diplomacy and urged Akbar to write an honest, transparent letter of apology to their father. Perhaps, as a daughter, Zinat was privy to Aurangzeb's truest nature and his vulnerability. Aurangzeb did eventually forgive Akbar for his treason and betrayal.[24]

Aurangzeb trusted Zinat-un-Nissa with the most delicate of diplomatic duties—assignments that required not just loyalty, but tact, discretion and a deep understanding of the empire's emotional undercurrents. One of the most telling examples of this trust was when he placed the care of two high-profile Maratha prisoners—Sambhaji's widow Yeshu Bai and her young son Shahu—in her hands.

Zinat wasn't just a passive custodian. Her relationship with the Marathas was personal: they had sheltered her brother, Prince Muhammad Akbar, when he rebelled against their father. Perhaps out of gratitude—or a deeper conviction about justice—Zinat took a far more empathetic approach than the imperial court usually allowed. When Shahu was released in 1707 and allowed to return to the Deccan, it was Zinat who quietly ensured his safe passage across the Narmada. Later, it was through her sustained influence that the harshness of his treatment was softened. In 1718, when the Maratha Peshwa Balaji Vishwanath marched into Delhi to negotiate the release of Yeshu Bai, Zinat again played a pivotal role in brokering her freedom.[25]

Zinat-un-Nissa's quiet diplomacy didn't just extend to external relations like the Maratha negotiations—it was deeply entwined with the inner workings of the imperial family. She remained a steady channel of communication between Aurangzeb and his sons, especially her beloved brother, Prince Muhammad Akbar. Even after Akbar was exiled to Persia in 1686 following his failed rebellion, Zinat continued to act as his emotional bridge to the Mughal court. When news of Akbar's death finally arrived in 1706 from the Persian frontier, a year before Aurangzeb himself died, the emperor informed her first.

Saqi Mustad Khan, chronicling the event, wrote:

> News came from informants on the frontier of Persia that Prince Muhammad Akbar, who had fled into the wilderness of disappointment and whose affairs have been described in previous years, had died. The Emperor consoled himself by reading the prayer and said, 'The great disturber of Hindustan has subsided.' He sent the news to Zinat-un-nisa Begam, and presented a mourning turban-end to Akbar's son Buland Akhtar.[26]

The formal tone of the announcement hides a deeper emotional register—Aurangzeb, ever the austere emperor, relied on Zinat to carry the personal weight of such moments. That he informed her before any court proclamation speaks volumes.

As her father waged relentless wars against the Marathas and suppressed rival claims to the throne, Zinat became his eyes, ears, and often, his conscience.

One of the earliest glimpses of her as a peacemaker emerges during Prince Mu'azzam's estrangement from

Aurangzeb. When he was captured by his own father, it was Zinat who softened the edges of imperial wrath. In 1691, when Mu'azzam's mother Nawab Bai passed away, Aurangzeb and Zinat jointly visited the mourning prince in his army camp. The record notes:

> Pavilions were spread from the courtyard of the Private Audience Hall to the Prince's quarters, and a screened lane formed. The Emperor, with Zinat-un-nisa Begam, visited the Prince and condoled with him. On Monday, the 20th July, 1691, the prince was granted an interview (with the emperor).[27]

The emotional nuance here is critical. In a court where appearances were everything, Zinat's presence wasn't ornamental. She was performing grief, reconciliation and familial restoration. Where Aurangzeb's authority created silences, Zinat built bridges.

She played the same role for her youngest stepbrother, Muhammad Kam Bakhsh—defying her blood brother Azam Shah's disdain to repeatedly secure imperial forgiveness. Saqi Mustad Khan records:

> On Wednesday, the 14th June 1693/20th Shawwal, Kam Bakhsh arrived at the Court, and through the mediation of Zinatunnisa Begum had an interview with the Emperor in the harem. He presented one thousand mohars as nazar and the same number of rupees as nazar.[28]

Zinat was the only sister trusted to escort such emotionally charged meetings. Her private influence, though rarely recorded in court bulletins, was vast—and deeply political. Every successful pardon she secured was a potential rebellion averted, a family fracture stitched shut. She even stepped into the ceremonial role of family matriarch. Much like her formidable aunt, Jahanara Begum, Zinat orchestrated the wedding of her brother Mu'izzuddin (later Jahandar Shah), ensuring every ritual and royal requirement was met with grace and grandeur. Saqi Mustad Khan notes:

> On Monday, the 8th September/8th Shawwal, the marriage entertainment of Mu'izzuddin took place ... The celebration was supervised by Zinat-un-nisa Begam (year 1684-85).[29]

Even in celebration, she was the quiet coordinator of peace and harmony. In a way, Zinat was the archetypal brown desi daughter: burdened with the task of keeping the family together, managing egos, smoothing over conflicts and making sure no one set the house on fire—even if the house was the largest empire in the world.

Zinat-un-Nissa's years in the Deccan weren't spent in perfumed palaces or idle leisure. She lived most of her adult life in army camps, tents and temporary forts, shadowing her father through the long, grinding campaigns against the Marathas. Unlike many Mughal women who stayed confined to the zenanas of Delhi or Agra, Zinat's life was mobile, militarized and filled with strategic responsibility. In 1700, for instance, she was summoned from the military base while the imperial army marched to Bhusangarh. And when Aurangzeb set off on an especially dangerous expedition after four years in Islampuri, it was Zinat who stayed back to anchor the harem's safety.

> The Emperor ... ordered that a cutcha wall ... be built around the small fortalice ... Zinat-un-Nissa Begam, the mother of the Prince, (i.e., Udipuri), and other ladies of the harem, and the families of all (common) people were let in this safe base under the care of Umdat-ul-Mulk ...[30]

Even in the midst of war, it was Zinat who was trusted to remain behind and provide stability. Her presence wasn't just emotional—it was logistical, strategic and deeply political. She was not merely accompanying the Mughal campaign—she was part of its command structure, entrusted with people, resources and decisions. It's striking that in a time of violent expansionism, Aurangzeb chose his daughter—not a general—to stand in for the imperial centre when he marched ahead.

Her role as Aurangzeb's emotional ambassador extended beyond the battlefield. When Hamida Banu Begum, the mother of Ruhullah Khan, passed away in 1704, Aurangzeb sent a formal condolence delegation to her son. The records tell:

> On Thursday, the 2nd November, Hamida Banu Begam, mother of Ruhullah Khan died. The Emperor graciously sent Muhammad Kam Bakhsh and Ashraf Khan, Mir Bakhshi, to Ruhullah's house to condole with him and

> bring him to Court. Robes were given to him and to
> his brothers. Zinatunnisa Begam visited his house by
> command.[31]

'Zinat-un-nisa Begam visited his house by command.' This wasn't just a polite gesture. It was a calculated message: Zinat represented the emperor in moments of private grief and public ceremony. In a court where power was shown through protocol, she became Aurangzeb's emotional and symbolic proxy, and stepped in on behalf of the royal family. Over the decades, Zinat-un-Nissa became far more than a daughter. She was the Mughal Empire's quiet diplomat, a stabilizing force in a fracturing dynasty, and a rare woman whose presence could simultaneously calm family tensions, preserve imperial dignity and express the one thing Aurangzeb seldom showed—compassion. As Aurangzeb's life neared its end, and the empire he built began to creak under the weight of its own contradictions, Zinat-un-Nissa remained one of the few constants—a daughter who carried her father's will, but tempered it with understanding.

What came next was the most solitary chapter of her life: the final years of a princess who had given her all to the Mughal court—only to retreat into quiet devotion as the world around her began to fade.

The final years

In the final, weary years of Aurangzeb's reign—when conquests had dragged on too long and the once-mighty empire was starting to splinter—it wasn't a son or a minister, but his daughter Zinat-un-Nissa who remained closest to him. Alongside his favoured concubine Udaipuri Mahal, Zinat was one of the few constants in his increasingly cloistered world. For years, she managed his household in the Deccan—quietly, efficiently and without ceremony— carrying the emotional and logistical burdens of a ruler who had exhausted both his armies and his soul.

Historians often complain about the silence around women in Mughal records—but in Zinat's case, the silence is occasionally broken. Year after year, the official accounts list the khan-i-saman—the officers who worked under Zinat to run her father's kitchen and groceries. It might seem trivial at first glance, but to be in charge of food, hospitality and daily life was to be trusted with the fabric of the emperor's existence. This was the domestic side of power—deeply gendered, often overlooked, but central to the rhythm of court life. Zinat didn't need a throne—she was already seated at the heart of her father's world.

And when that world came to an end in February 1707, Zinat was exactly where she had always been: by his side.

> The Qazi, scholars, and pious men engaged in furnishing and shrouding his corpse for burial … and kept his body in 'the khabgah,' till at last at the request of Zinat-un-nisa Begam, second daughter of the Emperor, Prince Muhammad Azam … arrived … and went into the deepest mourning.[32]

That moment—Zinat, standing watch over her father's shrouded body in the emperor's chamber—speaks louder than any imperial chronicle. It was her request that delayed the burial until her brother arrived. Her voice mattered even in death, not as a mourner alone, but as the one orchestrating the final rites of a man she had served, protected and loved in a way few others could understand.

Zinat-un-Nissa passed away in Delhi on 18 May 1721, at the age of seventy-seven. She had outlived her father by over a decade and watched the empire he had fought so hard to hold together begin to splinter. Yet, unlike so many others in the Mughal court, her legacy was never rooted in violence or ambition—it was in steadfastness. She left behind no children, no throne, no war—but something far more rare: a life of conviction, lived entirely on her own terms.

Like her sisters Zeb-un-Nissa and Zubdat-un-Nissa, Zinat was deeply learned in Islamic scholarship, trained by private tutors in scripture, jurisprudence and poetry. She never married, by choice—a radical act in itself in a world where women were political pawns in royal alliances. Instead, she anchored her life around faith, intellect and an unshakable commitment to her family. She served as a protector, mediator, confidante and stateswoman—often behind the veil, but never in the shadows.

Zinat, like many royal women of her time, also wrote poetry—though little survives today. Yet, even in what remains, her voice is unmistakable: quiet, dignified and devout. On her tomb, she left behind her own words—simple, elegant and filled with humility:

In my grave, the grace of God is my only help.
It is enough if the shadow of the cloud of mercy covers my tomb.

It's not the kind of epitaph you'd expect from a princess of an empire. And yet, it's exactly what makes her unforgettable. She didn't raise armies, but she kept peace at home. And in a dynasty filled with sons desperate to prove themselves, she proved that strength doesn't always roar.

Zinat-un-Nissa was a Mughal princess, yes—but she was also a classic eldest desi daughter: holding the family together, cleaning up royal messes and doing it all without ever asking for credit. That's not just rare. That's badass.

In the movie *Chhava* (2025) actress Diana Penty plays the role of Zinat-un-Nissa. However, the representation is incorrect. She is shown to walk around freely without a veil. Also, she is shown to support the torture of Sambhaji. Whereas, historically, she was sympathetic towards the Marathas for helping her brother.

9

The Fearless Tawaif

Mubarak Begum

I had just finished a heritage walk at Ghalib's popular haveli in Gali Qasim Jan, Ballimaran, and was making my way out of the area. I thought it would be faster if I walked rather than taking a rickshaw, which would ultimately get stuck in the narrow lanes of Old Delhi. My unrelenting fear is that one day my rickshaw will take a turn in these narrow, uneven gullies, and I will fall into a scalding cauldron full of oil in some halwai's shop! Armed with fear and pragmatism, I started walking, navigating the gullies, pushing people, jumping over potholes, and dodging bullock carts and rickshaws. When I reached Lal Kuan, I looked up to see the domes of the stunning Masjid Mubarak Begum rising above the shops. The mosque was painted red and had three smart domes. I clicked a photo of the mosque and continued walking towards my destination. The mosque soon became a memory and another image in my phone gallery.

In the year 2020, when the pandemic hit, the news was extremely grim and grave. Newspapers now contained more numbers than the alphabet; there were statistics and counts of lives lost due to COVID-19. Amidst this, Delhi experienced torrential rains. The government's funds were all diverted towards the health sector to maintain the state-run hospitals. Around this time, there was also news that the dome of the nineteenth-century Masjid Mubarak Begum was damaged in the rain.[1] Historians, scholars and art enthusiasts discussed the masjid to no end, and the name of the woman who brought it into existence was finally revealed.

In the beginning of nineteenth century, a young, innocent Mubarak Begum, a nautch girl, travelled from Pune to Delhi, where she fell in love with the much older Sir David Ochterlony, the British resident of the time. Not much is known about her earlier life, and the information passed down is mostly from British letters and documents that help us understand her role and position in society. Mubarak Begum became one of his thirteen wives, the youngest and by far the most beautiful, who enchanted David with her charms and coquettish mannerisms. She had converted to Islam even before she met David. While it cannot be ascertained why she converted, the prevailing theory is that since tawaif culture was embedded in Mughal culture, a Muslim name and fluency in Urdu and Persian languages would have commanded respect and guaranteed patronage by the rulers and noblemen.[2] Author William Dalrymple in his book *The White Mughals* notes that courtesan Mubarak Bagh was sold to David Ochterlony by a woman named Banbah, who resided with Mubarak al-Nissa in Ochterlony's house.[3]

Sir David Ochterlony was appointed lieutenant colonel and accompanied Lord Gerald Lake in the Anglo-Maratha war, which involved battles in Aligarh, Delhi and Koil. He fought valiantly and forced the Marathas to vacate the city of Delhi. He was appointed as the 'resident of Delhi', a position he held for the next three years.[4] In 1804, he managed to defend the city once again against Maratha chieftain and ruler of Indore, Yashwant Rao Holkar, which earned him the title of commander-in-chief; he was also given the title of Nasir-ud-Daula, the protector of the state, by the helpless yet proud Mughal Emperor Akbar Shah II, who was grateful he did not have to fight Marathas himself.[5] David Ochterlony was an interesting character in British colonial history. He was commonly known as 'Loony Akhtar' by the locals, amused by his eccentric nature, and a good example of what writer and historian William Dalrymple calls 'White Mughals'.[6] He was more than happy to dress and act like a native, having acquired thirteen wives to keep a proper 'zenana' of his own. A contemporary travel writer, Mrs A. Deane, writes that she saw Ochterlony on an elephant riding to Qutub Minar and showering silver coins like a Mughal nawab.[7] Another writer named Heber describes Ochterlony. He writes that Sir O was a pleasant-looking tall man wrapped in shawls, tunics and fur, and his face was barely visible. He was leading an entourage of horses, elephants and palanquins, carrying his family and servants' families. Even though Ochterlony earned around Rs 15,000 per annum, he maintained the appearance of an Eastern king.[8] Ochterlony was advised several times to go back to England, but he had left the country when he was very young and now had no one to call his own.

Scholar Savita Kumari adds that the East India Company government gave substantial funding to British residents to maintain a splendid court of their own—one to rival the Mughal emperor.[9] Near Kashmiri Gate of Old Delhi, Civil Lines became the focal point of British activities. There was a church, boarding school, cemetery, courthouse, garrison, British mansions, everything needed to make a home away from home. Initially, the British were given old Mughal mansions to suit their needs, but the growing European population ensured a separate township. Ochterlony was given the stunning but neglected Dara Shikoh library as his new residence. He retained most of the original structure, such as the five-cusped arch resting on balustrade columns in the central hall, but changed the outer facade of the house by adding a porch and European columns. The back of the house, too, was altered to add more European elements.[10] The British identity was becoming visible through the vocabulary of architecture. After the Anglo-Maratha war, Ochterlony repaired the fort's walls, added Martello towers, and became one of the first British residents to add to the city's architecture substantially.[11]

His home has been depicted in a famous early nineteenth-century watercolour painting by an anonymous Delhi artist. In the painting, Ochterlony is shown sitting on the floor and smoking hookah. A nautch performance is on in the room. There are natives behind him as he leans on a bolster. Musicians and women are accompanying the nautch dancer. The entire setting is very Indian, but European elements still exist, such as European vases, lamps and portraits. Such mixed households were prevalent in eighteenth-century India, where the British residents immersed themselves in the new culture and environment.

Although much younger than him, Mubarak Begum had a strong influence on David. One commentator writes that her hold on him was so strong that David was known as 'Generallee Begum' by his colleagues.[12] Another commentator wrote that the mistress is now 'mistress of everyone within the walls'.[13]

Mubarak Begum antagonized both the British and the natives. She insisted that she be addressed as 'Lady Ochterlony' or 'Qudsia Begum'. Titles such as 'Lady' and 'Sir' were reserved for pedigreed British, just as the title of 'Qudsia' was given to the Mughal queen mother.[14] By claiming titles that belonged to royalty and the colonial elite, Mubarak Begum didn't just blur the lines between ruler and ruled—she boldly redrew them, unsettling everyone who thought they knew their place.

Extending her influence on the household, Mubarak raised her daughters as Muslim and adopted a girl from the esteemed Nawab of the Loharu Muslim family who was married to a nephew of the famous nineteenth-century poet Mirza Ghalib.[15] Ochterlony was worried about his children's education. If he raised them as Muslims, he feared about them marrying into Muslim aristocracy and ending up as one of the many wives in the harem. And if he raised his children as Christians, they would forever be judged for their 'dark blood', despite having a fair complexion. In the end, it seems Ochterlony did choose to raise his daughters as Muslims—a decision that aligned more with the life he had built with Mubarak Begum and less with the judgemental gaze of British society. But his letters remain deeply revealing, not just as a father's dilemma, but as a window into the conflicted soul of the colonial elite.

Ochterlony, like many British men who had 'gone native', performed a delicate balancing act—emotionally rooted to India, yet constantly pulled back by the disapproval of a world that demanded distance, superiority and racial purity. His struggle was not just about how to raise his daughters; it was about whether one could ever fully belong to both worlds—or if, in trying, you ended up belonging to neither.

Ochterlony built a tomb and garden in the city, naming it after his wife, Mubarak Begum Bagh. He had bought the land from his assistant, William Fraser, especially for his wife. The land was close to Shalimar Gardens. He built a tomb inside the garden where he wished to be buried. The tomb dome was similar to St. James Church in Kashmiri Gate, topped with a cross. There were two wings to the tomb with multiple small minarets. The architecture was a fusion of his love for native culture and his Christian upbringing.[16] The Bagh was built during his second term as a resident around 1821–25. As official protocol demanded, he lived in the residency, and Mubarak Bagh was used as a place to stay at over the weekends. He wanted the Bagh to reflect the union of his marriage, and depict his and his wife's tastes in architecture and sensibilities. The only evidence of the Bagh is the painting we have of it. It is found in the 'Reminiscences of Imperial Dehlie', commissioned by Thomas Metcalfe, company agent and commissioner at Delhi.

For reasons unknown, Ochterlony died in Meerut in July 1825, and his tomb in Delhi remained empty.[17] He was buried in St John's Church in Meerut. After his death, Mubarak Begum inherited the Bagh. She used her wealth to build a haveli and a mosque in the Lal Kuan area near Hauz Qazi Chowk. She also remarried a Mughal amir, Vilayat Ali Khan.[18] In the early 1900s, Mirza Farhatullah Baig captured this very world in his celebrated novella *Dehli ki Aakhri Sham'a* (*The Last Light of Delhi*), imagining a grand 1845 mushaira, presided over by Bahadur Shah Zafar and graced by his son, Mirza Fakhru (pen name Ramz). In the book, it is mentioned that the mosque commissioned by Mubarak Begum in Lal Kuan had a printing press on the ground floor.[19] The masjid, however, had an ill reputation over the years because the natives and the British both hated Mubarak Begum as she overstepped her position as one of the wives of Sir David Ochterlony and held a strong influence on him. The masjid came to be known as 'Randi ka Masjid' or 'Whore's Mosque'.

The reason the begum's mosque acquired such a distasteful name has a lot to do with Mubarak Begum's role and involvement in the Revolt of 1857. During the ten months of the Revolt in Delhi, the sepoys took over the entire city. The elite and the clergy were not happy funding the sepoys, whom they saw as uncouth, ill-mannered ruffians and criminals. The tawaifs came to the rescue of these sepoys and ultimately funded a large part of the revolt. The tawaifs were the city's wealthiest women then, and the rulers and the aristocrats favoured them. They had amassed wealth through their skills and talent. The finest luxury was bought and held by the tawaifs—from exquisite pashmina to priceless porcelain, to the most expensive wine, to valuable jewellery that they often received as gifts. The tawaifs favoured the sepoys over the British, who did not respect their skill of dancing and singing; neither were they loyal patrons.

Mubarak Begum was, at that time, married to Vilayat Ali, a Mughal amir involved in the revolt. Her allegiance became more substantial to the rebels than the British, even if her late husband himself was an employee of the East India Company.

After the 1857 uprising, the British colonial administration intensified its efforts to suppress and marginalize the tawaif community, who had previously enjoyed significant cultural and social standing in Indian society. Their establishments, known as kothas, were frequently raided, and the women were labelled as mere prostitutes. Veena Oldenberg, who has extensively researched the topic, found Company tax records where the tawaifs have paid taxes, which run twenty pages long![20] Because feudal aristocracy was purged from the city and due to heavy taxation, tawaifs soon had little money and few prospects. The Anti-Venereal Act of 1868 and the Anti-Nautch Movement which gained momentum in the late nineteenth century, further deteriorated the condition of tawaifs in the city. The Anti-Venereal Act, part of the Contagious Diseases Act, enforced by the British in colonial India, allowed for the forcible medical examination and registration of women suspected of spreading venereal diseases.

Meanwhile, the Anti-Nautch Movement, which began in the 1870s and intensified by the 1890s, was led by colonial officials, Christian missionaries and Indian social reformers, who viewed tawaifs and devadasis as morally corrupt.

After Sir David Ochterlony's death in 1825, Mubarak Begum married Vilayat Ali, a Mughal soldier whom she backed financially and who rose to become a captain in Bahadur Shah Zafar's royal troops. When the 1857 uprising broke out, Vilayat Ali joined the Mughal side against the British—like many rebel officers, he appears to have been stripped of rank and estate after the revolt was suppressed. Contemporary British records make no further mention of him after 1858, suggesting he either perished during the fighting or faded into exile, leaving Mubarak Begum without his protection as colonial pressure on her household intensified.

Mubarak Begum's haveli in Hauz Qazi was more than a home—it was the beating heart of Delhi's classical arts. In his book, *Delhi ki Aakhri Sham'a*, Mirza Farhatullah Baig captures every detail in Mubarak Begum's richly appointed courtyard: divans draped with Kashmiri shawls, lanterns flickering against red sandstone walls, and the mingled scents of rose attar and incense hanging in the air. It is believed more than forty poets attended mushairas at her place—even when there was mounting colonial pressure to boycott salons and cultural gatherings. While the account is semi-fictional, most historians believe the nature of events did happen, as the book was written only around fifty years after the Revolt of 1857.

Mubarak Begum lived a fierce life even if she was sullied and vilified for being assertive and strong-headed. Her name remained attached to the mosque, though many people still call it 'Randi ka Masjid'. When I asked the caretakers about this, they became very uncomfortable, and their efforts to not associate this name with the masjid were apparent.

To enter the masjid, you climb a narrow staircase through a green arched doorway. Above it, a simple prayer is inscribed: 'O Allah! Open for me the gates of Your mercy.' At the final step, you're expected to remove your footwear. The caretakers are particular about this rule and don't hesitate to remind anyone who forgets. The masjid is always spotless and the stone floor stays cool even on the hottest afternoons. To the left, there's a shoe rack neatly arranged for footwear and a row of working taps where people squat to perform wuzu.

Built on the first floor, the masjid looks out to the congested road below. Its parapet serves as a resting spot, just high enough to lean back and take in the view. Across the street, a tea seller keeps a large saucepan bubbling with hot chai, and the air carries its sweet, spiced aroma. Down below, the usual chaos unfolds—rickshaws ringing their bells, cars inching through the tight lanes and, now and then, the slow clatter of a horse-drawn cart cutting through the noise like a remainder from another time.

The masjid itself is modest—a single-aisled structure with three simple archways. 'Allah' is written on both sides of the gateway and a small clock above the entrance keeps time for the daily prayers. Inside, a plain shelf holds the holy books and the qibla wall stands undecorated—its simplicity drawing the eye more than any ornament could.

There aren't too many visitors here, which makes it a peaceful place to sit quietly and watch the bazaar from above. Its name, Mubarak Begum Masjid, is painted boldly at the entrance—a deliberate attempt to erase the older, more scandalous name it once carried.

As you leave and descend the narrow staircase, another prayer is written above: 'O Allah! I beg of You Your Grace.'

At the bottom, I pause. An eight-year-old girl is performing on a tightrope stretched between two bamboo poles. An earthen pot rests perfectly balanced on her head as she walks the rope with the confidence of someone far older. Her mother and younger brother stand nearby, collecting coins from the small crowd. A stereo sits on the ground, playing an old song: *Mere haathon mein nau nau chudiya hain.*

Watching her, I can't help but think—women are always balancing something, aren't they? And one small distraction is often all it takes to slip. As she walks carefully across that thin rope, I find myself silently hoping she earns enough for her effort.

Mubarak Begum, better known as Generalee Begum, the consort of British resident Sir David Ochterlony, was once reported to have acted as if she had her own foreign policy! Contemporary accounts claim she filled Delhi's papers with notices of nizars (offerings) and khiluts (robes of honour) exchanged in her dealings with princely envoys. For a courtesan-turned-begum to publicly engage in such courtly rituals was seen as an extraordinary liberty in nineteenth-century Delhi.

10

Not Just Mumtaz

Shah Jahan's Begums Who Built Old Delhi

It was a Sunday morning, and I was tired—not so much physically, but in that emotional and mental sense of a burnout. The year 2024 had been a nightmare, leaving me financially drained. All my efforts had been spent running a heritage company I started when I was twenty-four. Because I bootstrapped it, it meant I had to be extra careful with funds. Yet, I've come to accept that if all my work goes towards paying employees and covering expenses, at least I'm doing something worthwhile. The company's entire purpose is to keep the conversation alive about India's heritage, especially in Delhi. But after six years of doing this, starting so young, I felt depleted. I was not a finance student nor a student of marketing. Still, here I was, checking balance sheets, making profit and loss statements, strategizing how to make the most of social media, and researching for the book and the walks. It was a tricky balance, learning to do all this by myself and being accountable for all the women in the company.

On days like these, when I felt I had spread myself too thin, I sought refuge in a monument. This time, Fatehpuri Masjid beckoned me. I am a non-practising Jain—one of the oldest religions in the world—yet, I believe equally in the power of all religions, or none. While my stance on religion is neutral and vague, I believe in a supreme being's presence. I am happy to appeal to any god if they are ready to listen to me amidst their hectic schedules. For me, nothing is heretic, and everything is sacred. With this mindset, I sought solace in the calm environment of Fatehpuri Masjid.

Fatehpuri Masjid lies west of Red Fort and is built at the end of Chandni Chowk road. If someone stood at the Red Fort's Lahori Gate holding one end of a thread, the other end would lead directly to Fatehpuri Masjid. This straight road is the city's central axis, with Lahori Gate and Fatehpuri Masjid acting as its two bookends. Outside the masjid, chaos rules. Rickshaws jam the roads, horns blare incessantly, queues form at food stalls and traffic for Khari Baoli starts swelling after 10 a.m. Escaping the mayhem, I reached Fatehpuri's entrance.

The masjid is painted red and decorated with green floral work at its entrance, while the inside is white. A rabdi wallah plies his trade outside the entrance, alongside dry-fruit sellers. Fatehpuri Masjid is famed for its chilled, condensed milk sweet served with dry fruits. Vendors keep the milky sweet on ice slabs, making it a delicious treat. Nearby is the iconic heritage shop Chaina Ram, dating to 1901, when it was first established in Lahore's Anarkali Bazaar; it was re-established in Old Delhi after Partition. The shop is celebrated for its chole bhature, sev pak, Karachi halwa, pinni, motichoor laddoo, kheer mohan, among other sweets. There's no seating, so people typically get takeaways for their families.

Stepping into Fatehpuri Masjid, my eyes had to adjust to the bright courtyard. The courtyard has a separate enclosure divided by marble and red sandstone railings. The enclosure is beautifully decorated with dense vegetation of tall plants and bushes. Several graves lie here, belonging to imams who cared for the masjid and madrassa instructors. In the centre stands a marble tank filled with water, equipped with taps and places for worshippers to squat and perform wuzu. There are also raised sandstone platforms in the courtyard where birdseed is scattered for the pigeons. Rooms and enclosures line three sides of the mosque; on the right is a madrassa where young boys study. I often see learned men in skull caps teaching groups of students. The kids have their heads bent, gently rocking as they recite passages.

Fatehpuri Begum was one of Shah Jahan's wives. Built in 1650, Fatehpuri Masjid is the second-largest mosque in Old Delhi after Jama Masjid. The masjid has a single limestone dome, unlike the Jama Masjid, which has three domes and is made from white marble. In earlier days, the wuzu tank was fed by the Faiz Nahr canal, which drew water from the Yamuna, but that channel was destroyed in 1857. An electric pump now does the job. It's possible that Jahanara's hammam near her serai was built so people could bathe and then visit Fatehpuri Mosque. Before 1857, the masjid was under a trust about which Ramki Das writes in his book *Zikr-e Umurat Am Zila-e Dehli*:

> This mosque was built by Fatehpuri [Mahal], also the wife of the above Badshah [Shah Jahan]. It was built during his reign [1650 CE] and like the Akbarabadi mosque this too is in the possession of a government trust and is made completely of red sandstone. It is situated adjoining the Lahori Darwaza [of the city].[1]

Another nineteenth-century writer, Sangin Beg in his book *Sair-ul-Manazil* beautifully describes the area around Fatehpuri Masjid. He writes:

> Here is the Chandni Chowk Police Chowki, which is connected to the Kotwali Chabutra. Near this is the Rewdiwalon ka Katra and the haveli of Nawab Hyder Quli which is the riyasat of coachmen. Here is the Masjid Fatehpuri Begam, which was constructed by Fatehpuri Begam, a wife of Emperor Shah Jahan. To the south of the mosque is a bazar where there are the Katra Ghulam Muhammad Khan, Katra Gondi and other buildings, the shop of Hafiz Ilahi Bakhsh the pedlar, and the shops of the Fatehpuri Masjid. Behind the mosque is a katra built by Fatehpuri Begam, which has shops of the maidagars, Kucha-e-Khari Baoli, shops of grocers and

batashawallahs, and shops of Muhammad Amin the attar. Also in this area are Kucha-e-Naya Bans, and the Chowki and thana building of the Lahori Gate Police, which is right next to the Lahori Gate. From the Lahori Gate of the Qila-e-Mubarak to the Fatehpuri Masjid the Faiz Nahar flows through the middle of the bazar: This is the interesting market of the chowk. One stops wherever the heart is captivated.[2]

Fatehpuri Masjid stands as more than a place of worship—it's a testament of Fatehpuri Begum's agency, carved into the very heart of Shahjahanabad. Built in 1650 and directly aligned with the Lahori Gate of the Red Fort, its position alone speaks volumes. Facing the imperial palace's main entrance, the mosque functioned as a daily reminder that Shah Jahan's wife commanded her own public stage. Pilgrims and courtiers exiting the fort saw her monument first, not the emperor's. This 'first impression' was a deliberate display of her status and influence. Sangin Beg's nineteenth-century sketch of the precinct reveals Fatehpuri Masjid as surrounded by bustling katras (market arcades), grocers' stalls, sweet shops, even a police chowki—an ecosystem she both shaped and served. Worshippers flowed seamlessly from prayer halls to bazaars, cementing the mosque not only as a spiritual hub but as the nucleus of everyday commerce and social exchange.

Circle the mosque, and you'll discover its hidden genius: it goes directly into Chandni Chowk's katras. Imagine finishing your prayers, stepping through the mosque's arches, and immediately diving into the pulse of trade.

Fatehpuri Masjid wasn't just a spiritual refuge; it was the hub of everyday Delhi life.

Despite their contributions to the city, Shah Jahan's other wives are but footnotes in history, literally, from a research point of view. Mumtaz Mahal's tale fits neatly into the romantic mould—an emperor's grief, a monument to devotion—so it becomes a universal parable of love and loss. The Taj Mahal sings that song perfectly, even though Mumtaz herself never saw a single brick laid. She is the inspiration rather than the agent. By contrast, Fatehpuri Begum wrote herself into Delhi's streets in living stone. She wasn't memorialized—she was *the* patron, the one who marshalled resources, chose the site and oversaw the mosque's construction. Yet, her mosque rarely makes it into popular lore, not only because it's less grand, but because it doesn't come wrapped in a ready-made romance. This is why women builders often fade from memory: the world loves a muse, but it's less comfortable celebrating a woman as an architect of power. Their legacies get overwritten, sometimes literally, with new names, new stories, new identities.

These structures weren't just places of worship; they were assertions of visibility, power and piety in a male-dominated world. While many of these mosques quietly shaped the city's spiritual and social landscape, Fatehpuri Masjid stood out—not just for its scale and architectural elegance, but for the woman behind it. Yet, history has been unkind to women builders. Structures built by them were often forgotten, stripped of their stories, or overshadowed by grander, male-commissioned monuments. Fatehpuri Masjid, surrounded by the bustling markets of Chandni Chowk and intricately woven into the everyday rhythms of the city, was not just a spiritual anchor—it became a political one too, playing a pivotal role during the Uprising of 1857.

By the time the Revolt of 1857 tore through Delhi, Fatehpuri Masjid was no longer just a mosque; it had become a symbol. Situated at the very edge of Chandni Chowk and close to the Red Fort, which was the heart of Mughal urban life, the mosque became an inadvertent witness to the empire's final unravelling. After the British crushed the rebellion, they launched a systematic campaign to dismantle not just Delhi's physical symbols of Mughal authority, but also its soul. Brij Kishan Chandiwalla, in his evocative 1964 book *Dilli ki Khoj*, recounts the aftermath:

> British soldiers stationed themselves inside Fatehpuri Masjid, turning this once-revered sanctuary into a debauched outpost. Liquor was served, drunken parties were held within its sacred walls, soldiers climbed the pulpit to deliver mock-sermons, and names were scratched into centuries-old stone—acts of desecration that were more than just disrespectful. They were deliberate erasures of power.[3]

In 1860, in one of the more bizarre footnotes of colonial policy, the mosque was *sold*—yes, sold—to Lala Chunnamal, a wealthy Khatri merchant, for Rs 19,000. The sale came with no strings attached; the British even gave him the legal right to tear it down and build a warehouse. But Chunnamal, perhaps out of reverence, perhaps foresight, did something extraordinary: he didn't destroy it. He simply locked up the mosque and waited.[4]

Seventeen years later, when the first Delhi Durbar was held in 1877 and Queen Victoria was proclaimed Empress of India, there was a shift. Muslim elites, long exiled from the city or silenced in it, returned to Delhi and petitioned to reopen Fatehpuri Masjid for prayer. Suddenly, the British were in a bind. The same mosque they had tried to erase had become a point of political sensitivity. They tried to buy it back, but Chunnamal, no longer just a trader but a shrewd negotiator, refused. Eventually, he agreed to sell—at nearly six times the original price, for Rs 1,10,000, along with procuring four villages in Mehrauli.[5]

Today, Fatehpuri Masjid stands at the centre of a bustling universe—one foot in history, the other in modern Delhi. The mosque has three gateways; the eastern gateway looks directly at the Red Fort—Shah Jahan's grandest effort at imperial urban planning.

Walk through the southern gateway, and you find yourself in Katra Baryan—a narrow artery that eventually leads to Lal Kuan, where Zeenat Mahal Haveli still stands, hidden behind spice-filled godowns. You can smell asafoetida, hear the clang of carts and catch fragments of Urdu floating from shopfronts. Meanwhile, the northern gateway opens into Khari Baoli, Asia's largest spice market, where trucks unload turmeric, saffron and cinnamon in heaps. Inside the Khari Baoli market is the iconic Gadodia Haveli, which shares its back wall with the mosque. The grand multi-level haveli with hundreds of rooms now houses godowns and wholesale shops. If you're lucky enough to climb up its narrow staircase, you'll find a rooftop that offers a breathtaking bird's-eye view of both Fatehpuri Masjid's dome and the swirling madness of Khari Baoli below.

Just a few steps away from the mosque's entrance, the scent shifts to that of sugar. Delhiites know this stretch by heart, especially the loyalists of Nagpal Dairy, Salamat Shah Ji Dairy and Jagat Dairy—local legends known for their thick, creamy rabri, malai-laden lassi and indulgent sweets served in kulhads. You can stand there, the taste of slow-cooked milk on your tongue, as Fatehpuri Masjid's red sandstone dome rises behind you, and feel how food, faith and history blend effortlessly in this corner of Old Delhi. When I stood here, amid the chaos of Delhi's commerce and the distant echo of the azaan, I couldn't help but think: this mosque isn't just architecture. It's a living story that continues to tell its tale— stubborn like the woman who built it.

Building a mosque offered a pious and dignified path to be remembered by posterity. Everyone knows Shah Jahan's partiality toward Mumtaz Mahal; yet, he had three other wives—Fatehpuri Begum, Akbarabadi Begum and Sirhindi Begum—all of whom erected mosques in Delhi to secure their own lasting commemoration. Abul Fazl writes that, since Akbar's reign, it was typical not to record a royal woman's name but instead to grant her a title—often referencing the region she came from or her faith. Thus, Fatehpuri Begum came from Fatehpuri near Agra, and Akbarabadi Begum came from Agra, which was known as Akbarabad then.

The names of women—daughters, wives, sisters—were freely mentioned in the early sources. Babur almost always gives the names of both parents whenever he refers to a child, son or daughter, in one context or another, but usually in the context of their marriage. Gulbadan too follows this format. From Akbar's time onwards, however, such names—particularly names of royal wives—begin to get omitted. Instead, as mentioned previously, their identities are established, if at all, with reference to the place of their birth or some other indicator. The historian of the reign of Akbar's grandson Shah Jahan, Inayat Khan, notes in his *Shah Jahan Nama* that:

> Ever since the reign of Akbar, it had been ordained that the names of the inmates of the seraglio (harem) should not be mentioned in public, but that they should be designated by some epithet derived either from the place of their birth or the country or the city in which they might have first been regarded by the monarch with the eye of affection.[6]

This practice of obscuring the real names of Mughal royal women and replacing them with epithets derived from geography or vague associations was not merely a matter of etiquette or privacy. It was, and remains, a systemic erasure. For historians, this poses multiple challenges: not just in tracing the biographies of these women, but in recognizing their agency, intellect and influence. For instance, when we encounter names like Fatehpuri Begum or Akbarabadi Begum, we're left guessing about the woman behind the title.

Was she a patron of the arts? Did she play a role in imperial diplomacy? What were her personal beliefs, ambitions or struggles? Much of this remains locked behind court conventions and historiographical silences. For historians, this creates a frustrating labyrinth: trying to stitch together a life from the architecture they built, stray references in court chronicles, family trees or inscriptions. It also means we often overlook significant figures simply because they weren't named, or because their legacy was subsumed into the identities of others. The challenge, then, is not just to recover names but to reconstruct them and to read silences as carefully as we read texts. And when we do, a richer, more complex image of Mughal women begins to emerge. As historian Harbans Mukhia notes, relationships within royal households were rarely simple. They weren't defined solely by hierarchy or romantic idealism, but often by emotional intimacy, companionship and mutual trust—even within polygamous settings.[7]

The historian further observes that relationships between Mughal husbands and wives were unique, passionate and intimate. Despite the fact that history clearly recognizes Shah Jahan's love for Mumtaz, among other Mughal emperors and nobles too there seems to be a level of affection, respect and worthy acknowledgement of the fairer sex. He writes:

What were, however, eminently permeable were the boundaries of personal relationships between husband and wife. Mughal India, much like the Delhi Sultanate, is teeming with moving stories of bonds between Emperors, Princes and their consorts that went beyond a passing affection. The bond was not conditional upon monogamy, although the conditions, such as they were, were asymmetrical for the male and the female consorts. The tales of Jahangir and Nur Jahan, and of Shah Jahan and Mumtaz Mahal, are the stuff of legends. Jahangir also notes the attachment of Itmad al-Daulla, Nur Jahan's father, to his wife. 'From the day on which his companion attained to the mercy of God, he no longer cared for himself but melted away from day to day... . After 3 months and 20 days he passed away.' ... Dara Shukoh had a wife, Nadira Begum, two concubines and a 'sweetheart'; but it was his wife who was his 'intimate friend'. In presenting the Album named after himself to Nadira, Dara inscribed upon it the words: 'To Nadira Banu Begum, my special and intimate friend, companion and sharer of secrets, I present this fine album: Muhammad Dara Shukoh, son of Shah Jahan Padshah Ghazi.'[8]

The relationship between husbands and wives in medieval times was more complicated than we might think today. It's important to understand those equations without judging them through the lens of modern marriages which are strictly formed by monogamy. Back then, especially among royal and wealthy men, it was common to have multiple wives. Each wife had her own unique connection with her husband, but there was usually one wife who held a special place in his heart, becoming his 'intimate friend'. This is what the above passage indicates—that we should view the relationship between Emperor Shah Jahan and Mumtaz, as well as with his other wives, such as Fatehpuri Begum and Akbarabadi Begum, with this broad understanding.

The lost queen of Shahjahanabad: Akbarabadi Begum

She wasn't Shah Jahan's favourite wife but she was formidable. Izz-un-Nissa, better remembered by her title Akbarabadi Begum, came into the Mughal court not through love, but alliance. As the granddaughter of the poet-warrior Abdul Rahim Khan-i-Khana, she was from a powerful lineage that Shah Jahan—then still Prince Khurram—could not afford to ignore. Their marriage in 1617 was likely political, but what she did with that position was anything but ornamental.[9]

She gave birth to Shah Jahan's son, Sultan Jahan Afroz Mirza, a child raised in the Deccan by her father, Shahnawaz Khan, but whose life was tragically cut short in 1621. He died young and was largely forgotten, just like his mother would be in the annals of history.

Yet, Akbarabadi Begum didn't fade quietly into the zenana. She built power with stone and brick.

In 1650, she commissioned a stunning urban complex just outside the Delhi Gate of the Red Fort: a majestic mosque of red, black and white stone; a hammam; a serai; and a sprawling square with canal-fed fountains. The bazaar that ran alongside stretched 1050 yards with 888 shops. Chandni Chowk may have been the jewel, but Faiz Bazaar (bazaar of plenty), as it came to be known, was her domain. This street became the beating heart of royal life. Every Friday, members of the imperial household would walk through it on their way to prayers.

In fact, Shah Jahan himself used her mosque regularly before the Jama Masjid was completed in 1656. And it's said that the scholar Shah Abdul Qadir Dehlavi translated the Quran from Arabic to Urdu within its very walls, which marked a massive cultural moment for the subcontinent's Islamic learning.[10]

Her mosque connected the community and the court to the city's spiritual and commercial lifeblood. And we know this because she left behind her own voice etched in stone. The mosque has been mentioned by Sangin Beg in his *Sair-ul-Manazil*, in which he notes there was an inscription at the entrance of the mosque:

This mosque is intended for the use of men only and it is such a place where the heart is at peace. The Hammam-e-Nizamat and Chauk-e-Dilkusho are located here. These are buildings where all seekers of truth observe prayers; and for the non-believers this place refreshes the soul. For the departed, it is a place of recreation, and for those of the mortal world, it is a place of gain. This mosque was built in Shihab-ud- Din Muhammad Shah Jahan's reign, in the name of his Begam Aza-un-Nissa, who was also called Akbarabadi Begam. It was meant with the intent and hope for reward and salvation. All the expenses related to the mosque (both internal and external spending) were met through the waqf (trust); so much so that when needed, its repairs could also be paid for through this trust. The rest of the money was put aside for the mosque, the hammam (tank), the students of the madrassa, and those who were in need, the poor (who have not been mentioned by name). These structures were built in two years, after an expense of 1.5 lakhs, and they were completed at the end of the month of Ramzan, from the twenty-fifth regnal year of the King, i.e. 1006 Hijri.[11] May God reward the King for this task. Amen.[12]

Its Persian inscription tells us the mosque was built for men and seekers of truth, for mourners and mystics, for the poor and the living. Every brick spoke of her vision—a woman crafting not just a monument, but a world. If Shah Jahan's reign is remembered for grandeur, Akbarabadi Begum quietly helped lay its foundations.

From the Akbarabadi Gate of the Red Fort to the Akbarabadi Gate of the city, she constructed a vast commercial strip: 1050 yards long, 30 yards wide, with 888 shops. That's nearly a kilometre of thriving trade. Alongside it flowed a branch of the Paradise Canal. At its head, she built her masterpiece: a striking mosque in red, black and white, named Ashat Panahi (Great Protection).

But Akbarabadi Begum didn't stop at places of worship. She added a serai for travellers, a hammam, and even laid out a grand square, to serve as a communal gathering space.[13]

So why don't we know of this mosque like we do the others?

Because the mosque was destroyed in 1857. The British razed it down after the revolt, part of their plan to flatten Mughal memory, especially spaces that inspired resistance or held symbolic power. Debris from her mosque was repurposed to build the Jama Masjid in Aligarh Muslim University.[14] Even its calligraphy, by Amanat Khan (the same artist who worked on the Taj Mahal), was salvaged. Akbarabadi's mosque lived on but only in fragments and footnotes. In 2012, the ghost of her mosque rose again. While digging for a metro station at Netaji Subhash Park, workers stumbled upon remnants of Mughal-era architecture. As rumours spread that this was the lost mosque of Akbarabadi Begum, locals began to pray there. Namaz turned into protest. Politicians joined in. For a brief moment, history pushed through concrete, demanding recognition. But the site was demolished again.[15]

What Akbarabadi Begum represents is larger than a lost building. She stands for the many royal women erased from textbooks, stripped of their names, remembered only through the cities they hailed from: Fatehpuri, Akbarabadi, Sirhindi, Udaipuri. And yet, these women built mosques. They founded schools. They shaped cities. They challenged the boundaries of what women could be, even within the zenana. But when their names vanished, their legacies began to crumble too.

Akbarabadi Begum was also an inherent player of the court's inner circle of power and diplomacy. After Mumtaz Mahal's death, Shah Jahan's attention, though forever partial to his daughter Jahanara, began to spread more evenly among his wives. During the grand Nauroz festival of 1650, court chroniclers recorded that while Jahanara was gifted jewels and fine garments worth over Rs 1 lakh and also the immensely profitable pargana of Panipat, Shah Jahan did not forget his queens. He gifted Rs 1 lakh each to Akbarabadi Begum and Fatehpuri Begum too.[16] According to Inayat Khan's *Shah Jahan Nama*, he referred to them with 'superior regard'—a phrase rarely used for consorts beyond the principal queen. Another instance narrates how Akbarabadi Begum presented Shah Jahan with a ring set with rubies that cost Rs 30,000 on his weighing ceremony.[17]

Her gift was political performance; she was securing her place in courtly favour, reminding the emperor (and those watching) that she was more than just a wife, she was also an investor in his image. It shows us a woman constantly curating her importance, navigating power with charm, wealth and strategic generosity.

In 1653, after the completion of Shahjahanabad and the Red Fort, Shah Jahan granted her a sprawling garden estate six miles west of the Lahore Gate. Known initially as Azzizabad Garden—after her title, Izz-un-Nissa—it was later renamed Shalimar Garden. It took four years to complete and cost Rs 10 lakh, with a serai built from her own funds, first in sun-dried brick, later upgraded to brick-and-mortar.[18] According to art historian Catherine Asher, such gardens weren't leisure retreats, they functioned as political thrones, modelled on the royal estates of Lahore and Kashmir. She writes:

> Akbarabadi Mahal, noted for building a mosque and serai within the city, in 1650 also provided a magnificent walled garden, today known as Shalimar Bagh, about 8 km north of the city. Contemporary texts indicate that it was modeled on Shah Jahan's gardens in Lahore and Kashmir that large terraced garden, which Bernier claims was Shah Jahan's country estate. This is probably true, for the layout and baluster columns of the largest remaining pavilion suggest that it was used as a throne room.[19]

It was here, in 1658, that Aurangzeb would be crowned emperor. In a way, Akbarabadi's garden hosted the empire's most controversial turning point.

This information is further proved by Inayat Khan in his book *Shah Jahan Nama*:

> A few years before this (1650), in conformity to the ever-obeyed farman, a royal garden had been founded outside Shahjahanabad at a distance of two and one-half ordinary kos from the precincts of the palace, on a plot of ground in the locality called Badli. This garden had been bestowed by His Majesty as a gift on his consort Akbarabadi Mahal and is now designated A'izzabad. In these days, after a lapse of four years and an outlay of 10 lakhs of rupees, the garden was now completed—together with its serai, which had formerly been erected of sun-

dried bricks, but was subsequently rebuilt with baked bricks and mortar at the Lady's own expense.[20]

What's even more striking is that Akbarabadi Begum wasn't building in isolation. Her choices reflected a pattern among Mughal royal women, especially queens and princesses like Jahanara and Fatehpuri Begum. All three invested in public spaces: gardens, mosques, serais, and hammams. These women were building a city. By creating these spaces, the begums were shaping how people saw the empire, one structure at a time. Catherine Asher points out that these buildings spoke a shared language: a clear, consistent message that Mughal women mattered, not just behind palace walls, but out in the open—as patrons, planners, and power players.[21]

We often forget this: while Shah Jahan was building for eternity in white marble, the women around him were crafting living, breathing cities. In many ways, Akbarabadi's works outlasted her memory. Her name was later erased, her mosque destroyed in 1857, her garden renamed. But her imprint on Delhi—and on the Mughal court—was never ornamental. It was foundational.

Maybe for the clearest sign of how important she really was, look at the map!

One of the main gates of Shahjahanabad—the entry and exit point for royals—was named after her. Her mosque wasn't hidden in some corner; it stood right next to the Red Fort, so close that Shah Jahan himself used it until the Jama Masjid was built.

As the evening namaz began, I got up to leave Fatehpuri Masjid. Twilight settled over Chandni Chowk, the sky glowing a brilliant orange. The masjid's reflection shimmered across the wuzu tank's water, softly rippling in the summer breeze. Once again, I stepped into the pandemonium of Chandni Chowk, allowing the river of humanity to carry me away.

Shalimar Bagh, located in north-west Delhi, is considered to have been laid out by Bibi Akbarabadi, one of Shah Jahan's wives. Originally known as A'izzabad after her name, Aziz-un-Nissa Begum, it was designed to resemble the famous Shalimar Garden in Kashmir. The highlight of this garden is the Sheesh Mahal, where Aurangzeb was crowned emperor on 31 July 1658. During the First War of Independence in 1857, Shalimar Bagh became the site of a fierce battle between British troops and sepoys, with the local residents of Shalimar village joining in the fight. Today, the garden is a more desolate place, though parts of it still feature majestic trees and shade.

Acknowledgements

I would like to thank Abhishek Panth, who contributed both in helping me write and finish this book. He held my hand during the toughest times and worked on many days for both of us. His keen observations, deep insights and hard work to assist me with the research for this book was instrumental in getting it published.

I would like to thank Trisha, my editor, who messaged me one day and suggested we should work on this book. Without her, this book would have been just an idea.

I would like to thank my sister Pakhi who read me so many stories when I was a child—my love for stories started at an early age because of her. I would like to thank my brother-in-law, Vaibhav, and my nephew, Yuvan (whom we dearly call Banku). They brought me joy on days when I was in deep despair.

I would like to thank my closest friend and confidant Prerana Das who patiently heard me vent on several days and acted as my unpaid therapist. I would like to thank my friends from school and college who went on several walks with me even before I started my company. I would like to thank the entire team of EIH, especially the people who supported the company and treated it as their own.

I would like to thank Dr Sonika Sandhu who was always the voice of reason and logic when I needed it the most.

I would like to thank Archana Upadhyay who helped me navigate the tedious world of publishing. I would also like to thank author Tanushree Podder who was generous in imparting her years of wisdom and knowledge as a writer.

Lastly, I would like to thank my Nani who always believed women are born to do big things in life.

Notes

Introduction

1. R.V. Smith, *Delhi: Unknown Tales of the City*, Roli Books, New Delhi, 2015, p. 94.

1: The Woman Who Built Chandni Chowk

1. Abdul Hamid Lahori, *Padshah Nama*, vol. 01, Part 01, ed. Kabir al-Din Ahmad and Abd al-Rahim, College Press, Calcutta, 1867–68, p. 391; Renuka Nath, *Notable Mughal and Hindu Women in the 16th and 17th Centuries A.D.,* Inter-India Publication, New Delhi, 1988, p. 118.
2. With due ceremonies, the newly born child was presented to Emperor Jahangir and the emperor gave the name 'Jahanara', or the 'Adorner of the World', to the baby. Originally given in Mirza Aminai Qazwini, *Shahjahan Nama or Badshah Nama*, MS. Asiatic Society of Bengal, Calcutta; cited in Nath, *Notable Mughal and Hindu Women in the 16th and 17th Centuries A.D.,* p. 119.

3. Nath, *Notable Mughal and Hindu Women in the 16th and 17th Centuries A.D.*, p. 119.

4. Lahori, *Padshah Nama*, vol. 01, Part 01, p. 96; Nath, *Notable Mughal and Hindu Women*, p. 119.

5. Nath, *Notable Mughal and Hindu Women in the 16th and 17th Centuries A.D.*, p. 119.

6. J.N. Sarkar, *History of Aurangzeb*, vol. 03, M.C. Sarkar and Sons, Calcutta, 1928, p. 58.

7. Rana Safvi, *Shahjahanabad: The Living City of Old Delhi*, Harper Collins, New Delhi, 2019, p.197.

8. François Bernier, *Travels in Mugul Empire A.D. 1656–1668,* tr. Archibald Constable, Archibald Constable and Company, Westminster, 1891, p. 280–281.

9. Niccolao Manucci, *Storia do Mogor or Mogul India, 1653-1708*, vol. 01, tr. William Irvine, John Murray, London, 1907, p. 221.

10. Today, this Kotwali Chabutra area is Gurudwara Shish Ganj.

11. Sayyid Ahmad Khan, *Asar-us-Sanadid*, tr. & ed. Rana Safvi, Tulika Books, New Delhi, 2018, p. 198.

12. Stephen P. Black, 'Contributors to the Urban Landscape: Women Builders in Safavid Isfahan and Mughal Shahjahanabad', in *Women in Medieval Islamic World: Power, Patronage, and Piety*, ed. Gavin R.G. Hambly, St. Martin Press, New York, 1999, p. 407–428, p. 422.

13. Black, 'Contributors to the Urban Landscape', p. 420.

14. Ibid.

15. Nath, *Notable Mughal and Hindu Women in the 16th and 17th Centuries A.D.*, p. 139–140.

16. Niccolao Manucci, *Storia do Mogor or Mogul India, 1653–1708*, vol. 02, tr. William Irvine, John Murray, London, p. 149–150.

17. Ibid. p. 150.

18. Jyoti Pandey Sharma, 'From Private Garden to a Public Park: The 1857 "Devil's Wind", The British Love for the Lawn and the Mutation of the Mughal Bagh', IASTE *Paper Series*, vol. 318, 2022, p. 55–74, p. 65.

19. Ibid. p. 65.

20. Ibid. p. 66.

21. 'A section of the Bagh on the east was carved out as a plot that was gifted in 1806 by the incumbent Mughal ruler, Shah Alam-II to Begum Samru, ruler of the principality of Sardhana, near Delhi. Begum Samru built a Kothi (stylistically hybrid mansion) on the plot that became a famous landmark of Delhi. Meanwhile the rest of the garden remained in a state of neglect.' Sharma, 'From Private Garden to a Public Park', p. 64.

22. Sangeeta Barooah, 'The Crowned in a Corner: The only statue of Queen Victoria in New Delhi lies unnamed in a cobwebbed corner of Delhi College of Art', *The Hindu*, 15 June 2014. https://www.thehindu.com/features/metroplus/society/the-crowned-in-a-corner/article6114957.ece

23. Manucci, *Storia do Mogor or Mogul India*, vol. 01, p. 216.

24. Shah Jahan, according to Manucci, bestowed the city of Surat upon Begum Sahib (Jahanara), and its revenue was reportedly utilized to fund the princess's betel leaf expenses. See, Manucci, *Storia do Mogor or Mogul India*, vol. 01, p. 216.

25. Nath, *Notable Mughal and Hindu Women in the 16th and 17th Centuries A.D.*, p. 125.

26. Manucci, *Storia do Mogor or Mogul India*, vol. 01, p. 220.

27. Robison, 'Jahanara Begum', p. 357.

28. Sarkar, *History of Aurangzeb*, vol. 03; Renuka Misra, *Women in Mughal India*, Munshiram Manoharlal, New Delhi, 1967, p. 66, 75.

29. Ira Mukhoty, *Daughters of Sun: Empresses, Queens and Begums of the Mughal Empire*, Aleph Book Company, 20 May 2018.

30. Carr Stephen, *The Archaeology and Monumental Remains of Delhi*, Gyan Publishing House, New Delhi, 2024.

31. Rana Safvi, *The Forgotten Cities of Delhi*, HarperCollins, New Delhi, 2020.

32. Mahboob-al-Rahman Saheb Kaleem, *Jahanara*, p. 63; Nath, *Notable Mughal and Hindu Women in the 16th and 17th Centuries A.D.*, p. 126

33. Manucci, *Storia do Mogor or Mogul India*, vol. 02, p. 239.

2: The Power Broker

1. *Delhi Urdu Akbar*, 22 November 1840, National Archives of India.

2. Aslam Parvez, *The Life and Poetry of Bahadur Shah Zafar*, tr. Ather Farouqui, Hay House India, New Delhi, 2021, p. 54.

3. R.V. Smith, 'The Sad Plight of Zeenat Mahal', *The Hindu*, 16 October 2011. https://www.thehindu.com/features/metroplus/the-sad-plight-of-zeenat-mahal/article2543190.ece.

4. Parvez, *The Life and Poetry of Bahadur Shah Zafar*, p. 55.

5. Delhi Commissioner's Office Archive, Delhi, File 65A, 7 December 1858, *Report on the Character and Conduct of the Attendants of the ex royal King*.

6. *Khulasa-e Akhbar*, 20 April 1849, National Archives of India. Cited in Parvez, *The Life and Poetry of Bahadur Shah Zafar*, p. 46–47.

7. Pavan K. Verma and Sondeep Shankar, *Mansions at Dusk: The Havelies of Old Delhi*, Spantech Publishers, New Delhi, 1992, p. 78.

8. R.V. Smith, 'The Sad Plight of Zeenat Mahal', *The Hindu*.

9. Parvez, *The Life and Poetry of Bahadur Shah Zafar*.

10. Punjab Archives, Lahore, Case I, 45, BSZ to James Thomason, 19 January 1849. Cited in William Dalrymple, *The Last Mughal: The Fall of a Dynasty, Delhi, 1857*, Penguin Books, New Delhi, 2007, p. 46.

11. Zahir Dehlvi, *Dastaan-e-Ghadar*, tr. Rana Safvi, Penguin Books, New Delhi, 2017, p.22–23.

12. Parvez, *The Life and Poetry of Bahadur Shah Zafar*, p. 50.

13. Ibid.

14. Ibid.

15. Spear, *Twilight of the Mughals*, p. 163.

16. Verma & Shankar, *Mansions at Dusk*, p. 81; 'A Case of Delhi Poisoning?', *The Hindu Archives*, 5 April 2004. https://web.archive.org/web/20041106184026/http://www.hindu.com/mp/2004/04/05/stories/2004040500720200.htm.

17. Spear, *Twilight of the Mughals*, p. 163.

18. *Mutiny Papers*, National Archives, No. 21, No. 23–24; Parvez, *The Life and Poetry of Bahadur Shah Zafar*, p. 123.

19. Dalrymple, *The Last Mughal*.

20. Dehlvi, *Dastan-e-Ghadar*, pp. 136–137; Arshad Islam, 'The Backlash in Delhi: Treatment of the Mughal Royal Family Following the Indian "Sepoy Mutiny" of 1857', *Journal of Muslim Minority Affairs*, vol. 31, No. 2, June 2011, p. 203.

21. Parvez, *The Life and Poetry of Bahadur Shah Zafar*, p. 103.

22. In Rangoon, her daily intake was somewhere around 10 grams. See, Parvez, *The Life and Poetry of Bahadur Shah Zafar*, p. 104.

23. Dalrymple, *The Last Mughal*, p. 482.

24. Brij Kishan Chandiwala, *In Search of Delhi: A Translation of Brij Kishan Chandiwala's Dilli ki Khoj*, tr. Jitender Gill and Namita Sethi, Routledge India, London, 2023, p. 235–236.

25. Verma and Shankar, *Mansions at Dusk*, p. 81.

26. Ibid. p. 82.

27. Ibid. p. 82.

28. Verma and Shankar, *Mansions at Dusk*, p. 81

29. Ali Fraz Rezvi, 'Zeenat Mahal: Where once a queen lived, girls are being groomed for the future', *The Patriot*, 21 June 2022. https://thepatriot.in/culture/zeenat-mahal-26141.

3: The OG Queen of Strategy, Sass and Survival

1. The area is now known as Bhagirath Palace.

2. A concubine is someone who was a courtesan and is now a personal concubine of a noblemen. She no longer performs for others. So, she was a courtesan who was taken as a concubine in the household of Asad Khan.

3. Brajendranath Banerji, *Begam Samru*, M.C. Sarkar & Sons, Calcutta, 1925, p. 15.

4. For more on the lives and culture of tawaifs of Delhi see, Anoushka Jain, *Bazar-i Husn: The Real History of Tawaifs and Kothas of Chawri Bazar*, forthcoming, Penguin Books.

5. John Lall, *Begam Samru: Fading Portrait in a Gilded Frame*, Roli Books, New Delhi, 1997, p. 16.

6. Ibid. p.19.

7. Ibid. p.19.

8. Ibid. p. 35.

9. It is said that Najaf Khan was very much impressed by the military skill displayed by Samru and his French officers. Najaf Khan started negotiations with the object of winning him over from the service of the Jat Raja. Samru was finally offered Rs 30,0001 a month. Banerji, *Begam Samru*, p. 7, p. 9.

10. Baillie Fraser, *Military Memoir of Lieutenant Colonel James Skinner*, *C.B.*, vol. 01, Amith, Elder and Co., London, p. 285.

11. Lall, *Begam Samru*, p. 46.

12. Samru was sent to Agra as its civil and military governor, and there he died on 4 May 1778. His remains were at first buried in his garden. Later on, they were removed to the consecrated ground in the Agra churchyard by Begam Samru. The Portuguese inscription, in raised letters, on his tombstone, in the Roman Catholic Cemetery at Agra reads, 'Aqui iazo Walter Reinhard morreo aos 4 de Mayo no Anno de 1778.' Cited in Banerji, *Begam Samru*, p. 12.

13. Banerji, *Begam Samru*, p. 16–17.

14. Sir William H. Sleeman, *Rambles and Recollections of an Indian Official*, vol. 02, ed. Vincent A. Smith, Asian Educational Services, New Delhi, 1995(originally published in 1844), p. 273.

15. For a full account of Begum Samru's income see, Banerji, *Begam Samru*, pp. 139–143.

16. Sleeman, *Rambles and Recollections of an Indian Official*, vol. 02, p. 274; Lall, *Begam Samru*, pp. 56–57.

17. Sleeman, *Rambles and Recollections of an Indian Official*, vol. 02, p. 276.

18. Cited in Banerji, *Begam Samru*, p. 23.

19. Lall, *Begam Samru*, p. 72.

20. See, Mrs A. Deane, *A Tour through the Upper Provinces of Hindostan; Comprising a period between the Years 1804 and 1814: With Remarks and Authentic Anecdotes, to which is Annexed Guid of the River Ganges, with a Map from the Source to the Mouth*, C&J Rivington, London, 1823, pp. 151 152; Lall, *Begam Samru*, pp. 101–102.

21. Colonel Skinner in his journal wrote that people of the Deccan who knew Begum Samru by her reputation, believed her to be a witch who destroyed her enemies by throwing her *chadir* at them. See, Fraser, *Military Memoir of Lieutenant Colonel James Skinner*, vol. 01, p. 286; also mentioned in Banerji, *Begam Samru*, pp. 145–146.

22. Deane, *A Tour through the Upper Provinces of Hindostan*, p. 149.

23. Ibid., p. 149.

24. Ibid., p. 169.

25. Ibid., p. 150.

26. Lall, *Begam Samru*, p. 128.

27. Deane, *A Tour through the Upper Provinces of Hindostan*, p. 150.

28. Thomas Bacon, *First Impression and Studies from Nature in Hindustan*, vol. 02, Wm. H. Allen & Co., London, p. 52.

29. Lall, *Begam Samru*, p. 161.

30. Bacon, *First Impression and Studies from Nature in Hindustan*, vol. 02, p. 54.

31. Ibid.

32. Cited in Banerji, *Begam Samru*, p. 187.

33. Banerji, *Begam Samru*, p. 191.

34. Lall, *Begam Samru*, p. 104n.

35. Lall, *Begam Samru*, p. 104n; Pavan K. Verma and Sondeep Shankar, *Mansions at Dusk: The Havelies of Old Delhi*, Spantech Publishers, New Delhi, 1992.

36. Verma & Shankar, *Mansions at Dusk*.

4: The De Facto Empress of Hindustan

1. Carr Stephen, *The Archaeology and Monumental Remains of Delhi*, Gyan Publishing House, New Delhi, 2024, p. 274.

2. Confirmed from a contemporary Persian source, *Tarikh-i Ahmadi*, see, J.N. Sarkar, *Fall of the Mughal Empire: 1739–1754*, vol. 01, M.C. Sarkar & Sons, Calcutta: 1932, p. 336.

3. Sudha Sharma, *The Status of Muslim Women in Medieval India*, Sage Publication, New Delhi, p. 145.

4. Sarkar, *Fall of the Mughal Empire: 1739–1754*, vol. 01, p. 334.

5. Mahmud al-Husayni, *Tarikh-i Ahmad Shahi*, 45b, cited in Sarkar, *Fall of the Mughal Empire: 1739–1754*, vol. 01, p. 335.

6. Ibid. p. 335.

7. See, Thomas William Beale, *An Oriental Biographical Dictionary*, ed. Henry George Keene, Baptist Mission Press, Calcutta, 1881, p. 28.

8. Ibid. p. 28.

9. *Tarikh-i Ahmad Shahi* by an anonymous author, from Sir H.M. Elliot and Prof. John Dowson, *The History of India, as Told by Its Own Historians: The Muhammadan Period*, vol. 08, Trubner and Co., London, 1877, p. 105.

10. Ibid. p. 112.

11. Sharma, *The Status of Muslim Women in Medieval India*, p. 145.

12. Sarkar, *Fall of the Mughal Empire: 1739–1754*, vol. 01, p. 336.

13. *Tarikh-i Ahmad Shahi* in Elliot and Dowson, *The History of India, as Told by Its Own Historians*, p. 115–116.

14. Shakir Khan, *Tazkira-i Shakir Khani*, mentioned in Sarkar, *Fall of the Mughal Empire: 1739–1754*, vol. 01, p. 335–336.

15. Sarkar, *Fall of the Mughal Empire: 1739–1754*, vol. 01, p. 335.

16. Ibid., p. 336.

17. Ibid., p. 336.

18. Ibid., p. 336.

19. Originally from Harcharan-das's *Chahar Gulzar-i Shujai* (1748), cited in Sarkar, *Fall of the Mughal Empire: 1739–1754*, vol. 01, p. 339.

20. A.S. Altekar, *The First Two Nawabs of Awadh*, Shiva Lal Agarwala & Co. Ltd, Agra, p. 196–197.

21. Ibid. p. 203.

22. See, Savita Kumari, 'Udham Bai: Glimpse into the Splendid Life of a Later Mughal Queen', https://www.academia.edu/36007480/Udham_Bai_A_Glimpse_into_the_splendid_life_of_a_Later_Mughal_Queen_by_Savita_Kumari.

23. Kumari, 'Udham Bai'.

24. Stephen, *The Archaeology and Monumental Remains of Delhi*, p. 274.

25. Cited in Muhmmad Umar, *Muslim Society in Northern India in the Eighteenth Century*, M.Phil Thesis, Aligarh Muslim University, 1998, p. 73.

26. Julie Codell, 'On the Delhi Coronation Darbars, 1877, 1903, 1911', *Branch*, https://branchcollective.org/?ps_articles=julie-codell-on-the-delhi-coronation-darbars-1877-1903-1911.

27. 'The State Entry into Delhi: Painting and Poetry at the Delhi Durbar of 1903', *The Heritage Lab*, https://www.theheritagelab.in/the-state-entry-delhi-durbar-painting/.

28. Yakin Kinger, '"Capturing" the Qudsia Bagh: Decoding the Colonial Lens', *Critical Collective*, 2022.; also, Tanuja Bhakuni, 'Bagh-e-Qudsia', *Zikr-e-Dilli*, 14 March 2021, https://zikredilli.com/delhi-depository/f/bagh-e-qudsia?blogcategory=Architecture.

29. Catherine B. Asher, *Architecture of Mughal India*, Cambridge University Press, Cambridge, 2001, p. 305.

5: The Kingmaker

1. See Nupur Binani, 'The Clock Towers of Delhi', *Enroute Indian History*, EHI Archives, 25 September 2024. https://enrouteindianhistory.com/the-clock-towers-of-delhi-2/.

2. Lahori, *Padshah Nama*, vol. 01, Part 01, p. 96; Nath, *Notable Mughal and Hindu Women*, p. 119.

3. François Bernier, *Travels in the Mogul Empire A.D. 1656–1668*, tr. Archibald Constable, Archibald Constable and Company, London, 1891, p. 14.

4. Ibid., p. 14.

5. Ibid., p. 280.

6. Cited in Lal, *The Mughal Harem*, p. 100.

7. Jean-Baptiste Tavernier, *Travels in India*, vol. 01, Oxford University Press, London, 1925, pp. 115.

8. Bernier, *Travels in the Mogul Empire*, p. 350–351.

9. Ibid., p. 372.

10. Ibid., p. 12–13.

11. Ibid., p. 132–133.

12. Niccolao Manucci, *Storia do Mogor or Mogul India*, 1653-1708, vol. 02, tr. William Irvine, John Murray, London, 1907, pp. 34–35.

13. Ibid., pp. 54–57.

14. Ibid., pp. 54–55.

15. C.M. Villiers-Stuart, Constance Marie, *Gardens of the Great Mughals*, Adam and Charles Black, London, 1913, p. 111.

16. See, Carr Stephen, *The Archaeology and Monumental Remains of Delhi*, Gyan Publishing House, New Delhi, 2024, pp. 260; Catherine B. Asher, *Architecture of Mughal India*, Cambridge University Press, Cambridge, 2001, pp. 203–204.

17. Stephen, *The Archaeology and Monumental Remains of Delhi*, p. 260.

18. Asher, *Architecture of Mughal India*, pp. 203–204.

19. Jyoti Pandey Sharma, 'From Private Garden to a Public Park: The 1857 "Devil's Wind", The British Love for the Lawn and the Mutation of the Mughal Bagh', IASTE *Paper Series*, vol. 318, 2022, p. 55–74, pp. 68–69.

20. Ibid., p. 69.

21. Mahendra Singh Vist, 'Heritage of Roshanara Bagh', *Journal de Brahmavart*, pp. 47–49.

22. Sharma, 'From Private Garden to a Public Park', p. 69.

23. James Dickie (Yaqub Zaki), 'The Mughal Garden: Gateway to Paradise', *Muqarnas*, vol. 03, 1985, pp. 128–137, p.136. http://www.jstor.org/stable/1523089.

6: The Power Behind the Throne

1. Soma Mukherjee, *Royal Mughal Ladies and Their Contributions*, Gyan Publishing House, 2001. New Delhi, p. 122.

2. For a list of Angas see, Gulbadan Begum, *Humayun Nama: The History of Humayun*, tr. Annette S. Beveridge, Royal Asiatic Society, London, 1902, pp. 203–301.

3. Atka Khan was like a father figure to Akbar and also served as the wazir, or prime minister, of the Mughal empire during the early years of Akbar's reign.

4. Abul Fazl, *Akbarnama*, vol. 02, tr. H. Beveridge, The Asiatic Society, Calcutta, 1907, pp. 453–454.

5. Ambreen Shamim, *Status of Women in the Mughal Empire During the 16th Century*, unpublished MPhil Thesis, Aligarh Muslim University, 2010, p. 27.

6. Abul Fazl, *Akbarnama*, vol. 02, pp. 91.

7. The *Tarikh-i Alfi* (Thousand Year History) is an historical work compiled by a committee appointed by Akbar in 990 Hijri, 1582 CE. The task of compiling this work was given to people like Mulla Ahmad Thattavi, Asaf Khan and Abdul Qadir Badauni. Cited in Ali Nadeem Rezavi, 'Sources for Akbar's Reign', *ASHA: Blast from the Past*, 30 March 2022. https://rezavisblastfromthepast.co.in/author/nadeemrezavi/page/3/.

8. Rezavi, 'Sources for Akbar's Reign'; also see Nawab Shams-ud-Daula Shahnawaz Khan and Abdul Hayy, *Maathir-ul-Umara*,

vol. 01, tr. H. Beveridge & Beni Prashad, Janaki Prakashan, Patna, 1979, p. 145.

9. Khan and Hayy, *Maathir-ul-Umara*, vol. 01, p. 384–385; also see, Mukherjee, *Royal Mughal Ladies and Their Contributions*, p. 123.

10. Mulla Abdul Qadir Badauni, *Muntakhab ut' Twarikh*, vol. 02, tr. W.H. Lowe, Asiatic Society of Bengal, Calcutta, pp. 30–32.

11. Abdul Qadir al-Badauni, *Muntakhab ut Tawarikh*, vol. 02, tr. George S.A. Ranking, Atlantic Publishers, New Delhi, 1990, p. 31.

12. Mukherjee, *Royal Mughal Ladies and Their Contributions*, p. 124.

13. Mukherjee, *Royal Mughal Ladies and Their Contributions*, p. 124; Khan and Hayy, *Maathir-ul-Umara*, vol. 01, p. 385.

14. Friedrich August Graf von Noer, *The Emperor Akbar: A Contribution towards the History of India in the 16th Century*, vol. 02, Thacker, Spink & Co., Calcutta, 1890, p. 94.

15. Rekha Misra, *Women in Mughal India*, Munshiram Manohar, New Delhi, 1967, p. 25; also, Dr R.P. Tripathi, 'Maham Anga and Akbar', *J.I.H.*, vol. 01, p. 326.

16. Fazl, *Akbarnama*, vol. 02, pp. 269; Mukherjee, *Royal Mughal Ladies and Their Contributions*, p. 125.

17. Khan and Hayy, *Maathir-ul-Umara*, vol. 01, p. 384–385.

18. Fazl, *Akbarnama*, vol. 02, p. 129.

19. Fazl, *Akbarnama*, vol. 02, pp. 221; Khan and Hayy, *Maathir-ul-Umara*, vol. 01, p.146–147; Shamim, *Status of Women in the Mughal Empire During the 16th Century*, pp. 29–30.

20. Badauni, *Muntakhab ut' Tawarikh*, vol. 02, p. 49.

21. Ibid., p. 49–50.

22. Khawaja Nizamuddin, *Tabaqat-i Akbari*, vol. 02, tr. B. De, M.A., I.C.S., Bibliotheca Indica, Calcutta, 1936, p. 264.

23. Nizamuddin, *Tabaqat-i Akbari*, p. 264; Khan and Hayy, *Maathir-ul-Umara*, vol. 01, p.147–148.

24. Badauni, *Muntakhab ut' Twarikh*, p. 60.

25. Khawaja Nizamuddin, *Tabaqat-i Akbari*, vol. 02, tr. B. De, M.A., I.C.S., Bibliotheca Indica, Calcutta, 1936, pp. 275–276. However, according to Abul Fazl's *Akbarnama*, this incident happened on Wednesday, the 28th Jumada-al-awwal, when His Majesty (Akbar) was returning from a visit to the shrine of Sheikh Nizam-ud-din Auliya. See, Abul Fazl, *Akbarnama*.

26. R.V. Smith, 'Gateway to medieval era: Delhi's historic entrances have witnessed several interesting incidents', *The Hindu*, 5 July 2015. https://www.thehindu.com/features/metroplus/society/gateway-to-medieval-era/article7389285.ece.

27. Smith, 'Gateway to medieval era'.

28. Carr Stephen, *The Archaeology and Monumental Remains of Delhi*, Gyan Publishing House, New Delhi, 2024, p. 200.

29. Ahmad Rahmani, 'Masjid Khairul Manazil', *The Milli Gazette*, https://www.milligazette.com/Archives/01082001/06.htm.

7: The Silent Architect

1. See Carr Stephen, *The Archaeology and Monumental Remains of Delhi*, Gyan Publishing House, New Delhi, 2024, p. 198.

2. 'Nizamuddin Urban Renewal Initiative', Nizamuddinrenewal.org, 2015, https://www.nizamuddinrenewal.org/conservation/isa-khan/.

3. 'Bu-Halima Gateway'. https://www.nizamuddinrenewal.org/conservation/buhalimas-garden-tomb/.

4. S.A.A. Naqvi, *Humayun's Tomb and Other Adjacent Monuments*, Archaeological Survey of India, New Delhi, 2002, p. 65.

5. The sturdy Archaeological Survey notice informs us that the incumbent is an unidentified commander and that the name is derived from the English word 'officer'. So it is the 'officer-wala's tomb'. They do not explain why anybody at the Delhi court would adopt and corrupt an English word as early as the sixteenth century, a time when most military vocabulary was derived from Turkish. But some painstaking research by the historian Subhash Parihar reveals that Afsar was a Persian tribal name, and that there were several Afsars employed at the early Mughal court, including one who assisted Humayun during his victorious return and recapture of India in 1555. See, Giles Tillotson, *Delhi Darshan: The History and Monuments of India's Capital*, Penguin Books, New Delhi, 2019.

6. Naqvi, *Humayun's Tomb and Other Adjacent Monuments*, p. 64.

7. It is given on an inscription on the gateway: 'In the name of God, the merciful and the compassionate. There is no God, but God and Muhammad is his prophet! O God! [His] kind [Miharbau] and old patron [is] Jahangir Shah.' Mentioned in Stephen, *The Archaeology and Monumental Remains of Delhi*, p. 199.

8. Sir Sayyid Ahmad Khan, *Asar-us-Sanadid*, tr. & ed. Rana Safvi, Tulika Books, New Delhi, 2018, p. 47.

9. Ibid., p. 49.

10. Gulbadan Begum, *Humayun Nama: The History of Humayun*, tr. Annette S. Beveridge, Royal Asiatic Society, London, 1902, p. 218.

11. See, Ishwari Prasad, *The Life and Times of Humayun*, Orient Longman, Calcutta, 1956, p. 21.

12. S.K. Banerji, *Humayun Badshah*, Oxford University Press, Milford, Humphrey, 1938, p. 232.

13. See, S.M. Azizuddin Husain, *Tazkiratul Umara of Kewal Ram: Biographical Account of Mughal Nobility from the Reign of Mughal Emperor Akbar to the Reign of Muhammad Shah*, Munshiram Manoharlal Publication, New Delhi, 2013; also, Banerji, *Humayun Badshah*, p. 232.

14. Gulbadan, *Humayun Nama*, p. 208.

15. Ibid., p. 143.

16. Ibid., p. 130.

17. Soma Mukherjee, *Royal Mughal Ladies and Their Contribution*, Gyan Publishing House, New Delhi, 2001, p. 42.

18. Ibid., p. 42.

19. Ibid., p. 42.

20. Ruby Lal, *Domesticity and Power in the Early Mughal World*, Cambridge University Press, Cambridge, 2005. p. 211.

21. Abdul Qadir al-Badauni, *Muntakhab ut Tawarikh*, vol. 02, tr. George S.A. Ranking, Atlantic Publishers, New Delhi, 1990, p. 308.

22. Abul Fazl, *Akbarnama*, vol. 03, tr. H. Beveridge, The Asiatic Society, Calcutta, 1939, reprinted in 2000, pp. 552–553.

23. R. Nath, *History of Mughal Architecture: The Age of Personality Architecture (Akbar, 1556–1605 A.D.)*, Abhinav Publications, New Delhi, pp. 247–248.

24. Glenn D. Lowry, *The Tomb of Nasiruddin Mohammad Humayun*, PhD Thesis, Harvard University, 1982, p. 135–136; also, Nath, *History of Mughal Architecture*, vol. 02, pp. 247–248.

25. Badauni, *Muntakhab ut Tawarikh*, vol. 02, p. 135.

8: Aurangzeb's Daughters

1. Abul Fazl, *Ain-i Akbari*, vol. 01, tr. H. Blochmann, Asiatic Society of Bengal, 1873, Calcutta, p. 44; Soma Mukherjee,

Royal Mughal Ladies and Their Contribution, Gyan Publishing House, New Delhi, 2001, p.16.

2. Cited in Mukherjee, *Royal Mughal Ladies and Their Contribution*, p. 36.

3. Nayanjot Lahiri, 'Commemorating and Remembering 1857: The Revolt in Delhi and Its Afterlife', *World Archaeology* 35, no. 01, April 2003, pp. 35–60, p. 41. https://doi.org/10.108 0/0043824032000078072.

4. Catherine B. Asher, *Architecture of Mughal India*, Cambridge University Press, Cambridge, 1992, reprint 2001, p. 255.

5. Stephen P. Blake, *Shahjahanabad: The Sovereign City in Mughal India* 1639–1739, United Kingdom: Cambridge University Press, 2002, p.58

6. Catherine B. Asher, *Architecture of Mughal India*, Cambridge University Press, Cambridge, 1992, reprint 2001, p. 255.

7. For a description of Aurangzeb's wedding to Dilras Begum see, Jadunath Sarkar, *History of Aurangzeb*, vol. 01 and 02, 2nd edition, Orient Longman Ltd., Calcutta, pp. 31–33.

8. Saqi Mustad Khan, *Maasir-i Alamgiri: A History of the Emperor Auarangzib Alamgir (reign 1658–1707 A.D.)*, tr. Jadunath Sarkar, Royal Asiatic Society of Bengal, Calcutta, 1947, p. 322.

9. Sarkar, *History of Aurangzeb*, vol. 01 and 02, p. 37.

10. Sarkar, *History of Aurangzeb*, vol. 01 and 02, p. 38.

11. Magan Lal and Jessie Duncan Westbrook collected and translated the first fifty ghazals of Zeb-un-Nissa from Persian to English in the *Wisdom of the East* series. See, *The Diwan of Zeb-un-Nissa*, tr. Magan Lal and Jessie Dunccan Westbrook, John Murray, London, 1913.

12. *The Tears of Zebunnisa: Being Excerpts from the Divan-i Makhfi*, tr. Paul Ernest Sutton Whalley, W. Thacker & Company, Berkeley, 1913.

13. These are three varieties of the Persian script (originally Arabic script) in common use in medieval times. Naskh is the base for type fonts and the typewriter; nasta'liq is the basic cursive script and the model for good handwriting. The third variety, shekaste, is actually a variant of nasta'liq, literally meaning 'broken' in which the dots (nuqtas) are not given. It is used by scribers to write quickly and also in coded ways.

14. Lal and Duncan, *The Diwan of Zeb-un-Nissa*, p. 9.

15. Jadunath Sarkar, *Anecdotes of Aurangzib and Historical Essays*, M.C. Sarkar & Sons, 1912, p. 49.

16. Renuka Nath, *Notable Mughal and Hindu Women in the 16th and 17th Centuries A.D.*, Inter-India Publication, New Delhi, 1957, p. 153.

17. Ibid., p. 153–154.

18. Khan, *Maasir-i Alamgiri*, p. 275.

19. Soma Mukherjee, *Royal Mughal Ladies and their Contribution*, Gyan Publishing House, New Delhi, 2001, p. 203. Also, Jadunath Sarkar, *History of Aurangzeb*, Vol. 01, p. 69.

20. Khan, *Massir-i Alamgiri*, p. 323; Nath, *Notable Mughal and Hindu Women in the 16th and 17th Centuries A.D*, p. 164.

21. Mukherjee, *Royal Mughal Ladies and Their Contributions*, p. 204.

22. Khan, *Massir-i Alamgiri*, p. 323.

23. Ibid., p. 323.

24. Nath, *Notable Mughal and Hindu Women in the 16th and 17th Centuries A.D.*, p. 166.

25. Ibid., p. 166.

26. Khan, *Maasir-i Alamgiri*, p. 288.

27. Ibid., p. 207.

28. Ibid., p. 217.

29. Ibid., p. 152.

30. Ibid., p. 248.
31. Ibid., p. 138.
32. Ibid., p. 309–310.

9: The Fearless Tawaif

1. Somya Lakhani, 'Delhi: 19th Century mosque damaged by lightning', *The Indian Express*, 20 July 2020. https://indianexpress.com/article/cities/delhi/delhi-19th-century-mosque-damaged-by-lightning-6514109/.

2. For more on this topic see, Anoushka Jain, *Bazar-i Husn: The Real History of Tawaifs and Kothas of Chawri Bazar*, forthcoming, Penguin Books.

3. For more on Mubarak Begum's background see the Mubarak Bagh Papers archived at Delhi State Archives, Delhi Commission Office, DCO F5/ 1861.

4. 'MHS Collections Online: Major General Sir David Ochterlony, Bt. K.C.B.', Masshist.org, 2025, https://www.masshist.org/database/822.

5. William Dalrymple ed., *Begums, Thugs and White Mughals: The Journals of Fanny Parkes*, Eland, London, 2002, p. 10.

6. Ibid.

7. Mrs A. Deane, *A Tour through the Upper Provinces of Hindostan; Comprising a period between the Years 1804 and 1814: With Remarks and Authentic Anecdotes, to which is Annexed Guide of the River Ganges, with a Map from the Source to the Mouth*, C&J Rivington, London, 1823, p. 161.

8. Bishop Reginald Heber, *Narrative of a Journey through the Upper Provinces of India*, vol. I, Carey, Lea & Carey, Philadelphia, 1829, p. 501.

9. Savita Kumari, 'Art and Politics: British Patronage in Delhi', *National Museum Institute of History of Art, Conservation and Museology*, New Delhi, pp. 217–229.

10. Ibid., p. 218.

11. Ibid., p. 218.

12. Gardner Papers, National Army Museum, Letter 90, 16 August 1821. Cited in William Dalrymple, *The Last Mughal: The Fall of a Dynasty, Delhi, 1857*, Penguin Books, New Delhi, 2007, p. 66.

13. Gardner Papers, National Army Museum, Letter 16, p. 42. Cited in William Dalrymple, *White Mughals: Love and Betrayal in Eighteenth-Century India*, Penguin Books, New Delhi, 2002, p. 183.

14. Unnati Sharma, 'An "Ambitious" Courtesan & a British Officer—the Tale behind Old Delhi's Mubarak Masjid', *The Print*, 21 July 2020, https://theprint.in/feature/an-ambitious-courtesan-a-british-officer-the-tale-behind-old-delhis-mubarak-masjid/465132/; also see, Dalrymple, *White Mughals*, pp. 183–184.

15. Private family papers in the haveli of the late Mirza Farid Beg, Old Delhi. Mentioned in Dalrymple, *The Last Mughal*, p. 66.

16. See, Jyoti Pandey Sharma, 'Cultural Hybridity in 19th-century Delhi: the architectural exploits of Resident Major General Sir David Ochterlony KCB Bt, Delhi's "Loony Akhtar" (crazy star)', *Transactions of the Ancient Monuments Society*, vol. 65, 2021, pp. 65–95.

17. Michael Edwardes, *Glorious Sahibs: The romantic as empire-builder 1799–1838*, Eyre & Spottiswoode, 1968, p. 226.

18. Dalrymple, *The Last Mughal*, p. 178.

19. Mirza Farhatullah Baig, *The Last Light of Delhi: Glimpses from a Golden Age of Poetry*, tr. Sulaiman Ahmad and Parvati Sharma, Penguin Books, New Delhi, 2022, p.11.

20. See, Veena Talwar Oldenburg, 'Lifestyle as Resistance: The Case of the Courtesans of Lucknow, India', *Feminist Studies* 16, no. 2 (1990): 259, https://doi.org/10.2307/3177850.

10: Not Just Mumtaz

1. Ramki Das, *Zikr-e Umurat Am Zila-e Dehli as Delhi and Its Environs Before 1857: The Account of Ramji Das*, Sarishtadar, tr. Shama Mitra Chenoy, Primus Books, New Delhi, 2023, p. 68.

2. Sangin Beg, *Sair-ul-Manazil*, tr. Nausheen Jaffery, ed. Swapna Liddle, Tulika Books, New Delhi, 2017, pp. 67.

3. Brij Kishan Chandiwala, *In Search of Delhi: A Translation of Brij Kishan Chandiwala's Dilli ki Khoj*, tr. Jitender Gill and Namita Sethi, Routledge India, London, 2023, p. 132.

4. Chandiwala, *In Search of Delhi*, p. 132; Nayanjot Lahiri, 'Commemorating and Remembering 1857: The Revolt in Delhi and Its Afterlife', *World Archaeology* 35 (01), April 2003, pp. 35–60, p. 41, 51. https://doi.org/10.1080/00438240320 00078072.

5. Lahiri, 'Commemorating and Remembering 1857'.

6. Inayat Khan, *Shah Jahan Nama*, p. 447; also see Harbans Mukhia, 'The World of the Mughal Family', in *The Mughals of India*, Blackwell Publication, Oxford, 2004, pp. 113–54, p.129.

7. Mukhia, *The Mughal of India*, p. 124.

8. Ibid.

9. Fergus Nicoll, *Shah Jahan: The Rise and Fall of the Mughal Emperor*, Viking, New Delhi, 2009, p. 103–104.

10. Rana Safvi, *Shahjahanabad. The Living City of Old Delhi*, HarperCollins, Noida, 2019.

11. Here, it seems the date for the compilation of the mosque is given wrong. The construction was completed in 1650 CE [which means 1060/1061 AH.] or by the line, from the twenty-fifth regnal year of the King which is 1652–1653 CE … I don't to understand what year 1006 CE will be as per the

Gregorian calendar. But it does not align with the date of the 1650s.

12. Sangin Beg, *Sair-ul-Manazil*, p. 54–55.

13. Stephen P. Blake, *Shahjahanabad: The Sovereign City in Mughal India, 1639-1739*, Cambridge University Press, Cambridge, 2002, p. 57.

14. Safvi, *Shahjahanabad: The Living City of Old Delhi*.

15. HT Correspondent, 'DMRC Stumbles upon 17th Century Mosque', *Hindustan Times*, 5 July 2012, https://www.hindustantimes.com/delhi/dmrc-stumbles-upon-17th-century-mosque/story-CaSyoulaPm0DlSo0C8jq5H.html.

16. Inayat Khan, *Shahjahan Nama*, p. 447.

17. Ibid.

18. Blake, *Shahjahanabad*, p. 63.

19. Asher, *Architecture of Mughal India*, p. 201, 203.

20. Inayat Khan, *Shahjahan Nama*, p. 451.

21. Asher, *Architecture of Mughal India*, p. 201.

About the Author

Anoushka Jain is a historian, author and founder of Enroute Indian History, a women-led initiative that brings the past alive through heritage walks, storytelling and research. She is a graduate in history from Hindu College, Delhi University and has a diploma in art history from the National Museum Institute. She has worked with the Indira Gandhi National Centre for the Arts and collaborated with the Ministry of Tourism as a knowledge partner to preserve India's Ramsar wetland sites.

Since founding Enroute Indian History in 2019, Anoushka has introduced thousands to Delhi's layered histories and India's diverse heritage. Her work has been widely featured in *The Hindu*, *The Indian Express*, The Print, *Travel + Leisure*, Feminism in India, and other platforms. Recognized among the 'Most Influential Women of 2023' by Women Listed and Her Circle (a Nita Ambani initiative), she was also awarded 'Emerging Entrepreneur in Heritage Sector' by *Hindustan Times*.

A regular speaker at Delhi University, O.P. Jindal, Chris and Amity, she is deeply engaged in making history accessib to wider audiences.

HarperCollins *Publishers* India

At HarperCollins India, we believe in telling the best stories and finding the widest readership for our books in every format possible. We started publishing in 1992; a great deal has changed since then, but what has remained constant is the passion with which our authors write their books, the love with which readers receive them, and the sheer joy and excitement that we as publishers feel in being a part of the publishing process.

Over the years, we've had the pleasure of publishing some of the finest writing from the subcontinent and around the world, including several award-winning titles and some of the biggest bestsellers in India's publishing history. But nothing has meant more to us than the fact that millions of people have read the books we published, and that somewhere, a book of ours might have made a difference.

As we look to the future, we go back to that one word—a word which has been a driving force for us all these years.

Read.